New Challenges to Understanding Organizations

KARLENE H. ROBERTS

University of California at Berkeley

Macmillan Publishing Company
New York

Maxwell Macmillan Canada
Toronto

Maxwell Macmillan International
New York Oxford Singapore Sydney

Editor: Charles E. Stewart
Production Supervisor: Helen Wallace
Production Manager: Roger Vergnes
Text Designer: Debra Fargo
Cover Designer: Cathleen Norz
Cover Illustration: © Douglas Fraser
Figure Illustrations: ECL Art Associates

This book was set in Caledonia by Americomp and printed and bound by Book Press.
The cover was printed by New England Book Components.

Macmillan Publishing Company
866 Third Avenue, New York, New York 10022

Macmillan Publishing Company is part
of the Maxwell Communication Group of Companies.

Maxwell Macmillan Canada, Inc.
1200 Eglinton Avenue East
Suite 200
Don Mills, Ontario M3C 3N1

Library of Congress Cataloging in Publication Data
Roberts, Karlene H.
    New challenges to understanding organizations / Karlene H.
  Roberts.
        p.   cm.
    Includes index.
    ISBN 0-02-402052-4
    1. Organizational effectiveness.   2. Organizational behavior.
  I. Title.
  HD58.9.R57   1993
  302.3'5—dc20   92-22771
                                                         CIP

Printing: 1 2 3 4 5 6 7 8   Year: 3 4 5 6 7 8 9 0 1 2

Preface

This volume is the result of a number of years of thinking about, engaging in research about, and reading about organizations that are successful and those that should have been successful in difficult circumstances. The Berkeley project, in which four of this book's chapters originated, provided a forum for heady discussions about how to think about organizations in which errors can lead to catastrophic consequences and about how best to insert a research effort into those organizations. I would like to thank the Berkeley team members as well as the other authors represented in this book for providing me with enormous insights. My thanks also go to my colleague Todd La Porte; to Ph.D. students Sigal Barsade, Maura Belliveau, Paula Consolini, Gina Gargano, Jennifer Halpern, and Alexandra Suchard, and to MBA student Jennifer Eccles.

People from other places also helped shape the direction and focus of the work. Some are represented in this volume. In addition, my thanks go to Sonja Haber, Charles Perrow, Denise Rousseau, and W. Richard Scott. I am fortunate to have elicited interest in this kind of research endeavor from Ph.D. students in other institutions. In addition to Suzanne Stout, who is represented in this book, my thanks go to Greg Bigley and Rochelle Klein from the University of California at Irvine, Carolyn Libuser from the University of California at Los Angeles, and Deborah Shurburg from Hofstra University.

The decision makers in the organizations who helped the Berkeley project come to life, who added insight upon insight to the work, and who often provided encouragement and opened doors when things looked gloomy, are many. My special thanks go to Michael Angus, William Crockett, Russell Cunningham, Bryant Giffin, James Schiffer, David Miklush, Mitchell States, John Townsend, all of Pacific Gas and Electric Company; Anthony Longo and Ralph Marsh at the Federal Aviation Agency's Oakland Regional Air Traffic Control Center; and to Vice Admiral James Service, Vice Admiral John Fetterman, Rear Admiral Robert Leuschner, Rear Admiral Thomas Mercer, Captain Lyle Bien, Captain Doyle Borchers, Captain Donald Scott, Captain Harry Rittenauer, Captain David Waggoner, Captain Richard Wolter, and Commander Robert Mantei, of the U.S. Navy. Many other people in each organization gave willingly of their time, energy, and insights.

Our editor at Macmillan, Charles Stewart, stayed with the project when it often appeared its authors would never produce their work or meet deadlines. He was encouraging and helpful, and most of all, always there.

Finally, the tasks involved in doing the research represented in the first part of this book required an intensity of research experience not required by most other organizations. This research necessitated either living in the organizations or coming close to living in them, often under conditions of some inherent danger. The tasks required to put the research together, by contrast, required something different: a place in which I could think unfettered and in which I could engage in collegial conversation.

For the first of these last named requirements I thank my parents, who often pitched in to help raise my son so I could be at sea with the Navy, and I thank my colleagues Todd La Porte, Gene Rochlin, and Paul Schulman for making sometimes bearable and often fun the treks into the field. For the second of these requirements I thank the dean and my colleagues at the University of California, Irvine, for allowing me four months with them—a time I will always remember as the first, and possibly only, time in my professional life in which my schedule was entirely dictated by my own research and writing needs. My special thanks to Dean Dennis Aigner, Jone Pearce, Lyman Porter, and Ann Tsui.

Karlene H. Roberts

Contents

New Challenges to Understanding Organizations

1

Introduction

KARLENE H. ROBERTS
University of California, Berkeley

Karlene H. Roberts is Professor of Business Administration at the Walter A. Haas School of Business, University of California, Berkeley. She is the author and co-author of numerous books and articles and has served on the editorial boards of the *Journal of Vocational Behavior, Journal of Applied Psychology, Organizational Behavior and Human Decision Processes, The Academy of Management Journal, California Management Review,* and the Academy of Management *Executive.* She is a fellow in the American Psychological Association, the American Psychological Society, and the Academy of Management. She has served on the Board of Governors of the Academy of Management and as chair of its Organizational Behavior Division. Roberts' research interests are in cross-national management, research methodology, organizational communication, and the design and management of reliability-enhancing organizations.

The Berkeley research was supported in part by Office of Naval Research contract N-00014-86-k-03123, National Science Foundation grants SES-8708804 and SES-891105, the Institutes of Governmental Studies and Transportation Studies, University of California, and by Brookhaven National Laboratory contract no. 459427. The papers from the Berkeley group in this volume draw on discussions of the High Reliability Organization project research team which includes Todd R. La Porte, Political Science; Karlene H. Roberts, Haas School of Business; Gene I. Rochlin, Energy and Resources; Principal Investigators, University of California, Berkeley. Other contributors are Denise M. Rousseau, Northwestern University; Paul R. Schulman, Mills College; and Karl E. Weick, University of Michigan. Student members included Paula Consolini, Douglas Creed, Jennifer Halpern, Barbl Koch, Edward Lascher, Suzanne Stout, Alexandra Suchard, and Craig Thomas.

*I*n the summer of 1984, an interdisciplinary group of Berkeley researchers met with high-level managers in three organizations. While functionally very different, these organizations have in common a potential for making operational errors that can result in catastrophe. They all operate complex and potentially hazardous technologies. This kind of organization is generally brought to the attention of the public and the research community only after an accident occurs. In many respects this Johnny-come-lately attention is similar to shutting the barn door after the horse is gone. It is difficult to gain an objective view of any organization that has just suffered the trauma of a fiasco, and at such times the organization is likely to be quite defensive about outsider scrutiny.

The three organizations that initially participated in the research were chosen because of their excellent records of safe operation.[1] Over time, their top-level managers helped us zero in on research issues that posed challenges to the organizations; this enabled us to focus on processes that would help us understand how these organizations are similar to and different from "garden variety" organizations.

Since all organizations are social phenomena designed to produce a good or provide a service, it is not likely that organizations characterized by sophisticated, potentially dangerous technologies, and charged with operating those technologies so as not to hurt themselves or their environments, are very different from other organizations. The problem facing the Berkeley team was to identify those operations that are different from what is usually observed in organizations, and to address the issue of how well existing theory helps in either designing or managing such organizations.

THE ORGANIZATIONS IN THE BERKELEY PROJECT

The three organizations in the initial phases of the project were the Federal Aviation Administration's Air Traffic Control System; Pacific Gas and Electric Company's nuclear power plant at Diablo Canyon, California; and the U.S. Navy's nuclear powered aircraft carriers. A brief description of each organization conveys both its complexity and the unusual level of safety found in its operations.

The United States air traffic control system spans the U.S. mainland, Hawaii, and Alaska. It is comprised of airport, local, regional, and national control centers. The system is knit together by radio, radar, and telephone. In 1990 there were 44,450 U.S. highway and 827 aviation fatalities. In that year

---

[1] Originally these organizations were labeled High Reliability Organizations (HROs) or reliability-enhancing organizations. Problems that emerge because of labeling are thoroughly discussed by Rochlin (Chapter 2). While some research is still being done in these organizations, the group has moved on to study other kinds of organizations in an attempt to identify other characteristics of reliability-enhancing organizations and to extend observations along the dimension of organizations requiring more and less reliable operations. Examples of the kinds of organizations now being explored are nuclear power plants in Europe, marine shipping, and toxic waste management.

the American air route traffic control centers handled 37,547,000 aircraft, and airport towers handled 63,912,000 aircraft (U.S. Department of Transportation, 1991).

Diablo Canyon nuclear power plant operates two Westinghouse pressurized water reactors and employs 1200 people. It ranks as one of the best-run power plants in the world. Generating capacity is a commonly used efficiency measure in power generation. Diablo Canyon's two units combined operated 86 percent of their generating capacity in 1990, which ranked them as number one in the United States for two-unit nuclear power plants and compared favorably to the industry average of 66 percent. Unit one ranked eighth in the world, and the units that were better are 20 percent larger. An indicator of economic performance is time between unscheduled outages. In 1992 unit two enjoyed the longest run between scheduled outages of any light water reactor in the world. This long run reflected the excellence of maintenance at the last scheduled outage as well as employee performance since that time. The Nuclear Regulatory Commission rated plant safety performance as the best of any plant in the western region of the United States in 1991.

Nuclear powered aircraft carriers are also large, technologically complex systems that engage in sustained high tempo operations. Nimitz class carriers displace 96,000 tons of water (compared to the *Queen Elizabeth II's* displacement of 67,000 tons). Their power plants could supply the electrical needs of a city the size of Minneapolis. They carry 6000 men (and no women) and fly ninety aircraft of seven different types. Planes are launched and recovered at intervals from 48 to 60 seconds from the 4.5 acre flight deck. Four steam catapults accelerate aircraft from a complete standstill to 140 knots in just over 2 seconds. Planes are recovered at speeds of 130 knots and decelerate to zero in approximately 2 seconds within 315 feet of touchdown. On the flight deck, planes are refueled and fitted with ordnance while their motors run and their crews change.

None of the Nimitz class carriers has had a serious reactor or weapons magazine accident, and the last major deck fire (an accident most feared by carrier personnel) attributable to anything other than the cost of doing battle on any U.S. carrier was aboard USS *Enterprise* in 1969. The aircraft accident rate is also exemplary. In 1991 the Navy had 2.94 class A accidents (involving a fatality or property damage equal to or greater than $1,000,000) for every 100,000 flight hours (Navy Safety Center, personal communication).

As these three brief descriptions suggest, these complex organizations could offer ample opportunities for mishaps, loss of life, or at the extreme, widespread carnage. They operate safely, however, a fact not predicted by existing organizational theory.

RESEARCH APPROACH

A number of methodologies are employed by the project (Roberts and Rousseau, 1989). Much organizational research is conducted by researchers who go into organizations with preconceived notions about their processes, take either a static or dynamic short look at these processes, and return to the Ivory Tower to write about what they have seen and measured. Some researchers have never actually observed the organizations they write about. A good deal of the rest of organizational research takes existing data, usually collected for some other purposes, to test some preconceived notion about the processes these data should reflect.

Our research took a very different approach. Preconceived notions were kept to a minimum for reasons discussed below. During the first year of the work, quarterly workshops were held with managers in the initial three organizations in order to help us understand their challenges, to frame those challenges within the language of organizational research, and to work out with insiders approaches to the most productive data gathering. A considerable amount of time was devoted to gaining the trust of participants—people at all levels of the organizations—because such organizations are understandably extremely cautious about who they allow to observe them.

Paper and pencil and archival data were collected (e.g., Koch, this volume; Roberts, Rousseau, and La Porte, in press) and the researchers spent many months living in and otherwise gaining as much experience as possible with the organizations. Some of this in-depth organizational experience is represented in this volume (Rochlin and Schulman). Detailed knowledge of the organizations is also discussed elsewhere (e.g., La Porte and Consolini, 1991; Rochlin, La Porte, and Roberts, 1987; Roberts, 1990b, 1992).

The structures of these organizations are difficult for the uninitiated to understand, and because of this the team felt that we should begin the work with as few preconceived notions about their processes as possible: "A priori categories would have been unable to capture qualitative substantive revisions in groups. . . . Category systems may be used for specific hypothesis testing but are inappropriate for inductive discourse analysis in theory development (Gersick, 1988, p. 14)."

When reporting on the potential dangers and problems of such organizations, the press often decries the wrong issues precisely because it has preconceived notions about how they operate. Most organizations that are subject to research are relatively more open to laypeople and are accessible to lay comprehension. For example, we have all been in schools, banks, hospitals, and so on, and most of us think we understand how they work. Organizations that possess potentially hazardous aspects are much more difficult to comprehend, although that greater mystery does not deter often damaging oversimplification in the media. The public is insufficiently trained to understand what constitutes danger in such organizations and is generally loathe to think about potential risks. Likewise, the organizations want to be left alone due to vulnerability to negative public sentiment and to an often well-founded distrust of the uninitiated (researchers) who can "stand them into harm's way."

The carriers present a good example of the inadvisability of researchers carrying into the organization many preconceived notions about processes. For the neophyte, aircraft carriers are simply gigantic, strange, discombobulating, disorienting places. Nimitz class carriers are twenty-four story high organizations, comprised of 6000 men and 3360 compartments and spaces, in which every passageway looks like every other and in which it is initially impossible to find one's way from place A to place B. In addition to the disorientation caused by the physical plant, there is additional disorientation caused by the fact that many activities engaged in are potentially very dangerous; the environment is often extremely noisy; and evolutions of activities often happen very rapidly. Often more than one plane launches at any one time, and launches and recoveries frequently happen simultaneously.

Aviators and others with experience at sea aboard the carriers are obviously not confused by such operations. Over the years, their training is so extensive that the organization seems second nature to them. However, because the training required for this to happen is so intense and long, and because officers and enlisted men are not selected for their jobs based on their skills in articulating organizational processes, the processes and their meanings are difficult, and sometimes impossible, for participants to convey. In addition, most carrier personnel are trained in depth with regard to the skills required to do their jobs, rather than in breadth with broad knowledge about the whole organization. Only a few are trained to have the "big picture." Thus, the process of discovery requires extensive, lengthy interaction among researchers and operators if they are to develop the requisite trust and rapport with participants needed if the observers are to garner familiarity with the range of processes.

In addition to engaging in workshops with managers from the organizations, the Berkeley group became involved in similar activities with scholars from other universities. Their aim was to broaden their thinking about organizational processes that should be included in the research. Finally, we felt that yet other scholars' contributions to the organizational literature should raise for us concepts and issues that should be included in future research. Some of these scholars contributed to this compendium. They are as varied in background and approach to the study of organizations as is the Berkeley group.

THE BOOK

In the first paper from the Berkeley research project (Chapter 2), Rochlin deals directly with the problem of defining high reliability organizations (HROs) and setting forth characteristics that must exist if an organization is to be a member of that set. Many organizations have some of the characteristics Rochlin highlights; HROs must have them all. He points out that it is impossible to separate the physical–technical, social–organizational, and social–external aspects of these organizations for they are inextricably woven together. He describes why the phenomenon is something other than an expanded risk management scheme and points out that these innately risky technologies are effectively managed to the extent that the organization can control both hazard and probability of hazard. Finally, he states that managers seem to live easily with the paradoxes inherent in their organizations.

Schulman presents a dimensionalized model of reliability-seeking organizations. He describes decomposable and holistic systems as falling at opposite ends of the dimension of reliability. This model might be nicely contrasted with Meyer and Starbuck's contribution that focuses on political and structural underpinnings of organizational demise. Eisenhardt's notion of fast decision-making organizations offers another perspective from which to compare the organizations Schulman describes.

Creed, Stout, and Roberts focus on the metaphor of construct space, thus placing reliability squarely as a sector in effectiveness research. They comment that the main concern in a reliability-seeking organization is "avoidance of errors that can result in catastrophic consequences for its participants, and the surrounding population and environment." And they add to this the requirement to reduce errors of less consequences that can nevertheless contribute to more serious problems.

These authors point out that, above all else, high reliability organizations try to avoid ineffectiveness which is more clearly understood in them than is effectiveness. "Reliability is a value oriented against 'ineffectiveness' rather than toward effectiveness and as such enjoys no equilibrium state—no stopping rules" (see also Rochlin and Schulman, this volume). These authors call our attention to the need to think about the dynamic simultaneous evolution of technology, culture, and effectiveness.

Koch focuses specifically on the safety aspect of reliability. She presents the development of a valid and reliable static measure of safety consisting of a number of subscales. She discusses the meanings of her subscales as consistent with other findings from the Berkeley work and from other research. She states that the scales represent cultural norms to which members of high reliability organizations must adhere. Koch and Bea and Moore offer the most technical and applied approaches in this volume.

The remaining seven papers in this volume present additional ideas drawn from other research and observation. They each focus on different issues. They are not meant to present a logical unfolding of issues but rather are as diverse a set of ideas as could be found. The goal was to bring forth issues from the Berkeley work that might be provocative in other contexts and to bring to the Berkeley work concepts, issues, and concerns raised in those other contexts.

Meyer and Starbuck tell a story about the impact of ideology on behavior, and the near impossibility of changing that ideology in the face of changing environmental conditions. HROs are also based on strong ideologies. The authors discuss the origins of ideologies and show that as the ideologies grow they become more tightly integrated, making the process of change even more difficult. Ideologies develop both auras of objectivity and specific languages for their expression. These authors point out that visualizing strategic reorientation is always difficult because of the uncertainty about what will result. This would be particularly difficult in organizations for which strategic reorientation may be the last trial before the final error or catastrophe.

When the need for reorientation reaches a certain point, managers construct safeguards for their cherished ideologies. This phenomenon may be related to the continual development of procedures identified in HROs in which there are apparently no stopping rules. Meyer and Starbuck point out that modifying ideologies requires finding leaders who are capable of helping organizations change their stories, myths, sagas, symbols, and rituals. The difficulty of achieving this in any organization is apparent, and reification of reigning procedures is probably more characteristic of HROs than of other types of organizations. People in them are frightened that change will result in destabilization (see also Hirschhorn). The first story one hears upon entering an air traffic control center is about President Reagan's firing of the controllers *in 1980*. Meyer and Starbuck conclude with lessons learned, not the least of which is that success and failure have the same roots.

Eisenhardt focuses on protean and volatile environmental characteristics rather than on technology as the source of uncertainty in milieus requiring fast decision making. Like much of the high reliability work, her research is inductive; again the existing literature offers little precedence as guidance. Her work suggests that research in high reliability organizations should attempt to characterize better the environments in which those organizations operate. Meyer and Starbuck's tale of organizational demise suggests the same thing. Both of these perspectives recall the notion of organizations as requisite variety suggested by Weick (1987). Eisenhardt focuses on real time activities, constant environmental assessment, the distribution of accountability, and the use of a great deal of information in successful organizations. Research in high reliability organizations finds the same factors (Roberts, Stout, and Halpern, in press).

While in Eisenhardt's organizations strategic decisions are not made in matters of minutes and seconds as is often the case in operational decisions in high reliability organizations, an implicit suggestion from the Eisenhardt work is that strategic decision making be a new focus in high reliability research. Eisenhardt notes the use of redundancy through the availability of multiple decision alternatives and the integration of a number of decisions in fast-decision organizations. Redundancy is a key factor in high performance in reliability-enhancing organizations (Roberts, 1990a, b). She notes three similarities among the two kinds of organizations: job specialization, thick webs of communication, and a balance of centralization and decentralization.

Hirschhorn discusses conflicting, often inappropriate, and certainly dysfunctional procedures and structures for workers at the Ocean Reactor nuclear power plant. Here, checks and balances replace unity of command, rules replace roles, and politics undermines team work. This is in stark contrast to Schulman's findings in a similar work situation. Hirschhorn's plant could easily have profited from developing the kind of communication glue Eisenhardt discusses in her evaluation of high performance organizations. Creed, Stout, and Roberts note that the technology of HROs demands minimization of political activity if they are to obtain their performance goals. Here is an example of politics interfering with those goals.

Hirschhorn presents a four-part model of organizational success that is consistent with the Berkeley findings: (1) the organization is hierarchical in structure; (2) delegation is broad and deep; (3) management develops guiding and detailed procedures; and (4) emergency procedures integrate these two classes of procedure. Hirschhorn's nuclear power plant has much to learn from Schulman's.

The next two papers take a more micro perspective of organizational life than any of the preceding papers except for Koch's. Foushee and Lauber discuss an interesting experiment that began with one goal and ended up with another. They were interested in the impact of fatigue on flight crew performance. After they began the experiment they suspected that crew familiarity might be a positive override to fatigue in predicting crew performance. Their results support this hypothesis.

Foushee and Lauber's experimental findings are consistent with the various communication and trust outcroppings that appear in Koch's safety scales. The HRO researchers discuss the importance of trust that must operate in their organizations (as do many other researchers, e.g., Fulk and Mani, 1986). Foushee and Lauber identify one underpinning to the development of trust (crew familiarity). Schulman also discusses the necessity of constantly renewing trust: "Credibility and trust are perishable properties in any organization. They have to be continually nurtured and renewed if they are to survive. . . . Every day is a new day in interrelationships and in holding on to trust. It never gets institutionalized." Eisenhardt, too, uncovers the importance of trust in her findings about the use of counselors by top decision makers in fast-decision organizations.

Weick discusses the Tenerife air disaster in which a KLM and a Pan Am 747 collided resulting in the loss of 583 lives. He identifies as culprits the interruption of important routines between and within interdependent systems; interdependencies that became increasingly tight over time; loss of cognitive efficiency; and communication breakdown. A rapid diffusion of multiple errors created a feedback loop that magnified minor errors into major problems. Bea and Moore might have been able to tease out of their case studies many of the same culprits.

Weick provides some practical implications that can be applied to many of the discussions in this volume. First is the necessity for talk and a culture that values talk. All the other authors in the book allude to this factor in one way or another. Second is the cultivation of interpersonal skills, a factor that would surely have helped in the situation described by Hirschhorn or in any of Bea and Moore's cases. Third is that stress is additive and that workers should be alert to it in themselves and others. Fourth is that controllability is important and is created by a generous distribution of discretion throughout the system. Hirschhorn, Schulman, and Meyer and Starbuck would applaud this recommendation. Finally, organizations should treat chaos as a resource and should reframe crises into opportunities to demonstrate and reaffirm competence. While not discussed by any of the authors, HROs use simulation to play this out.

Bea and Moore present an applied research program, and thus come full circle from the earlier papers. Most organizations are designed and some are even operated by people coming more from the tradition these researchers come from than from psychological-sociological-political science traditions (Perrow, 1983). It is interesting that Rochlin, the physicist, presents the first and most theoretical of papers, while Bea and Moore, the engineers, present one of the last and most applied of the papers.

Probabilistic risk assessment (PRA) is the underlying tool in Bea and Moore's research. PRA is applied to the problem of attempting to reduce offshore (tanker and platform) accidents. Bea and Moore's research program focuses on five tasks and includes the development of extensive case histories. Included here are cases based on three platform accidents that illustrate how most marine accidents can be attributed to compounded human and organizational error (HOE). Bea and Moore's categories of types of errors are interesting in that these categories provide a vehicle for comparing the kinds of errors we see in reliability-enhancing organizations and elsewhere.

Event tree modeling (a form of PRA) is used to identify the overall failure probability of a system. Three steps are involved. The first phase identifies key subsystems and the elements of their reliability. The second phase analyzes the process of identifying potential problems and their probabilities for each subsystem. The third phase analyzes organizational procedures and incentives to determine their influence on the occurrence of error, and the probability that they are observed, recognized, communicated, and corrected in time. Bea and Moore apply their model to the installation of an emergency shut down valve in an existing pipeline. While Bea and Moore provide a general model, the specifics uncovered in the other papers in the book might be fed into such a map to provide a finer-grained network of understanding.

Finally, Roberts and Moore present one of the case studies developed as a basis for PRA analysis, an analysis of the Exxon Valdez accident. This paper examines the activities of Exxon Shipping Company, the Coast Guard, and the Alaska state pilot that are relevant to the spill. Over the years the organizations that should have been responsible atrophied. It is also a story of failure to institutionalize appropriate training, reward, and control systems in a situation in which safety should have been paramount. The analysis is similar to Weick's analysis in that here the breakdown of appropriate interdependence among organizations tasked to insure safe activities is clearly shown.

In the Exxon Valdez situation, none of the factors discussed as important in HROs were attended to. Effectiveness is thought about almost entirely in terms of revenue rather than in terms of avoiding ineffectiveness. Rules and procedures only vaguely guided behavior in a situation very much like the disagreeable situation Schulman discusses.

Together the eleven chapters in this volume raise many issues. These issues are important in describing and understanding the intricacies of complex organizations in which behaviors can have catastrophic consequences, and in organizations that may not be quite as subject to catastrophic self-destruction (Meyer and Starbuck, Eisenhardt). This book should suggest additional, intriguing questions for researchers and should raise managers' awareness of various factors they should monitor to prevent failure in their organizations.

REFERENCES

Fulk, J., and Mani, S. (1986). "Distortion of communication in hierarchical relationships." In McLaughlin, M.L., ed., *Communication Yearbook 9*. Newbury Park, CA: Sage; 483–509.

Gersick, C. J. G. (1988). "Time and transition in work teams: Toward a new model of group development." *Academy of Management Journal*, 31, 9–41.

La Porte, T. R., and Consolini, P. M. (1991). "Working in theory but not in practice: Theoretical challenges of high reliability organizations." *Journal of Public Administration Research and Theory*, 1, 19–47.

Perrow, C. (1983). "The organizational context of human factors engineering." *Administrative Science Quarterly*, 28, 521–541.

Roberts, K. H. (1990a). "Some characteristics of high reliability organizations." *Organization Science*, 1, 160–177.

———. (1990b). "Managing hazardous organizations." *California Management Review*, 32, 101–113.

———. (1992). "Structuring to facilitate migrating decisions in reliability enhancing organizations." In Gomez-Mehia, L. and M. W. Lawless, eds., *Top Management and Executive Leadership in High Technology: Advances in Global Technology Management*, 2. Greenwich, CT: JAI Press, 171–191.

Roberts, K. H., and Rousseau, D. M. (1989). "Research in nearly failure-free, high reliability systems." *IEEE Transactions*, 36, 132–139.

Roberts, K. H., Rousseau, D. M., and La Porte, T. R. (in press). "The culture of high reliability: Quantitative and qualitative assessment aboard nuclear powered aircraft carriers." *Journal of High Technology Management Research*.

Roberts, K. H., Stout, S., and Halpern, J. J. (in press). "Decision dynamics in two high reliability military organizations." *Management Science*.

Rochlin, G. I., La Porte, T. R., and Roberts, K. H. (1987). "The self-designing high-reliability organization: Aircraft carrier flight operations at sea." *Naval War College Review*, 40, 76–90.

U.S. Department of Transportation (1991). *Federal Aviation Administration Administrator's Handbook*.

Weick, K. E. (1987). "Organizational culture as a source of high reliability." *California Management Review*, 29, 112–127.

2

Defining "High Reliability" Organizations in Practice: A Taxonomic Prologue

GENE I. ROCHLIN
University of California, Berkeley

Gene I. Rochlin is Professor of Energy and Resources and Research Policy Analyst at the Institute of Governmental Studies, University of California, Berkeley. His research interests center on large-scale sociotechnical systems. His recent research interests, in addition to high reliability organizations, include cross-national studies of power plant organization and management; electrical and other energy systems and their relation to global environmental problems; the use and abuse of information and computer technologies in large technical organizations; the proliferation of nuclear weapons; and the use and control of both nuclear and conventional weapons systems.

Professor Rochlin has been the recipient of a John Simon Guggenheim Memorial Foundation Fellowship and a John D. and Catherine T. MacArthur Foundation Individual Fellowship for Research and Writing in International Security. He is a Fellow of the American Physical Society. Professor Rochlin's published works include *Plutonium, Power and Politics: International Arrangements for the Disposition of Spent Nuclear Fuel* (University of California Press, 1979), *Science, Technology, and Social Change* (W. H. Freeman & Co., 1974), and numerous articles, chapters, book reviews, and editorial works.

> . . . *the capacity of the human mind for formulating and solving*
> *complex problems is very small compared with the size of those*
> *problems whose solution is required for objectively rational behav-*
> *ior in the real world . . . or even for a reasonable approximation to*
> *such reality . . . Herbert Simon*[1]

Were the literature not replete with alternative definitions of effectiveness (Cameron, 1983; Vance, 1989; Scott, 1992, Chapter 13) the organizations in the Berkeley research project might best be characterized as "highly effective" in their delivery of the social and technical goods they produce.

More reflective of the dynamic by which they constantly seek to improve reliability and intervene to prevent organizational errors or failures, they might also be characterized as "demanding of perfection"—perfection in their understanding of the technology in detail and as a system; perfection in their ability to perform individual tasks; and perfection in their ability to monitor, detect, prevent, and anticipate operational and systemic errors and failures. From the perspective of performance as an activity, rather than as a static measurable variable, these organizations might be characterized as "reliability-seeking," whereas from the point of view of the public they might instead be labeled as "reliability-enhancing." The ambiguity of language and multiplicity of viewpoints are, of course, phenomenological and contingent; the problem of using static descriptors for a fundamentally dynamic set of properties, activities, and responses is not.

The organizations have nevertheless come to be labeled as *high reliability organizations* (HROs) both in our own writings (e.g., Rochlin, La Porte, and Roberts, 1987; La Porte, 1988; Roberts and Gargano, 1990) and those of others (e.g., Eisenhardt, this volume; Weick, 1987). In retrospect, this choice of compact, acronymic terminology was both necessary and unfortunate. Necessary because some label is needed to identify organizations which, as is argued below, are indeed clearly distinguishable from those that have been the subject of most historical study and analysis in the organizational literature. Unfortunate because the term implies that our evaluation is based on some absolute, and static, standard of performance rather than on a relative evaluation of the dynamic management of a difficult and demanding technology in a critical and unforgiving social and political environment.

This threatens to create an interpretive problem that is as much epistemological and ontological as terminological. For this reason, more than usual care must be exercised both in using the label for the organizations under study and in applying it to other organizations and phenomena that appear to be similar until one can be quite certain that they are members of the same organizational subset.

While Schulman (this volume) addresses differentiation within a set of

---

[1] From: *Models of Man, Social and Rational: Mathematical Essays on Rational Human Behavior in Social Settings*, New York: Wiley, 1957, p. 198.

high reliability organizations, Koch (this volume) begins to think about how one might differentiate and compare reliability-enhancing and non-reliability-enhancing organizations. Eisenhardt (this volume) points to some similarities between her fast-decision organizations and the organizations in the Berkeley project. Thus, the issue of comparability among "high reliability" and other organizations is improving over time.

Given the present social trend toward the development and deployment of ever-more complex technologies; increasing perceptions of the nature and extent of social, personal, and environmental hazards; and a persistent tendency to increase the size, scope, and integration of plant operations (which increases both hazard and complexity), it would be easy, based on the present literature, to despair of our future ability to control and manage the risks entailed. The literature is replete with stories of high-technology "failures" (e.g., Three-Mile Island, Bhopal, Chernobyl, *Challenger*). They make up the larger portion of extant case studies and analyses of near or actual catastrophes and "man-made disasters" (e.g., Hirschhorn and Weick, this volume).

The three organizations in the Berkeley project are similar to those described in the "failure" literature—yet to date they have not failed. While the present study does not and cannot present recipes for designing organizations in such a way that they can operate safely and reliably, it does at least address some criteria which, if not present in an organization's form or design, make it unlikely that it will in fact perform at a high level over long periods of time.

PROBLEMS OF DEFINITION

The study of organizations that succeed in meeting these manifold challenges poses a prior threefold analytic problem:

○ The organizations studied must be defined with sufficient precision to allow for disciplinary rigor in developing descriptive and theoretical models.

○ The definition must be sufficiently unambiguous to avoid confusion between these organizations and others that are either similar on the surface or have been assigned similar labels for other reasons.

○ An analytic framework must be constructed through which empirical observations can be used to construct theoretically sustainable explanations of how these organizations are able to operate at the observed levels of performance when so many others in our society, given similar tasks, have failed.

In order to follow the preceding agenda, it is necessary to identify those factors that distinguish the organizations analyzed here from the more conventional ones addressed in most of the organizational literature. Among the characteristics we have noted to date are:

1. They manage technologies that are increasingly complex, requiring specialized knowledge, specialized management, and a variety of esoteric skills at the operational level.

2. The public consequences of technical error in operations have the potential for sufficient harm such that continued success (and possibly even continued organizational survival) depends on maintaining a high level of performance reliability and safety through intervention and management (i.e., it cannot be made to inhere in the technology).

3. Public perception of these consequences imposes on the organizations a degree of formal or informal oversight that might well be characterized as intrusive, if not actually comprehensive.

The second-order effect of the preceding points imposes on management a complex role in which it must balance internal and external demands for safety not only against internal capacity, but also against external demands for responsiveness and reliability in the delivery of timely services. To operate at all well under these conditions requires a degree of internal organizational complexity that itself is an observational indicator of their differentiation from other organizations (Perrow, 1986; Mohrman and Von Glinow, 1990; Demchak, 1992). The benchmark for doing better than "just operating well" must be set by the "expected" failure rate as well as the degree of potential risk—and both risks and expectations are a moving target.

Our organizations are therefore also distinguished by a set of dynamic indicators that span far more than static indicators can measure.

○ While they perform at very high levels, their personnel are never content, but search continually to improve their operations.

○ They set goals beyond the boundaries of present performance, while seeking actively to avoid testing the boundaries of error.

○ Their search for performance and suspicion of quiet periods continually regenerates operational challenges even during times when things seem to be working quite well.

Although much of what we see is covered piecemeal by one existing study or another, the central integrative features of these organizations are not well covered by existing organizational literature (see, for example, Perrow, 1986; Scott, 1987; La Porte and Consolini, 1991). Much of it does not address matters of safety and reliability at all or treats them as exogenous, marginal, or essentially fungible characteristics.

The study of organizational failures or organization-induced disasters (e.g., Perrow, 1984; Turner, 1978; Shrivastava, 1987; Romzek and Dubnick, 1987; Reason 1988; Vaughan, 1990; Medvedev, 1991) is of considerable use, particularly in enabling us to screen out factors common to the "successful" organizations under study. But it complements the research described here and does not subsume it. Our central purpose is to identify and characterize both static and dynamic characteristics of organizations that have not just "avoided" failure through good fortune or the vagaries of probability, but actively who have managed to control and reduce the risks of technical operations whose inherent hazards make them prone to join the list of classical failures. In other words, these organizations have not just failed to fail; they have actively managed to avoid failures in an environment rich with the potential for error.

HOW ARE OUR ORGANIZATIONS TO BE CHARACTERIZED?

An external, quasi-public definition of organizational "success" is the acceptance and acknowledgment by the public, and by regulators or other social overseers, that the organization in question performs its assigned tasks effectively, efficiently, and reliably while adequately protecting public and worker health and safety.

In these terms, the organizations in the Berkeley project are rare exemplars of large, complex organizations that successfully manage and/or operate and/or directly control advanced technological activities or services that meet three defining criteria:

1. The activity or service is inherently complex, in that tasks are numerous, differentiated, and interdependent (Thompson, 1967).

2. The activity or service meets certain social demands that require performance at the highest level of service obtainable within present safety requirements, with both a desire for an even higher level of activity and a penalty (explicit or implicit) if service slackens (La Porte and Consolini, 1991; Roberts and Gargano, 1990).

3. The activity or service contains inherent technological hazards in case of error or failure that are manifold, varied, highly consequential, and relatively time-urgent, requiring constant, flexible, technology-intrusive management to provide an acceptable level of safety to operators, other personnel, and/or the public (Rochlin, La Porte, and Roberts, 1987).

As stipulated at the outset, the organization must not only meet service and safety goals simultaneously, but must also be perceived to have done so. Therefore:

> The activity or service cannot be provided at the required level of reliability of service and safety unless the managing and/or operating organization exhibits a high level of performance in both task and integration. If it does not, the activity or service will be judged to be inadequate and/or socially unacceptable (Vaughan, 1990).

There is one further, more inclusive categorical definition:

> It is impossible to separate physical-technical, social-organizational, and
> social-external aspects; the technology, the organization, and the social
> setting are woven together inseparably (La Porte, 1975; Perrow, 1986).

These defining criteria place certain boundaries on organizations that are
candidates to join the list of those the Berkeley group studied:

1. The organization is required to maintain high levels of operational
reliability and/or safety if it is to be allowed to continue to carry out its tasks (La
Porte and Consolini, 1991).

2. The organization is also required to maintain high levels of capability,
performance, and service to meet public and/or economic expectations and
requirements (Roberts, 1990a, b).

3. Because of the consequentiality of error or failure, the organization
cannot easily make marginal tradeoffs between capacity and safety. In a deep
sense, safety is not fungible (Schulman, this volume).

4. As a result, the organization is reluctant to allow primary-task related
learning to proceed by the usual modalities of trial-and-error for fear that the
first error will be the last trial (La Porte and Consolini, 1991).

5. Because of the complexity of both technology and task environment,
the organization must actively manage its activities and technologies in real
time, while maintaining capacity and flexibility to respond to events or circumstances that can at most be generally bounded (Roberts, 1990a, b).

6. The organization will be judged to have "failed"—either operationally
or socially—if it does not perform at high levels. Whether service or safety is
degraded, the degradation will be noted and criticized almost immediately
(Rochlin et al., 1987).

These organizations must therefore maximize their operational capacity
along at least three dimensions. First, and most obvious, is maximization along
the axis of safety (see Koch, this volume). Second, and necessary for delivery of
services, is maximization of performance along the axis of technology. Third,
and a consequence of a highly social nature of the service, is the need to
maximize perceptions of performance along a "political" axis scaled by sociopolitical criteria such as acceptance and reward (see Schulman, this volume).
The organizations under study firmly believe that the three criteria cannot be
traded off at the margin or elsewhere.[2]

A highly reliable organization is often defined as one that has already been
judged on empirical or observational grounds to provide a desirable activity,
product, or service at a desired or demanded level of performance while maintaining a very low rate of error or accident. However, since both reliability and

---

[2] Meyer and Starbuck in Chapter 6 provide a nice example of organizational collapse because of the
failure of appropriate political response. The lack of tradeoff among all three criteria differentiates
the organizations in the Berkeley study from theirs.

error rate are subjective criteria, and since neither specifically includes the type of activity in which the organization engages or the nature and frequency of the risks involved, many other organizations performing tasks that are essentially trivial, inherently low risk, or whose consequences develop so slowly that post-event hazards are easily managed, also tend to get lumped in. As a result, and despite our efforts, *high reliability* remains more an organizational bricolage than an analytically distinguishable category.

Because "high reliability" is generally defined by social and perceptual criteria, no truly objective measure is possible. From the utility's point of view, for example, an electrical grid would be considered *very* highly reliable if the failure rate were less than one part in ten thousand (.0001, or .9999 reliable); from the public's point of view this translates into power outage of about 50 minutes per year. Whether this is reliable or not depends upon whether the electrical service is for home lighting and cooking or for running a hospital; in anticipation, hospitals have backup power systems while most homes do not. Moreover, it may make a great difference to specific users whether the reliability is distributed as one long outage per year or a power loss for one minute every week.

To the extent that its service exceeds the level of adequacy, an organization may be rewarded for its performance. However, there is generally no reward for safety and reliability in excess of acceptable levels. Indeed, as a general rule, the expectations of consumer/users will "rachet" so that, over time, no net degradation from any previously achieved and sustained level is acceptable. Furthermore, the task environment is an actively hostile source of new error so that the organization perceives itself as facing increasing demands without the ability to control or diminish exogenous sources of error.

What distinguishes reliability-enhancing organizations is not their *absolute* error or accident rate, but their effective management of innately risky technologies through organizational control of both hazard and probability, thereby making possible the social exploitation of an activity or service whose social and/or human costs would otherwise be unacceptable at effective levels of performance. There is, therefore, no a priori way to evaluate where any given operational condition in the valuative space (that is, the mathematical or statistical performance of the organization) is relative to any theoretical optimal condition. Such an evaluation is inherently static, while both the performance and the valuation of the organizations in the Berkeley project constitute a continuous, interactive dynamic.

IS THE PHENOMENON NO MORE THAN AN ELABORATE RISK-MANAGEMENT REGIME?

In the risk-analysis literature, specific risk (risk per unit time) is defined as the sum of the products of individual hazards due to specific failures and/or errors, multiplied by the probability for each to occur in the specified time interval: that is,

$$\text{Specific risk} = \sum_i x_i p_i$$

where x_i are the severities (consequences) for individual events arising from equipment failures, and p_i are the probabilities *per unit of activity* that any given event will occur. However, where the possibility of anthropogenic error is significant (whether due to operator error, representational or systemic error, or to contextual errors, for example, failure to properly inspect a part), the equation needs to be expanded as:

$$\text{Specific risk} = \sum_{i,j} (x_i p_i + x_j p_j)$$

where x_j and p_j are the magnitude and probability of anthropogenic events.

In any risk-management regime, the assumption is that the overall risk of some activities, performed at the rate or level required or demanded by consumers, is too high to be acceptable to those same consumers (or their political agents). The organization must therefore act upon its own environment. Several strategies are available. The level or type of activity or service may simply be reduced to a level that the public finds acceptable, or it may be canceled or substituted for entirely; companies and agencies may intervene to try to redefine the acceptability criteria to allow the activity to continue; or technical remedies may be sought that redefine the technical activity itself in such a way as to considerably reduce either the hazard or its probabilities.

The questions of risk perception, risk acceptance, and the cultural, social, and political responses to both are too broad and too complex to analyze in this essay (see, for example, *Daedalus,* 1990). We note only that organizations cannot reduce risk by reducing external demand for services. Nor can they act to modify the sociopolitical environment in which they are situated. Therefore, their only choice is to seek to manage risk within the external framework in which both risk and demand are defined.

There is insufficient space here to summarize the extensive literature on probabilistic risk assessment, automation, and attempts at replacing human operators (and their presumed failings) with automated systems (see, for examples: Ralph, 1988; Dougherty, 1990). It is sufficient to say that the underlying assumptions are that inherent (physical-technical) and anthropogenic causes are both separable and fungible. The goal is often to engineer the system so that either (a) all possible anthropogenic sources of error, x_j, are small, or (b) discretion is removed and/or external (often technical) control and monitoring systems are added to drastically reduce the probability, p_j, that operator action can trigger error—barring extreme malfeasance or deliberate intent. Thus, only the "technical" and therefore presumably controllable sources of risk will remain.

This approach is not suitable or appropriate for the organizations in the Berkeley study. All of them assume they operate equipment whose complexity and inherent vulnerabilities are such that technical and/or physical failures will occur, regardless of engineering solutions or methods applied. The role of the operators is not just to operate the equipment, but actively to seek to anticipate, detect, and correct technical failures as they occur. The undetected malfunction of some part (e.g., a bolt in an aircraft landing gear) is therefore seen not as an equipment error but as a *systemic* failure. Technical and anthropogenic causes merge.

These organizations attempt to reduce the x_i and x_j as much as possible. But they further assume that their central strategy must be to organize around deliberate and systematic search for and control of both the p_i *and* the p_j. Risk is seen not as a set of passive probabilities to be coped with or restructured, but as an operational variable whose coefficients must be dynamically managed. The underlying belief, and the foundation of organizational reliability, is that only through its own performance and behavior can the organization control the coefficients; that it can continue to operate only if both the probabilities and, to some extent, the risks themselves are effectively managed and controlled through its own training, skills, and error-detection and correction mechanisms (Rochlin et al., 1987). The alternative is probably the external imposition of intrusive regulation or increasingly stringent operational requirements, both of which are seen by our organizations as having a decidedly negative impact on safety (see Hirschhorn, this volume).

WHY IS TECHNOLOGY CENTRAL TO OUR CHARACTERIZATION?

The triple whammies of technological complexity—high potential consequence, tight functional coupling, and potentially rapid evolution of untoward events— are all part of the defining technical environment. Technological complexity is a determining factor because an organization created to manage or oversee a single, defining activity can be sufficiently narrow in scope and purpose, and can be sufficiently stable over time, that the process and results of trial-and-error learning can be recast as fairly rigid organizational forms. Historical examples include boiler safety (a case of historical importance) and vehicle safety inspection.

High potential consequence is central, since without it the degree of risk remains low even if the probabilities are not effectively controlled. If consequences are low, the organization can afford to experiment with management techniques, seeking to minimize probabilities through a variety of strategies for testing at the margin. It can also afford to attempt to manage risk on the margin since the consequences of strategic error are most likely small and containable—and can be written off as part of the cost of acquiring knowledge.

Tight functional coupling and rapid evolution of events are also central since they prevent or preclude the development of event-containment mechanisms as an insurance policy. When errors propagate slowly or impacts develop only over long periods of time, effective containment mechanisms can make the effective cost of experimentation or error low. When they propagate rapidly, each individual organizational failure or error is irreversible and consequential, making it difficult, if not impossible, to shift to trial-and-error as a primary mode of individual and organizational learning.

For most of the functional service activities performed by the organizations under study by the Berkeley "HRO" group, tight coupling and rapidity of error propagation is matched by technical demands for quick and accurate response both for the provision of service *and* for the preservation of safety. Both assigned missions and operational "surprises" consist of rapid and complex sequences and superpositions of events that require not only organizational response, but often an "on-the-fly" organizational reconfiguration to meet contingencies (Rochlin, 1989).

However, it should be noted that the notion of what constitutes "rapid" and, therefore, what defines "tightness" of functional coupling varies widely both within and among organizations. For air traffic controllers, margins of performance, or of error, may be measured in minutes, or tens of seconds; for carrier flight operations, perhaps seconds; for grid management, many minutes. The definition of "rapid" is an event that unfolds in a time comparable to or shorter than the ability of the system (organization plus operators plus technology) to respond to even if the problem is clearly and correctly identified. Thus, a large ship headed for a rock may be known by all to be on a physically "inevitable" path for collision many minutes before the disaster occurs. The fact that the operators know what is about to happen does not empower them to change the outcome (Roberts, in press).

The physical and operational characteristics of the kinds of technologies being managed determines the time frame and imposes real constraints on operators and managers—just as they define and shape the nature of the hazards involved and the risks that might be entailed. Events, event chains, and consequences have a certain technical core that can neither be ignored nor argued away. Few if any potentially risky activities that do not involve complex, quite advanced, technologies meet these criteria. Therefore, the organizations managing them, however well they perform, do not fit our category. They have a degree of flexibility in response and elasticity in a crisis that make the stringent conditions of our "perfection-demanding" organizations unnecessary, and perhaps inefficient.

CAN CASES BE IDENTIFIED AND DEFINED BY INDEPENDENT OBSERVATION?

If we are to avoid the haphazard application of labels such as *reliability* or *effectiveness* to any and all organizations that would like to be nominated, we must demonstrate that the class of organizations to be included can be defined unambiguously. From our work, and the preceding discussion, there emerge three relatively compact yet major distinguishing *static* empirical descriptors that at least bound the definitional region in which we are interested—one external and two internal to the organizations.

The first is primarily observational and judgmental, social rather than technical in nature:

> The organization must be judged to be not only effective, but "successful,"
> in the sense that it performs with high levels of capacity and safety, both by
> its own criteria and by those of outside regulators and the public.

This first criterion sums over the three dimensions of performance; sociopolitical, technical, and safety. However, due to the difficulty of determining "how much" of each set of criteria is "enough," let alone represents excellence, the criterion is highly dependent upon both the nature of the organization under study and the nature and difficulty of its task.[3] That an organization performing critical tasks with high-hazard technology "survives" is not quite enough, since accidents may be avoided by pure luck or may be neglected or overlooked by historical circumstance. Unless the organization in question performs its tasks in a socially and politically critical environment of adequate scrutiny, it has simply not been tested. The chemical industry, for example, is only now just beginning to be held accountable to the standards commonly applied to air traffic control or the nuclear power industry (Meshkati, 1992).

The other two static criteria are more susceptible to direct organizational analysis:

> Exogenously, the technology must be sufficiently complex and demanding
> so that relatively simple technical and organizational fixes will not suf-
> fice—the technology must be such that the organization has to intervene
> actively.

This criterion excludes passively successful organizations, such as telecommunications, and passive or accepting rather than questing organizational strategies, such as "garbage cans" (March and Olsen, 1976). For technologies that are relatively simple, or relatively free of major hazard, active and directed management of risk is not required.

> Endogenously, the notion of safe and reliable operation and management
> must have become so deeply integrated into the culture of the organization
> that delivery of services and promulgation of safety are held equally as in-
> ternal goals and objectives: neither can be separated out and "marginalized"
> as subordinate to the other, either in normal operation or in emergencies
> (Roberts, Rousseau, and La Porte, in press; Schulman, this volume).

This criterion excludes organizations whose technology or environment is such that the limits of performance can be tested on the margin and adjusted

---

[3] Schulman in Chapter 3 addresses the problem of "how much is enough."

by a feedback process to gain or maintain acceptance—for example, the U.S. railroad industry, which has a long record of marginalizing safety and making changes only in reaction to manifest failures or unusually serious accidents (see also Bea and Moore, this volume). Such industries generally operate reasonably simple or straightforward technologies, and present hazards that the public usually considers to be self-limiting in space and time. There are no organizations that present the complex and consequential demands sketched here, but that operate successfully and credibly without internalizing the goals of safety and reliability.

As described later by Koch and by Creed (this volume), the internalization of the twin goals of safety and reliability is difficult to measure through static observables. Nor is it created through rhetorical exhortation or symbolic, but contextless, management slogans ("Quality is Job One."). Evaluation depends on a field interpretation of the in-context actions and interactions of operators, managers, and administrators. Thus, from the three static descriptors, we generate a further condition in the form of a hypothesis about the organizational dynamic that matches well our empirical observations:

> In the described context, reliability arises from and is defined in terms of an interactive dynamic of management, intervention, anticipation, and surveillance.

Furthermore, based upon our empirical work:

> The processes for pursuing safety and reliability are often more important to the organization's success than the forms in which they are encapsulated.

Based on our observations, these dynamic conditions are necessary. But they cannot be demonstrated as sufficient unless at least one failed organization operating under the specified conditions with internalized reliability can be identified. Moreover, it must also be shown that the reasons for failure did not arise from exogenous factors outside the organization's possible range of control (e.g., through an "act of God" or a technical failure in an area of design or implementation not within its power to identify or correct). Proof of sufficiency seems elusive: It is in the nature of logical proof that no accretion of lists of successful organizations can constitute *deductive* proof of sufficiency, so the question of whether other conditions are also necessary remains open.

WHAT RELEVANT CHARACTERISTICS HAVE WE OBSERVED?

As is clear from the preceding discussion, the organizations studied by the Berkeley group cannot easily be characterized by static descriptors. The locus of reliability is in the dynamic of execution and the mobilization of organizational resources more than in any snapshot of organizational form. For this reason, the characteristics described below were determined by extensive, interactive field work. Continual involvement with the organization and its tasks is necessary if one is to understand it well enough to ascertain its internal dynamics. In this sense we are like traditional cultural anthropologists, sharing both the demanding analytic requirements and the professional cautions and caveats that have been so well characterized in that domain (see also Roberts and Rousseau, 1989; Edgren, 1989; Van Maanen, 1988).

Based on our research to date, it is nonetheless possible to list some of the organizational characteristics (intervening variables) that set these organizations apart while setting aside for the moment the more profound questions of whether they are independent of one another or the degree to which any individual characteristic may be required—independently or in combination with some other.

1. An *ab initio* assumption that errors are omnipresent and insidious and that eternal vigilance is the price of success.

2. A parallel assumption that the sources of error are dynamic, not static, so that the monitoring mechanisms themselves must be constantly renewed and re-invigorated.

3. As a result, the operational assumption that the operating environment is a constant source of threat, requiring constant vigilance, even (and especially) at times when things seem to be going well.

4. Maintenance of redundant modes of problem solving at the operational level, and resistance to pressure to resolve or "rationalize" the process by adopting a single "best" approach.

5. The creation, maintenance, and exercise of multiple simultaneous informal organizational structures adapted to contingencies (structural variation according to the nature of the problem) (Rochlin, 1989; Roberts, 1992).

6. An organizational commitment to anticipatory as well as reactive modes of dealing with real and potential problems.

7. A relative empowerment of organizational units dedicated to searching for incipient or latent error (Reason, 1989).

8. The inability or unwillingness to test the boundaries of reliability (which means that trial-and-error learning modes become secondary and contingent, rather than primary) (Schulman, this volume).

9. The absence of "stopping rules" for self-improvement and self-regulation, as long as organizational resources and time remain available, so that additional information is always cost-effective at the margin as a means of controlling and bounding uncertainties (Schulman, this volume).

10. A particular kind of obeisance to formal regulations and codes ("going

by the book")—extended with accepted standard operating procedures (SOPs) based on tradition.

11. Acceptance of the proposition that even if a complete formal history
    and analysis were available, the task of actively maintaining perfor-
    mance and searching for error would only be simplified, and not
    removed or reduced in importance.

In short, these organizations seek an ideal of perfection but never expect
to achieve it. They demand complete safety but never expect it. They dread
surprise but always anticipate it. They deliver reliability but never take it for
granted. They live by the book but are unwilling to die by it. If these beliefs
seem wonderfully contradictory, those who express them are under no particular pressure to rationalize their paradoxes; indeed, they seem actively to resist
such rationalization (see also Roberts, Creed, and Stout, this volume). We
often hear the whole spectrum expressed by a single individual over the course
of an interview or series of discussions.

This lack of goal rationalization extends to the organizational as well as the
individual level. The observed deliberate, and often self-conscious, effort to
create and maintain multiple modes of decision making and duplicative error-
searching regimes, and to hold differing perspectives and rank-ordering of
preferences by different groups is a manifestation of collective organizational
response rather than individual behavior. Such representational ambiguity is
implicitly (and sometimes explicitly) acknowledged and accepted by the organization, not just as part of the cost of maintaining performance levels, but as
an active contributor to problem solving.

RELATION OF OUR STUDY TO EXISTING LITERATURE(S) ON ORGANIZATIONAL FAILURES

Most of the extant literature on complex organizations managing complex,
high-hazard technologies tends to focus on questions of organizational failure—
where failure may be defined either in terms of compromising public safety, or
of declining levels of performance, as a necessary price of continuing to be
allowed to operate (see, for example, Bea and Moore; Hirschhorn; Meyer and
Starbuck; Weick: all this volume). The first type of failure represents an immediate threat to the organization, the more so to the extent that its charter is
predicated on protecting the public. The Chernobyl disaster is a classic, if not
totally unique, example. The second type represents an equally potent threat
to the extent that the organization's charter is predicated on the delivery of
necessary services. The *Challenger* disaster is perhaps the classic example.
NASA did not compromise or threaten *public* safety but was nevertheless
constrained thereafter to operate at much lower operational levels until the
public (and the government) could be persuaded of its operational safety
(Romzek and Dubnick, 1987).

In general, the extant case studies refer to organizations that can be categorized as follows:

○ Those that failed to adapt to changing technology, and retained traditional modes of decision making (Meyer and Starbuck, this volume; Shrivastava, 1987; Reason, 1989).

○ Those that adapted too rigidly or shifted over too rapidly from traditional to "modern" (engineering-oriented) modes while casting off their experiential base. (Examples, rarely analyzed in the literature, include the General Electric nuclear fuel reprocessing plant in Tennessee, which was closed down on safety grounds before it even opened; and the Rancho Seco nuclear reactor in California, which was shut down after a few years of operation. See also Bea and Moore, this volume).

○ Those that failed to understand how changes in mission or organizational goals could undermine or render ineffective previous mechanisms for error control (NASA, especially in the case of the *Challenger*—see, for example, Romzek and Dubnick, 1987).

○ Those that adopted the rhetoric of reliability but never really understood the implications of following through (Chernobyl, Three-Mile Island).

○ Those that simply failed, either because they neglected reliability or because they underestimated impact or consequence (the Exxon Valdez—Reason [1989] and Turner [1978] cite many such cases in their extensive work).

The question then arises: Given that a failure occurred or was perceived to have occurred, at what conceptual and systemic level did it take place? Systemic parsing is straightforward; errors and/or failures can occur at the individual level, at the group level, or at the administrative/managerial level. In traditional analysis, the central problematique is the determination of error. Current literature and most newspaper or media reports of accidents or disasters have asked who caused the event, and what were the underlying causes (poor training; impaired judgment; tension; and so forth).

Conceptual parsing is more difficult and is rarely performed in the constant search to treat errors as moral lapses and to seek to place the blame. Weick (1991) points out the need to carefully distinguish *errors* from *mistakes*: "An 'error' occurs when a person strays from a guide or a prescribed course of action, through inadvertence, and is blameworthy, whereas a 'mistake' occurs when there is a misconception, misidentification, or misunderstanding." Errors, in this lexicon, are lapses in judgment or performance in a decision environment rich in time and low in ambiguity. Mistakes arise from specific, individual judgments made in a context in which the information was presented poorly, or in such a way as to preclude the operator from exercising informed, expert judgment in the time, or with the information, available.

Turner (1978) adds a third category in his studies of "man-made disasters." In his lexicon, "disaster equals energy plus misinformation." That is, since organizations are by nature "negentropic"—designed to order, structure, and manipulate their environments—when information is faulty the very processes of assembling energy and information to achieve a desired goal or perform an action can result in a very good organization organizing to produce a very bad effect (Schulman, 1980). In general, Turner argues, organizations are more susceptible to such effects when a large, complex problem is dealt with piecemeal by different units or sub-units, even when they belong to the same organization or organizational unit—very much like the "resident pathogens" proposed by James Reason (1989).

Moreover, for each of these categories, one may also follow Landau's (1973) argument that organizations are primarily seekers of knowledge—constantly constructing hypotheses about themselves, their tasks, and their environments. Errors (or mistakes, or faulty constructs) are the result of disjuncture between hypothesis and reality; they may be either Type I (rejection of a true hypothesis) or Type II (acceptance of a false one). The resulting typology is admittedly quite complex (Rochlin, 1991), yet there remains some common factors.

Whichever model is applicable, in almost every case of failure the organization(s) seem to have been "surprised" by the outcome. Their anticipation was that their hypotheses were sound, their operations safe, and/or their operators and managers capable of detecting and correcting in time any errors or deviations that might be detected. Moreover, in some of these events (most notably Bhopal and Chernobyl) complacency about safe operations and equipment reliability was a major contributing factor in turning an accident into a disaster (Meshkati, 1992; Medvedev, 1991).

ARE "HROs" DIFFERENT?

While it might be convenient to reconstruct a typology or taxonomy of organizational "successes" to parallel the rather exhaustive existing classifications of failures, such an exercise is fruitless. Success is usually multiply-determined, and causal factors overlap and interact. Every actor, and every analyst, seeks to assert the validity and importance of his or her own approach or contribution. It is difficult even to determine or count the number of times the organizations in the Berkeley study could have failed but did not. It is necessary, therefore, to go beyond the matter of whether failures occurred and consider the strategies by which highly reliable organizations comprehend the nature of their risk environment.

These organizations differ from those analyzed in most of the literature on hazard, risk, and organizational failure in their explicit or tacit understanding that organizational failures can be the result not only of individual shortcomings or faults but also of mistaken representation (Weick, this volume) or well-guided but misinformed actions, at the individual, group, or organizational level.

They seem to have designed their operations around the idea that their task environments present a continual, active threat to safety, that errors are imminent, and that they must scan constantly to monitor incipient error. Surprises are expected; the absence of any surprise over a long period of time creates not a feeling of complacency but of anxiety that their error-seeking mechanisms are decaying. Moreover, for each of the organizations we studied, there is at least one mechanism for intertask and intergroup coordination to prevent the sort of fragmentation of information analyzed by Turner. When the task environment is most complex, the organization may even develop a whole repertoire of coordinative mechanisms, tested and drilled against the hour (minute or second!) they are needed (Rochlin et al., 1987).

In addition, our organizations self-organize to encourage and reward the self-reporting of errors (Roberts, 1991; Roberts, Stout, and Halpern, in press), on the explicit recognition that the value to the organization of remaining fully informed and aware of the potentiality for the modality of error far outweighs whatever internal or external satisfaction might be gained from identifying and punishing an individual and/or manufacturing a scapegoat to deflect internal or external criticism (Rochlin et al., 1987).

Indeed, one primary mode of response seems at variance with almost all the literature except a small body recently developed for analyzing risk in situations similar to those described here. Rasmussen's (1986) work emphasizes the notion of scanning for errors in advance—of anticipating failures and exogenous developments—by a mechanism he characterizes as "feed-forward." In contrast, the primary mode of error detection and correction in ordinary organizations is strictly "feed-back," whether the error-correction process is described as trial-and-error or comprehensive. In all three of the organizations in the Berkeley study, operators and managers alike emphasize the need to scan ahead, to anticipate rather than react to probable failures.

During quiet and stable periods, the primary concern of most technology-managing organizations is to avoid boredom and inattention. In contrast, members of reliability-enhancing organizations use the time to construct, reconstruct, and rehearse a variety of errors, mistakes, and even exogenously driven calamities that might present some future danger. When ordinary organizations accept a period of calm as a sign of success and a benign environment, the personnel of the organization we studied remain deeply suspicious that the environment is malign and tricky and that at best they are having a stretch of good fortune. This is an attitude and approach that has never been reported for most organizations, and certainly not for those that are the subject of the extensive analyses of failures.

CONCLUSION

Any three-letter acronym (TLA), however eloquently descriptive, is only a label. Properly used, such a label invokes a set of generally accepted, relatively invariant, static descriptors. In our case, however, the lack of any widespread consensus as to the meaning of "reliable" or "effective" makes it unusually dangerous to assume a commonality of meaning among our colleagues or across varying literatures. Moreover, as discussed above, the organizations we study are also characterized by a number of dynamic parameters involving operating conditions, and anticipation and modes of organizational as well as individual response that are not easily captured by any simple set of static indicators, let alone any fixed label. Whatever conversational merits follow from having a quick-and-easy term to bandy about are more than canceled by the resulting lack of precision and clarity.

As is argued at the outset, this is more than a terminological problem. Any description that characterizes our organizations solely in terms of their evaluated performance misses the essential characteristic of attempting to reduce or control risk by dynamic management of probabilities and circumstances, and the relativity of social evaluation of outcomes. Naval flight operations do kill and injure people from time to time; the accepted condition of success is that the number of people killed or injured is far less than one would expect given the nature of the inherent hazard (although even here the perhaps unachievable goal is zero–zero). On the other hand, air traffic controllers would consider themselves to be very threatened if even a few of the dozens to hundreds of deaths and injuries in commercial air travel were to be attributed directly to them.

One of our colleagues suggests that our organizations can be viewed as members of the intersection of two logical sets of complex technology-managing organizations.[4] Traditional organizational literature tends to address that set for which static descriptors are thought to be adequate. Organizations in this set may for one reason or another be *judged* to have achieved some degree of high reliability or effectiveness on the basis of statistical or other indicators, even when they operate under conditions in which risks of error or failure are small or easily contained.

The set that interests us consists of those organizations that operate, manage, or regulate complex, advanced technologies that embody sufficient inherent hazard to pose a significant public risk if they are not properly administered. As we point out, a great deal of the literature that focuses on these organizations addresses itself primarily to the causes and consequences of failure or serious error, particularly for those cases where the risks are not so readily contained. Indeed, a quick reading of the literature could easily lead one to the conclusion that no member of this set can permanently belong to the

---

[4] Paula Consolini, personal communication.

other, that sooner or later the organization will (and perhaps must) fail (Perrow, 1987).

We argue in contrast that the intersection does exist—perhaps as an extension of the traditional static set—and that the three organizations in the Berkeley project manage to stay in the "highly-reliable" category by a dynamic process not easily captured by the usual static descriptors. In a sense, we thereby argue that through an interactive management dynamic and an enormous self-awareness of their own vulnerability, these organizations seek successfully to contain "resident pathogens" (Reason, 1989) even if they cannot exterminate them, and to control "normal accidents" (Perrow, 1984) even while accepting their normality. What we do not know, and what guides our further inquiry, is how stable this dynamic is as environment, task, and technology change over the long term.

Here is sufficient motivation to study any of these organizations. But their similarities run deeper, suggesting a causal link between safety and organizational structures, forms, beliefs, and cultures whose characterization forms the core of our empirical studies. Perhaps the most surprising observation (to us) was the remarkable similarity among three apparently quite disparate, task-differentiated, and organizationally and conceptually independent organizations—a similarity that they themselves noted quickly (with some amazement) when we shared our research results.

Safety is not just a code to avoid public punishment, nor solely a matter of organizational survival; it has become a completely internalized operational imperative. It cannot be completely measured by abstract indicators, even by the organizations in question. It must be evaluated in the context of the social returns to operation, demands placed on operational capacity and tempo in order to realize them, and the internal as well as external consequences if the organization does not perform at the levels we observed. As discussed above, organizations cannot afford to fall short along any of the three dimensions—sociopolitical evaluation, technical performance, or safety—and still be judged effective.

Those organizations in the extant literature that have "failed" while operating under similar c nditions and performing similar tasks all lacked one or more of the characteristics we identify. That they became the common examples in general social parlance points to both the exceptional nature of the organizations studied by the Berkeley group and the abiding importance of ascertaining how and why they differ from those that have failed. In this, the pre-existing body of literature and empirical work, with its focus on specific explanations of failure and general arguments for success, lacks the specificity necessary for generalization, let alone for policy.

As Perrow (1987) acerbically points out, what the field of organizational studies lacks is ideas, not data. Describing these organizations and collecting data on their performance has proved less troubling than generating definitions that can be generalized to explain what underlies what we have been observing.

In the final paragraph of his book on organization theory, summarizing the literature on organizational effectiveness, W. Richard Scott (1989) says:

> Criteria for evaluating organizational effectiveness cannot be produced by some objective, apolitical process. They are always normative and often controversial, and they are as varied as the theoretical models used to describe organizations and the constituencies that have some interest in their functioning. . . . We should not seek explanations for organizational effectiveness in general, since such general criteria are not available (361–362).

The criteria for and evaluation of reliability, whether defined positively by the dynamic of organizational structure and culture or negatively as the avoidance of seemingly inevitable errors and failures, are even more demanding than the traditional search for definitions and models of organizational effectiveness. Seen in this light, the problem of arriving at a consensual definition becomes a primary research issue rather than a disciplinary side-alley.

For the moment, attempts to construct a complementary or counter-conventional body of organizational theory seem wasteful of time and energy. At the theoretical level, the question of terminology is subordinated to that of contingent, ontological taxonomy. If the resulting epistemological framework drifts towards the antitheoretical and postmodern (Jameson, 1990; Turner, 1989), this drift reflects the state of the literature when applied to modern, large-scale, complex, high-risk technological systems.

To the extent that we observe our organizations to have grown their own organizational cultures of safety and reliability rather than to have grafted them on or adapted them from other models or from expert advice, they have become not only self-organizing but also self-defining, properly the objects still of study and classification and not of recommendation and manipulation. "Working in practice but not in theory" (La Porte and Consolini, 1991), the organizations studied by the Berkeley group continue to exist, to adapt, and to perform superbly in defiance of traditional analysis.

REFERENCES

Cameron, K. S., and D. A. Whetten, eds. (1983). *Organizational Effectiveness: A Comparison of Multiple Models*. New York: Academic Press.

Demchak, C. C. (1992). War, Technological Complexity, and the U.S. Army. Ph.D. dissertation, Department of Political Science, University of California, Berkeley. Cornell University Press, forthcoming.

Dougherty, E. M., Jr. (1990). "Human reliability analysis—Where shouldst thou turn." *Reliability Engineering and Systems Safety*, 29: 283–299.

Edgren, L. D. (1989). "The 'Commando' model: A way to gather and interpret cultural data." In B. A. Turner, ed., *Organizational Symbolism*. Berlin: De Gruyter, 173–187.

Landau, M. (1969). "Redundancy, rationality, and the problem of duplication and over-lap." *Public Administration Review*, 29, 346–358.

———. (1973). "On the concept of a self-correcting organization." *Public Administration Review*, 36, 533–542.

La Porte, T. R., ed. (1975). *Organized Social Complexity*. Princeton: Princeton University Press.

La Porte, T. R. (1982). "On the design and management of nearly error-free organizational control systems." In D. S. C. Wolf and V. Shelanski, eds., *The Accident and Three-Mile Island: The Human Dimensions*. Boulder, CO: Westview Press, 185–200.

———. (1984). "Technology as social organization." IGS Working Papers on Public Policy. Berkeley: Institute of Governmental Studies, University of California.

———. (1988). "The United States Air Traffic System: Increasing reliability in the midst of rapid growth." In Hughes, R. M. and T. P., eds., *The Development of Large Technical Systems*. New York: Martinus Nijhoff, 215–244.

———. (1991). "The challenge of understanding large technical systems." In T. R. La Porte, ed., *Social Responses to Large Technical Systems: Control or Anticipation*. Dordrecht: Kluwer Academic Publishers, 1–4.

La Porte, T. R., and P. M. Consolini (1991). "Working in practice but not in theory: Theoretical challenges of high-reliability organizations." *Journal of Public Administration Research and Theory*, 1, 19–47.

Mayntz, R., and T. P. Hughes, eds. (1988). *The Development of Large Technical Systems*. Boulder, CO: Westview Press.

Medvedev, G. (1991). *The Truth About Chernobyl*. New York: Basic Books.

Perrow, C. (1984). *Normal Accidents: Living with High-Risk Technologies*. New York: Basic Books.

———. (1986). *Complex Organizations: A Critical Essay*. Third Edition. New York: Random House.

Ralph, R., ed. (1988). *Probabilistic Risk Assessment in the Nuclear Power Industry: Fundamentals and Applications*. New York: Pergamon Press.

Rasumssen, J. (1986). *Information Processing and Human-Machine Interaction: An Approach to Cognitive Engineering*. New York: North-Holland.

Reason, J. (1989). *Human Error: Causes and Consequences*. New York: Cambridge University Press.

Risk. Daedalus: Journal of the American Academy of Arts and Sciences. (1990). 119, No. 4.

Roberts, K. H. (in press). "Bishop Rock dead ahead: The grounding of the USS *Enterprise*." *Naval Institute Proceedings*.

———. (1992). "Structuring to facilitate migrating decisions in reliability enhancing organizations. In L. Gomez-Mehia and M. W. Lawless, eds. *Top Management and Effective Leadership in High Technology Firms*, 3, Greenwich, CT: JAI Press.

———. (1990a). "Managing hazardous organizations." *California Management Review*, 32, 101–113.

———. (1990b). "Some characteristics of high reliability organizations." *Organization Science*, 1, 160–177.

Roberts, K. H. and G. Gargano. (1990). "Managing a high-reliability organization: A case for interdependence." In M. A. Von Glinow and S. Mohrman, eds.

Managing Complexity in High Technology Organizations. New York: Oxford University Press, 146–159.

Roberts, K. H., D. M. Rousseau, and T. R. La Porte (in press). "The culture of high reliability: Quantitative and qualitative assessment aboard nuclear powered aircraft carriers." *Journal of High Technology Management Research*.

Roberts, K. H., S. K. Stout, and J. Halpern (in press). "Decision dynamics in two high reliability military organizations." *Management Science*.

Rochlin, G. I. (1989). "Informal organizational networking as a crisis-avoidance strategy: US Naval flight operations as a case study." *Industrial Crisis Quarterly*, 3, 159–176.

———. (1991). "Iran Air Flight 655: Complex, large-scale military systems and the failure of control." In T. R. La Porte, ed., *Social Responses to Large Technical Systems: Control or Anticipation*. Dordrecht: Kluwer, 95–121.

Rochlin, G. I., T. R. La Porte, and K. H. Roberts (1987). "The self-designing high-reliability organization: Aircraft carrier flight operations at sea." *Naval War College Review*, 40, No. 4, 76–90.

Romzek, B. S., and M. J. Dubnick (1987). "Accountability in the public sector: Lessons from the *Challenger* tragedy." *Public Administration Review*, 40, 227–238.

Scott, W. R. (1992). *Organizations: Rational, Natural, and Open Systems*. Third edition. Englewood Cliffs, NJ: Prentice-Hall.

Shrivastava, P. (1987). *Bhopal: Anatomy of a Crisis*. Cambridge, MA: Ballinger.

Schulman, P. (1980). *Large Scale Policy-Making*. New York: Elsevier.

Thompson, James D. (1967). *Organizations in Action*. New York: McGraw-Hill.

Turner, B. A. (1976). "The organizational and interorganizational development of disasters." *Administrative Science Quarterly*, 21, 379–397.

———. (1978). *Man-Made Disasters*. London: Wykeham Publications.

Turner, B. A., ed. (1989). *Organizational Symbolism*. Berlin: De Gruyter.

Van Maanen, J. (1988). *Tales of the Field: On Writing Ethnography*. Chicago: University of Chicago Press.

Vance, M. A. (1989). *Organizational Effectiveness: Bibliography*. Monticello, Ill.: Vance Bibliographies.

Vaughan, D. (1990). "Autonomy, interdependence, and social control: NASA and the space shuttle *Challenger*." *Administrative Science Quarterly*, 35, 225–257.

Von Glinow, M. A., and S. A. Mohrman, eds. (1990). *Managing Complexity in High Technology Organizations*. New York: Oxford University Press.

Weick, K. E. (1977). "Organizational design: Organizations as self-designing systems." *Organizational Dynamics*, 31–46.

———. (1979). *The Social Psychology of Organizing*. Second edition. New York: Random House.

———. (1987). "Organizational culture as a source of high reliability." *California Management Review*, 29, 112–127.

———. (1991). "The nontraditional quality of organizational learning." *Organization Science*, 2, 116–124.

Wolf, D. S. C., and V. Shelanski, eds. (1982). *The Accident and Three-Mile Island: The Human Dimensions*. Boulder, CO: Westview Press.

3

The Analysis of High Reliability Organizations: A Comparative Framework

PAUL R. SCHULMAN
Mills College
Oakland, CA

Paul R. Schulman (Ph.D., Johns Hopkins University) is Professor of Government at Mills College in Oakland, California. He is a specialist in organization theory and management, particularly on the management of complex technologies. He has written *Large-Scale Policy-Making* (Elsevier North-Holland, 1980), a comparative analysis of the Apollo project, the "War-on-Poverty" and the "War-on-Cancer," and has just completed *Disorder By Design*, an analysis of the instability of deductive designs in technology, organization, and social policy. In addition, he has written monographs on technological innovation and federal budget policy, and has published numerous articles in journals such as the *American Political Science Review*, *Administration and Society*, *Journal of Politics*, and *Liberal Education*.

Special thanks to Todd La Porte for his very helpful suggestions regarding this chapter.

*T*he Berkeley research project has analyzed organizations committed, both by choice and environmental forces, to live within the low error tolerances of complex technical systems. Further, they are committed to a continual reduction of possible causes of error. Their commitment to reliability is, in the context of day-to-day decisions, at least as compelling as their commitment to operational efficiency (La Porte and Consolini, 1991).

The analysis of these organizations reveals a number of unusual properties. Concern for reliability (or "availability" in the case of the fossil fuel plant that serves primarily as a peak-load rather than a base-load component of its power system) has become intensive and wide-ranging throughout each organization. For most of these organizations, the antithesis of reliability is risk, risk so consequential that it defies the boundaries of rank or function. The entire organization could through failure lose that "niche" of environmental acceptance or support within which it operates. The technical hazard is such that not only the careers, but also the lives, of its participants (and a significant number of outsiders) can be at risk because of errors or system breakdowns. Further, virtually any employee in the organization can put in jeopardy the future of the entire organization through failure or error. This brings home the immediacy of reliability as both a collective and an individual objective.

In important respects, reliability has become for these organizations a widely accepted proxy for organizational health. Nearly error-free performance is assumed by both managers and a surprising number of their subordinates to be inextricably connected to the integrity of fundamental organizational processes and to the well-being of the organization and its stakeholders. Indeed in a number of instances, reliability assumes an importance that is literally incalculable at the margins. This is quite different from the way in which reliability is treated conventionally as an organizational asset.

RELIABILITY AS A NON-MARGINALIZABLE PROPERTY

Most organizations function under a basic economy of resource commitments in relation to outputs. Under norms of intendedly rational behavior, when resources (or organizational effort) reach points of diminishing marginal returns in relation to valued outputs, their consumption is likely to be reduced or rationed. This adjustment process requires, however, some agreed-upon model of causation that provides members of the organization with an understanding of the connection between a given resource or effort and an organizational outcome. For marginal adjustments to be rational, the understanding of causation must be fine-grained enough to resolve outcome differences made by both increments or decrements of committed resources. In most organizational settings, such fine-grained understanding of causality and marginal cost/benefit tradeoffs depends on organizational learning through trial-and-error.

It is precisely these calculations, or even estimations, that are difficult for high reliability-demanding organizations to perform. Reliability demands are so intense, and failures so potentially unforgiving, that only a sharply reduced amount of trial-and-error learning about causal relationships is permitted. Managers are hardly free to reduce investments and arrive at conclusions about the marginal impacts on reliability. In fossil-fueled power plants, for example, there are suspicions that some expenditures have long since passed the point of diminishing returns for reliability, but there is a great reluctance to test this proposition at the risk of disruptions to the grid, outages to customers, and complaints to utility commissioners. In the case of nuclear plants, this reluctance is many times greater due to both the potential magnitude of the consequences and the scrutiny of regulators.

Managers of reliability-centered enterprises are caught atop both technically and sociologically complex structures. Because they are not convinced they understand fully a precise causal model for the provision of high operating reliability (indeed, it might be organizationally dangerous to assume so), they attack the reliability demand on a variety of fronts. In the research conducted by the Berkeley group, virtually every manager interviewed appeared to believe that there is not a steady-state or a stable "resting point" for the high performance systems under their management. Unless continual reinvestments are made in improving technical systems, procedures, reporting processes, and employee attentiveness, those performance standards that have already been attained are likely to degrade.

The treatment of reliability as a holistic, nonmarginalizable property can make a big difference in managerial strategy. Most prominently, a kind of "motion mania" is promoted. Constant efforts at improvement, clarification, and learning seem to be the norm. Relatively little activity is so routinized or rigidified as to be beyond the reach of re-evaluation and critical reassessment.

These characteristics are observable across all the organizations studied—organizations that literally must maintain, as a requirement for survival, unusually high levels of reliability in their everyday performance. But research also teaches us that these organizations are not identical; there are alternative approaches to the achievement of high levels of reliability. Some differences appear in everyday institutional practice; others are rooted more fundamentally in organizational design. Certainly many of these differences can be accounted for by variations in organizational culture and individualized organizational histories and experiences. But some differences seem strategic—the outcome of contingent requirements of technology, environment, resources, or scale. In particular, this essay examines how the technical character of hazard influences the approaches taken by an organization to the management of risk and the attempted maintenance of high reliability.

THE DISTINCTIVENESS OF FAILURE

One of the most important features of highly complex, high performance technologies is the large discrepancy between the state of the system in operation as opposed to its behavior and character in failure. This is true not only for the physical state of the system and its parts, but also for the knowledge required to understand its behavior. As one analyst describes it, "Knowing how a system works is not the same as knowing how it can fail" (Majone, 1978).

In organizations committed to high reliability, there is widespread recognition that the technical systems under management are capable of producing surprises. Events can occur that cannot be anticipated by simple extrapolation from existing understanding of how such systems work, whether that understanding is derived from formalized models, procedural handbooks, or informally acquired experience.

While organizational analysts might recognize that these organizations routinely maintain unusually high levels of nearly error-free performance, it is important to note that their members often are not attentive to the "normal" or routine of their performance. Instead, many administrative and technical features and many aspects of the organizational culture focus attention upon failure and its consequences.[1] While these organizations run with seemingly relentless constancy and predictability, in many respects their members are running scared—always alert to the possibility of failure and its costliness, if not its worst-case ramifications.

The consistent, preventative preoccupation with failure seems to be a distinguishing feature of the high reliability organization. That is why the conditions under which failure can occur and the counter-strategies required to contain its consequences have such an important impact upon so many organizational features. It is the character of what can go wrong—the architecture of failure—that influences their design and behavior as much as the routine requirements for success. In fact, while there are explicit and agreed-upon definitions of failure (sometimes societally imposed), there are fewer similarly agreed-upon definitions of "success." A fundamental asymmetry between the recognition of failure and that of success is dramatically evident. This assymetry is recognized in Creed, Stout, and Roberts' (this volume) discussion of organizational effectiveness.

High reliability is rather like good health—hard to define in its own right but easily identified in its absence. For organizations that must function continually at high levels of reliability, it is quite difficult to offset a failure with previously successful performances. Reliability is not a "bankable" asset to husband like other assets against a future offset. These organizations, both to their critics and their members, are only as reliable as the first error ahead of them—their reliability is not contingent on the many failure-free performances that lie behind.

Disparities in the architecture of failure can account for important differences in organizational characteristics. In this respect it is important to recognize the incompleteness of organizational analyses that are based upon features of organizational technology such as interdependency, complexity, or

---

[1] Meyer and Starbuck's discussion in Chapter 6 in part focuses on the dynamics of lack of attentiveness to potential failure by NCR.

component-coupling (Thompson, 1966; Perrow, 1984) under *normal* operation. To focus upon the intended design of a technical system is to underestimate the consequences of critical differences between its modes of operation and its modes of failure. The managers and operators of high reliability organizations generally do recognize the radical differences. Understanding modes of failure and their mitigation strategies can help the rest of us account for a wide range of organizational features and practices.

The disparity between operational and failure modes for hazardous technologies can be analyzed along two dimensions: behavioral and analytical. Behaviorally, an important question is whether the technical system can decompose or degrade safely into uncoupled components or whether system integration and interdependency must instead be maintained among the parts in order for it to fail safely. In other words, is the technology "inherently" safe, with safety a passive property inhering in the rapid termination of its operation, or does safety instead require the continued operation of a set of interdependent parts?

Organizationally, this question can be expressed in terms of specific human actions required to ensure safety in the face of failure and the location of responsibilities to ensure these actions. Does maintaining safety in the face of technical failure require coordinated, organization-wide actions, or can it be achieved by organizational decomposition, that is, by devolving action responsibility down to the level of detached departments or individuals?

Secondly, system failure can be described in terms of the analysis required to maintain safety. How broadly gauged a perspective is necessary on the problem at hand? Must synoptic information covering the entire technical system be brought to bear to guarantee safety, or can localized "real-time" monitoring and analysis serve to guarantee safety during failure?

These diverging sets of requirements in the face of failure yield as Figure 3-1 illustrates, a rudimentary classification of high reliability organizations.

Figure 3-1
A Classification of High Reliability Organizations Based on Safety Requirements Under Failure

		Level of Action Required for Safety	
		Localized	**System-wide**
Level of Analysis Required for Saftey	**Localized**	Decomposable orgainization	Clearance-focused organization
	System-wide	Action-focused organization	Holistic organization

A DECOMPOSABLE HIGH RELIABILITY ORGANIZATION

The first circumstance is one in which safety under failure is maximized by a capacity for decoupling dependencies and interactiveness among administrative and technical systems. We call this a *decomposable organization*.[2] Maximum safety in relation to a hazardous technology is attained when the integration among tightly coupled systems can be sharply diminished or broken during times of breakdown or failure. These systems are characterized by decomposable or nearly decomposable complexity (Simon, 1962). Analytic boundaries can be sharply contracted or localized. In addition, the responsibility for execution can also be localized in a way commensurate with these analytic boundaries. In its purest form, the decomposition can run all the way down to a single individual who is both the actor and analyst. The Air Traffic Control system of the Federal Aviation Administration might be characterized in this way. It features both analytic and action decomposability.

Air Traffic Control

The Air Traffic Control (ATC) system is divided into twenty air route traffic control centers. The air traffic monitoring and clearance functions of the centers are divided into sectors based on either geography or altitude. Individual controllers are in charge of radar displays (CRTs)—one for each sector. Supporting the controller at each station is another controller whose function is to help keep track of flight plans for each of the planes in the sector by means of strips of papers arrayed vertically on a board adjacent to the CRT. Next to each station is another station to whose contiguous coverage planes are handed off.

The ATC system features an assortment of integrative structures. The FAA Air Traffic Directorate in Washington sets a variety of policies that apply to all the centers—from personnel issues to course content in the air traffic and tower controller training academy in Oklahoma City; from the design and procurement of new equipment to maintenance standards for the old. There is also a national air traffic flow center from which all traffic patterns over the country can be monitored and from which route restrictions in times of overcrowding can be imposed. Finally, coordination agreements are negotiated between centers for handling traffic handoffs and jurisdictional overlaps.

Despite the existence of these elements of administrative and technical integration, however, safety resides in the decomposability of larger, integrated systems. The network of air routings can be closed off sector by sector in the case of equipment failure. Air traffic controllers can direct pilots to increase the distance separating airbound planes, the "in-flight separation," as a way of loosening the coupling among elements of the network. Planes can even be denied clearance to take off as a means of limiting network complexity.

---

[2] Weick's organizations, this volume, were also potentially decomposable.

Organizationally, safety resides at the most basic level of decomposition— the individual air traffic controller (and the pilot of the aircraft under control). The controller is expected to untangle overly complex or dangerous air traffic patterns in his or her sector. This is done by extending to the controller a great degree of analytical and behavioral autonomy. By enlarging aircraft separation or by modifying or refusing requested routings, controllers can safeguard the system from dangerous traffic formations (e.g., extreme congestion).

Controller activity is seen by many in the FAA as similar to the visualization and problem-solving processes employed in a game of chess. Self-confidence is an important element in the problem-solving process; self-doubt or "paralysis in analysis" is a condition that will radically shorten the career of a controller. "Decisiveness and the ability to take risks are necessary qualities" in an air traffic controller, according to the FAA training academy superintendent. (These very qualities, it will soon be apparent, are viewed as highly threatening in the context of a holistic high reliability organization.)

To be sure, intersectoral cooperation is essential. For example, coordination is necessary for safe air traffic control when an aircraft flies from one section to another; controllers must perform a handoff of responsibility for the craft. But in interviews with both controller supervisors and higher FAA officials, it was clear that at all levels the individual controller is regarded as the ultimate safeguard of the system. This ultimate decomposability of the organization's highest-reliability demanding function is an important buffer against a great deal of turbulence and uncertainty that has beset its overall structure and environment.

The major turmoil of the controllers' strike and mass firing in 1981 still haunts the organization. Personnel have not been restored to pre-1981 levels and there are no real controls over the increase in traffic density that loads the system. Instead of careful efforts to regularize the environment and limit increasing traffic loads, the FAA has relied primarily on the individual controller to take up the slack.

The system is also buffeted by turbulence in the controller training process. Significant political influences contribute to the design of curriculum for controllers offered at the FAA's Oklahoma City training academy. The pressure to contract out for governmental goods and services, emanating from both Congress and the executive branch during the Reagan and Bush administrations, has led to a significant amount of contracted course design in the controller's curriculum. Academy instructors who have to teach these courses complain about the quality of their design and the course materials.

Criticisms abound throughout the system about the type of training offered at the academy—that it is neither practical nor up-to-date, and that major gaps remain between formal training and field operation requirements. Here again the individual controller serves as the primary buffer against risk and uncertainty introduced elsewhere in the system. A large proportion of controller training occurs in the field at air traffic control facilities. Operating controllers, serving as mentors, fill in gaps in the controller candidates' training. Indeed, the full certification of a new controller requires that an existing controller sign off on this supplementary training.

Finally, the individual controller provides a buffer against yet another source of error and uncertainty: the introduction of new technologies into the organization. In one case controllers acted to safeguard the system from risk associated with introducing a new computer technology. The "ocean sector" at the Oakland Center Regional ATC facility covers thousands of miles of Pacific Ocean flyway for transcontinental flights whose destination or point of departure is the San Francisco–Oakland area. Because of its size and the absence of satellite communication, this sector has no real-time radar scanning of the air traffic under its control. Instead, controllers rely on pilots' own reports of their positions, keeping track of them by written notations, which are updated periodically by subsequent communications with the pilots. The pace of coordination for ocean sector controllers is much slower than the real-time, rapid-fire control process associated with the overland sectors. Much larger in-flight separations are maintained. One controller likened the difference in speed and response to that between chess and basketball. Some controllers, accustomed to the greater responsiveness of the overland sectors, want no part of the ocean sector. "You have to watch your mistakes play out in slow motion, and there's not much you can do about them," one overland controller complained.

In order to assist ocean sector controllers, a new computer system was developed to take reported aircraft positions, directions, and airspeeds, keep track of them, and plot the ocean sector traffic minute by minute through extrapolation of these parameters. An attempt was made to introduce the new computer system before it had been fully debugged and tested. On the day of its introduction, now referred to as "Black Saturday" by ocean sector controllers, they were required to feed in all aircraft location information through computer keyboard. Twice the system "crashed," leaving the sector display blank and requiring the controllers to retype all of the previously supplied information. This was time-consuming and distracting in relation to the job of controlling aircraft. Finally, controllers informed center managers that if the computer trial were to continue, they would no longer accept responsibility for the maintenance of aircraft separation in their sectors. This ended the experiment.

The ability of controllers to refuse responsibility for maintaining separation is a major constraint on higher management within the centers, and indeed throughout the air traffic control system. Managers cannot make changes or allow conditions to develop that give rise to conditions their controllers consider unsafe. Reportedly, a survey of controller reactions to continued increases in air traffic flow indicated that significant numbers of them would ultimately refuse responsibility for separation of traffic if their workloads continued to increase.

The fact that safety-stabilizing analysis and action can be decomposed to the level of the individual controller provides a major reliability buffer against system-level error in air traffic control, whether those errors are in training, traffic loads, or the design and maintenance of new technology. Of course, the individual controller can in fact be the source of devastating error. This occurred recently in the fatal ground collision between a commuter plane and a 727 aircraft at the Los Angeles airport, apparently caused by a ground controller who erred in clearing two planes for the same runway simultaneously. In many respects, the controller safeguards the air traffic control system more than the system safeguards the performance of the controller.

This role for controllers appears to affect significantly the character of the supervision they receive. A shift supervisor is in charge of a cluster of four to five sectors and can unilaterally relieve any controller whose performance is questionable. But the supervisor appears to exercise carefully rationed formal authority over individual controllers. The accepted approach seems to be to collaborate to some degree with other controllers in the performance monitoring process. Controllers, as well as their supervisors, are alert for signs, sometimes quite subtle, that one of their peers might be "in trouble." A change in conversation pattern, a silence, or an edge in the voice might cause increased watchfulness. If further evidence suggests that a controller is indeed in trouble, both the supervisor and another controller might consult with one another. As a consequence, the supervisor might send the individual in question on a break or even home.

Both controllers and supervisors who were interviewed readily admit that controllers tend to have highly individualistic personalities, dislike formal supervision, and even distrust the motives of their supervisors. Supervisors are former controllers, but given the relative flatness of air traffic center organization and the pay levels accorded controllers, they have few promotional opportunities beyond the supervisory level and do not make very much more income than those they supervise. Many controllers suspect, as a consequence, that supervisors take their positions because they are burned out as controllers or that they are seeking a "power trip" over their former colleagues.

In general, the administrative framework surrounding the air traffic control function appears to moderate environmental turbulence and even internal uncertainty and conflict less effectively than in other organizations committed to high performance reliability and low error rates. In one ATC center, an experimental ten-hour, four-day-a-week shift was introduced to accommodate long commute distances for the controllers—agreed to by higher management over the objection of supervisors. Contradiction, controversy, and uncertainty appear to be tolerable in ATC organizations as a consequence of the decomposability of safety analysis and action responsibility down to such a fundamental level.

A HOLISTIC HIGH RELIABILITY ORGANIZATION

At the opposite end of the spectrum from the decomposable high reliability organization is the holistic one. Here safety in the face of failure requires maintaining the highest level of organizational integration—both in analysis and in action. The Diablo Canyon Nuclear Power Plant is such an organization.[3]

Located just west of San Luis Obispo, California, the plant commands a view of the Pacific Ocean that would be a tourist's delight. The access road from the outer gate to the plant site winds seven miles through 10,120 acres of beautiful ocean-front canyon land. There is a farm along the way, complete with beef cattle and crops under cultivation.[4] All of the land, however, is fenced, monitored, and protected by the Pacific Gas and Electric Company. Managing the land is simply one part of a complex technical and organizational challenge connected with the nuclear generation of electric power.

The Diablo Canyon plant has two separate units, each of which is capable of generating approximately 1100 MW of electricity for a combined total at full output of 2190 MW (enough to meet the electric power needs of an average American city of two million). There are 1250 employees on site and over 1100 outside consultants, staff augmentation, and service contract workers employed during scheduled maintenance overhauls or "outages."

Diablo Canyon is organized into Operations, Maintenance, and Engineering departments. Operations has senior control operators, control operators, and assistant and auxiliary operators. Maintenance personnel are divided into Mechanical, Electrical, and Instrument and Control departments.

In addition, the plant has a Nuclear Power Generation support group in the General Office of Pacific Gas and Electric in San Francisco (NPG/GO). Despite its location three hundred miles to the north, this group is actively involved in the plant's operations. Its director is a senior vice-president of the company.[5] NPG/GO has approximately 711 employees, 387 alone in Nuclear Engineering and Construction Services (NECS), which does construction work at Diablo Canyon on an assignment basis. It also has a wide variety of nuclear engineers, systems analysts, regulatory compliance specialists, and emergency planners.

For nuclear power plants there is really no passive-mode safety. Complexity cannot be decomposed readily to achieve stability through simplification. Anytime there is nuclear fuel in a reactor, a variety of systems must operate to monitor and control its reactivity, dissipate its heat, control water pressures and flows, as well as maintain a variety of backup systems that safeguard these primary functions. Even when fuel has been removed from the reactor, highly radioactive components must still be monitored, shielded, and contained.

The technology of nuclear power in existing plant designs does not readily allow itself to be simplified for safety. An air traffic control network as we have seen can be decomposed to reach safety, as when traffic is kept out of a sector,

---

[3] Compare this organization to Bea and Moore's holistic organizations that have focused on reliability-enhancing strategies (this volume).

[4] The cattle are used to monitor radiation levels in the area and are consequently one element of reliability-enhancing processes.

[5] The plant manager at Diablo Canyon is also a company vice-president.

separations are increased, or planes are denied clearance to take off. An automatic reactor shut down or "trip," however, is in many respects a riskier mode than is continuous operation of the reactor. The full operational integrity of a variety of valve and pumping systems is necessary to relieve pressures and carry off heat from the core.

When failures occur in a nuclear power plant, neither analysis nor action can be safely decomposed. Both must be maintained, if not extended, to encompass a fully integrated system of parts and interdependencies. Analytically, it is important that failure diagnostics include all possibilities. A truncated analysis—limited to too few components of the technical system or subject to too early an analytic closure—can lead to misdiagnosis of what has gone wrong (Weick, 1988; this volume).

Narrowly focused actions, founded in misdiagnosis of a problem, can lead to even worse consequences, as happened at Three-Mile Island (Perrow, 1984). The responsibility for action, if too localized, can be dangerous. Remedial actions need to reflect a system-wide perspective of the consequences of what is being done. Actions taken too soon, in too narrow a context, can jeopardize other parts of the system. The closure of one valve, for example, may increase pressure on others. Even actions taken in separate generating units might affect one another. In one case at Diablo Canyon, a test requiring the brief shut down of an instrument air pressure system on one reactor during its scheduled maintenance overhaul was postponed due to worry that perhaps the instruments might somehow be connected to the air pressure system of the other operating unit. Even the engineering drawings of the units were not taken as definitive evidence of the independence of the air systems. Only after a personal inspection or "walk-down" of the entire system by a supervising engineer were maintenance workers authorized to act to initiate the air shut down on the nonoperating unit.

At Diablo Canyon, great effort is undertaken to maintain levels of integration in both analytic and action capabilities as a method of containing failure. These efforts have an important influence on the structure and culture of the organization. They are designed to prevent the compounding of failure by actions taken in ignorance, haste, or shortsightedness which, while they may be locally rational or maximizing, might lead to hazardous consequences at a system level. The organization guards against this by mobilizing a truly impressive arsenal of integrating structures. Sorting out the surprisingly complex set of administrative powers proved to be a very challenging task. It was hard even for employees of the plant to describe organizational responsibilities and authority relations in a summary statement. It took scores of interviews and an extended set of observations over many different activities to begin to understand the complex, organic network of interdepartmental relationships.

The most differentiated set of administrative actors and the most frequent intersection of responsibilities occurs within the safety domain, and this domain is very extensively defined. Where error, oversight, or failure have foreseeable consequences that threaten individual or environmental safety, administrative procedures are likely to be most elaborated and the interdepartmental inter-actions most intense.

Given the multiplicity of sub-organizations at Diablo Canyon, a variety of interorganizational committees and groups function to coordinate their activ-ities and gain the necessary clearances required for work to proceed. A weekly managers' meeting is held that includes not only department managers from Diablo Canyon but also senior managers from the nuclear power support group in the general office (NPG/GO).

A Plant Staff Review Committee (PSRC) meets at least weekly to approve procedural and equipment modification and design changes. Its membership includes representatives from all of Diablo's sub-units. Technical Review Groups (TRGs) are investigative groups formed to discover the cause of any regulatory nonconformances that occur. Their membership typically includes representatives from the major departments. The same is true for Event In-vestigation Teams (EITs), formed to investigate and report on forced outages or "trips" that occur in either unit, and for Safety System Outage Modification Inspection groups (SSOMIs) that meet to appraise proposed design changes from the standpoint of their potential impact on unit shut down and other plant safety systems.

Additionally, for scheduled outages, an Outage Control Center (OCC) coordinates maintenance work, materials, and clearances. It includes repre-sentatives from each of the departments assigned full-time to the center. Fi-nally, a Work Planning unit is responsible for planning jobs, gaining necessary clearances, and distributing relevant procedures to appropriate foremen. The assembling of a work "package," while coordinated by the Work Planning Department, requires review and sign-off by many of the plant's departments, giving them veto power over work performed.

Negotiating Organizational Integration

A classic organizational study (Strauss, Schatzman, Ehrlich, Bucher, and Sab-sin, 1963) describes a complex pattern of reciprocal, yet unstated, agreements among doctors, nurses, aides, orderlies, and even patients that govern opera-tion of a psychiatric wing of a large urban hospital. This "order" underwent continual renegotiation—renewal, revision, or rejection—as day-to-day life at the hospital proceeded. The authors attributed most of these fluctuations to the medical indeterminacy associated with psychiatric care. The uncertainty was sufficient that each patient needed to be treated as a special case.

The same phenomenon is observable at Diablo Canyon, a radically dif-ferent setting in which technical knowledge is hard, not soft, and where the need for *standardization* in the character and quality of job performance is a pre-eminent organizational requirement. Here, not only are a wide range of informal interorganizational agreements observable, but their negotiation and continual renewal are also recognized and embraced *formally* in the organization as an integral foundation of its safe and reliable operation. This is consistent with Eisenhardt's (this volume) description of the use of counselors in fast-decision organizations.

At the foundation of this strategy is a recognition of the need to maintain constant organizational integration, both analytically and in coordinated action, to maximize safety in case of failure. There is widespread recognition that all of the potential failure modes into which the highly complex technological systems of the plant could resolve themselves have yet to be experienced. Nor have they been exhaustively anticipated in formal protocols and procedures. In this respect, the technology is still capable of surprises.

In the face of this potential, there is an aversion to what might be termed *aggressive hubris*. The culture of the organization supports this aversion and is reflected in an "organizational personality" that predominates. Coolness and caution are repeatedly mentioned as personality traits desirable among employees or co-workers. "People who are not excitable, who analyze before they act," or "people who are willing to back off at times" were cited as desirable "types" for Diablo Canyon. Perhaps more importantly, a surprising variety of interviewees specifically volunteered the *un*desirability of one trait: hubris or "bullheadedness." A radiation protection general foreman asserted, for example: "There is a real danger in having very headstrong people intent on their own way." A quality control inspector volunteered that "people who have a belief they are infallible can have a very negative impact here." Contrast this with the "decisiveness" and risk-taking qualities cited as desirable in air traffic controllers. (Roberts, Rousseau and La Porte [in press] highlight additional cultural characteristics required for safe operations in reliability-enhancing organizations.)

What is sought in personality is expressed in organizational structure. The requirement for integrating differentiated organizational authority is a structural insurance against thoughtless or hasty action. The variety of "sign-offs" required makes it less likely that sins of hubris will be committed, particularly where sign-offs imply careful analysis and coordinated action from a variety of perspectives. But the array of differentiated powers throughout the plant that must be integrated requires constant adjustment and accommodation to make the system work. Integration depends upon the continual reinforcement of key values at the plant: credibility and trust. These are constantly mentioned in all departments as essentials for successful operation. They are also acknowledged to be exceedingly perishable and evanescent factors.

Credibility among departments means that skill levels must be mutually recognized. It also means that a given department's inconveniences to another must be understood as based on legitimate concern, and not the result of arbitrariness or incompetence. For example, it took some time for the Non-Destructive Examination department to establish credibility for its indirect method of testing, particularly before it could confront plant managers with proposals for costly or time-consuming repairs or replacements, the need for which could often be established only on the basis of probabilistic measurements. As one of its members noted, "At best I'm going to cost them money and impact their schedule."

Similarly, the Chemistry Department has to maintain credibility of instrumentation in order to get rapid responses from operators when indicators reveal impurities or imbalances in water or condensate chemistry. The Quality Control Department needs maintenance foremen to accept that quality control inspectors know what they are talking about when they question the way a job is done. Maintenance has to establish its own credibility with Operations so that preventive maintenance, which requires operator clearances, can be done in a timely manner. Operations, in turn, has had to convince maintenance and the outage manager that their planned reactor shutdown procedures are right and cannot be significantly speeded up. The Regulatory Compliance office has had to establish a credible image to convince all departments that it is attempting to solidify the plant's position vis-a-vis its regulators and has not become a hostile regulator itself.

Trust, described by one assistant plant manager as "the lubricant of the organization," refers to the expectation that prior agreements and negotiated arrangements will be upheld and honored over time. The importance and fragility of such trust was amply demonstrated in one incident during a refueling outage. A radiation protection inspector stopped a maintenance job because the scaffolding erected for it protruded over the reactor vessel in violation of the NRC's Foreign Materials Exclusion (FME) regulations. The maintenance foreman accused the Radiation Protection Department of reneging on its agreement that the scaffolding design would be acceptable. "They're changing the rules in the middle of the game," he complained bitterly.

Later it was discovered that a new agreement had been negotiated between the radiation protection officer and the night shift foreman to make minor modifications in the design of the scaffolding in order to comply with FME requirements. The night shift foreman had neglected to update his day shift counterpart. Seeing the scaffolding, the radiation protection inspector for his part believed that Maintenance had reneged on the agreement. Both the radiation protection officer and the maintenance general foreman took special pains to clarify the situation and restore amicable relations between the two departments.

Credibility and trust are perishable properties within any organization. They have to be continually nurtured and renewed if they are to survive. As the Diablo Canyon Operations Manager put it, "Trust is important. You have to talk to people a lot to hold it." The Chemistry Department manager agreed: "Every day is a new day in interrelationships and in holding on to trust. It never gets institutionalized." This picture is very different from Hirschhorn's (this volume) account of behavior in a different and less successful nuclear power plant.

Credibility can vanish with departmental error, misunderstanding, or miscommunication. A constant stream of meetings seems to nurture credibility and trust. Every Friday there is a plant manager's meeting at 10 A.M. and a plant staff review committee meeting at 1 P.M. (often running several hours). There are almost daily Technical Review Group (TRG) meetings to conduct error investigations. A given TRG may meet several times before it is able to draft a Non-Conformance Report, a License Event Report, or a Justification for Continued Operation. There are Event Investigation Team meetings after an automatic plant shutdown as well as briefings conducted for special visits by General Office officials or external officials such as Institute of Nuclear Power Operators (INPO) representatives. During outages there are outage updates and briefings twice a day for all departmental representatives, as well as inter-disciplinary work team meetings throughout the day.

Such meetings are all interdepartmental (there are also a variety of departmental meetings such as the crew briefings or "tailboards" held at the start of each shift). They serve not only to help coordinate interdepartmental activities but also to maintain lines of communication, clarify or redress misunderstandings, and ease strain that might have developed between two or more departments in the course of everyday work. It is perhaps no surprise that qualities frequently mentioned as highly valuable for plant personnel are friendliness and skill in interpersonal relations. These qualities facilitate the development of credibility and trust needed among departments to effect the coordination of complex tasks. They are important elements in preventing jurisdictional antagonisms that could threaten operations at the plant.

Even in the face of failure or error, system integration is maintained through constant interaction. Indeed, when faced with failure, members of the plant's departments can be readily observed in meetings, where they question the interpretation of other departments and add their own perspective on what's at risk in a proposed course of action. In effect, interacting with one another, employees generate hypotheses about what is going on, what can be done, and what the long-term, system-wide consequences of proposed actions might be. This is their way of coping with the potential for surprise within the enormously complex technology they are trying to control. It is their way of ensuring safety in the face of failure. (At another level of analysis, Foushee and Lauber [this volume] describe a different foundation for building trust and credibility—flight crew familiarity.)

Decomposable and holistic high reliability organizations lie at the extremes of approaches to the reliability problem. Between these extremes lie mixed organizations, again heavily dependent on what their core technology requires in the way of stabilization activities in failure. We call these intermediate types *action* and *clearance-focused* organizations.

ACTION-FOCUSED HIGH RELIABILITY ORGANIZATIONS

Command and control are the primary products of some organizations. They exist in a mediating relationship with other organizations that need to be linked together in pooled interdependency (Thompson, 1966). The function of these organizations is to provide continuous monitoring and coordination. Reliability means maintaining this role under a variety of conditions with a minimum of error.

An organization that fits this model is the power control center for an electric utility grid. Our study included the power control center for the northern California utility grid of the Pacific Gas and Electric Company. This center monitors the state of the grid including electric power generating units (many of whose output it can control directly through a computerized system called Direct Digital Control), and the power flow over the transmission lines of the utility. In addition, power control must also monitor the utility's linkage to the Pacific Intertie, a set of large, high voltage lines crossing the Pacific Northwest through which different utilities buy or sell power to one another (a process known as "wheeling").

In power control, system-wide analysis is conducted in real time as part of the organization's monitoring function. The purview needs to be system-wide because of the pooled interdependency of the network. At the same time, however, action responsibilities are generally focused in a single individual whose authority is not unlike that of an air traffic controller—the system dispatcher. The dispatcher is expected to give orders to the plants regarding their output levels. He or she must also give clearances for individual plants (with the exception of Diablo Canyon) to take units off line or even to initiate maintenance on units that might need to be called into service.

The dispatcher must constantly monitor voltages and frequencies on the grid to guard against overload or underload. He or she must also monitor the import or export of current through the intertie. An additional person in power control, the "power broker," has responsibility for determining the optimum mix of generating units to operate, fuels to be burned by them, and electricity to be bought or sold from the intertie, given projected demands for the day. This is done by solving a series of optimizing equations. The dispatcher can use this information in the daily plan of operations, but will at times depart from it based on his or her judgment of the state of the grid and knowledge of special circumstances of the constituent elements of the system. The concentration of these action responsibilities in the dispatcher stems from the need for rapid action lest fluctuations in the grid get out of hand. The dispatcher must always be one step ahead of the actual situation, or else irretrievable problems may develop that could lead to the grid's collapse.

While action responsibility is highly individualized in power control, it is not exactly localized in the same sense as that of the air traffic controller or a flight crew. The system dispatcher is positioned to take actions that have "global" reach in terms of the network of other organizations under his or her coordination. At the same time, the dispatcher has a much more integrated analytic picture of the entire grid than the controller has of the air traffic control network. The organization of power control combines both an integrated analysis of the entire technical system and the decisiveness important for proper coordination. Errors of omission or inaction are the real danger in a coordination-dependent system; the organization in charge of this coordination must guard against them.

As one supervisor put it, a good dispatcher is "someone who believes he's right and sticks by it." Again, it is interesting to note that these same qualities are greatly feared in a holistic high-reliability organization such as Diablo Canyon.

A CLEARANCE-FOCUSED ORGANIZATION

The last type of organization is only partially a high reliability organization. It is one which relies in failure on localized analysis but does not commensurately decompose or decentralize action responsibility. The organization stresses localized analysis because it must manage relatively detachable, unstandardized, idiosyncratic technical units. At the same time, it upholds system-level authority because it seeks to maintain an administrative hold tighter than the coupling of its technical elements—in pursuit of goals other than the reliability of its technical core. These goals may be efficiency, managerial "crispness," or other values that compete with reliability as organizational objectives. The use of generalized authority serves a clearance function, reconciling reliability requirements to those of other competing objectives. An example of this is a conventional fossil-fueled electric power plant in which "availability" and efficiency rival operational reliability as organizational objectives.

The Pittsburg Power Plant is a fossil-fueled power plant located about 35 miles east of San Francisco. It too is owned by the Pacific Gas and Electric Company. The plant consists of seven independent generating units that together can produce about 2002 MW of electricity. The units are differentiated into three sets. Units 1 to 4 are relatively small 156 MW units and are the oldest, placed in operation in 1954. Units 5 and 6, placed in operation between 1960 and 1961, generate 325 MW each. Finally, Unit 7 is the newest and largest. It can generate 720 MW and began commercial operation in 1969.

The three types of Pittsburg units are decoupled physically and functionally. Physically, each set of units is self-contained, with a separate control room and separate building arrayed in a line according to age, away from the administration building. Functionally, the units are also differentiated. The massive Unit 7 is a baseload unit, the economics of which call for its continuous operation, whereas Units 1 to 4 are brought on and off line frequently, depending upon the supplemental power needs identified by the utility's central power control dispatcher. Units 5 and 6 have an availability status in between the other two sets. Administratively, each set of units has its own shift supervisors and control operators.

The Pittsburg plant, with the exception of its large Unit 7, is described by its manager as a marginal operation to the utility's main office. Its main importance is maintaining available power when needed. This power demand fluctuates according to three external factors:

1. demand fluctuations on the northern California power grid;
2. breakdowns elsewhere on the grid;
3. fuel price fluctuations (the utility is in the "spot" oil market and large oil inventories are stored at the plant; on some days it is more cost effective to sell oil than to burn it to generate electricity).

These externally required fluctuations in output place a great demand on the plant to maintain full availability. Such fluctuations pose challenges distinct from and at times contradictory to operational reliability. Availability means readiness, but without the predictability and release of ongoing operation. In fact, bringing units on-line from a cold start puts more strain on materials and personnel than does simply operating them continuously. Also, as a maintenance general foreman noted, "The plant can get into more trouble from a unit shutdown than one that is running."

Availability is a less visible property to those outside the plant than is operational reliability. Personnel at the plant complain frequently that the utility's general office undervalues Pittsburg's availability as a company resource. The manager noted that in the past ten years the plant has assumed increasing importance in absorbing uncertainty and error elsewhere in the power system. A larger number of other PG&E plants have lessened flexibility in their power production levels (for example, the Diablo Canyon nuclear plant must run at full power for as long as possible given its reliability requirements as well as a performance-based pricing agreement reached with the California Public Utilities Commission). As operating margins become narrower system-wide, the uncertainty absorbing functions of Pittsburg take on new, if under-appreciated, significance. Indeed, senior plant managers at the time of our visits were working on a management incentive report that would highlight statistically the financial importance of availability to the utility.

Structural Units at Pittsburg

The plant is divided into four departments: Operations, Maintenance, Engineering, and a newer department called Business Planning. Operations is considered the most important, if not the central, department of the plant. Operations must grant clearances for virtually all activities, even for those indirectly involving the generating units. Operations personnel have the primary responsibility for identifying problems at the plant. Monitoring all systems 24 hours a day is a departmental responsibility.

If Operations is the "client" department for the rest of the plant, it too has a customer to which it must always be responsive: power control. Power control determines by its own economic logic which units will be on-line (and at what power output), which will be maintained as "hot" or "spinning" reserve, and which will be shut down with boilers allowed to cool. Any maintenance to units must first be approved by the dispatcher at power control. Under a Direct Digital Control (DDC) system, the Pittsburg units can actually be operated from power control and their outputs adjusted as needed. (It is interesting to note that power control exerts hardly any influence on Diablo Canyon. The nuclear plant simply runs according to its own technical capacities and requirements. The idea of a DCC-type system controlling nuclear reactors from a distance, incorporating a perspective other than the pre-eminence of plant reliability and safety, is unthinkable both to the utility and its external regulators.)

Under its general foreman, Operations is organized by units, with a separate operating foreman for units one to four, five and six, and unit seven. There are also unit-based senior control operators, assistant control operators, and auxiliary operators.

The Maintenance Department at Pittsburg is subdivided under its supervisor into mechanical, electrical and instrument, and control divisions. Each division has a general foreman and shop foremen who, in the mechanical and electrical divisions, are also assigned to specific sets of units. As noted above, Operations must grant clearances for all maintenance work on or affecting the generating units.

The Engineering Department consists of three types of engineers: project, results, and operations engineers. Project engineers oversee the planning of capital and large maintenance projects. Results engineers test for unit efficiency and do component testing and performance monitoring. Operations engineers add engineering support to Operations or Maintenance when needed on a day-to-day basis. For example, chemists test boiler water quality, and an environmental coordinator checks for compliance with regulatory requirements.

The relatively new position of business planner reflects recent cost/effectiveness evaluations now being done throughout the utility. In an engineering-dominated culture, the role of financial analyst is still evolving at plants like Pittsburg.

Foundations of Localized Analysis

An important reality at Pittsburg is the age of many of its generating units. Even the newest one, Unit 7, has lasted longer and is run at much higher outputs than its designers had envisioned. As a consequence of their age, the units have evolved different life histories—including repair and modification differences. "Gerry-rigging" is a fact-of-life in the maintenance of these units, and great improvisational efforts are often required to keep them operating.

As a result, the units are idiosyncratic, with elements of uniqueness in their technical properties. This means that when failures occur, experienced-based, even tacit, understanding of how they work is often more important than formal, theory-based analysis. Here again, the stress is on localized over system-wide analytic perspectives. One of the major objectives of the plant's Engineering Department is to bring more formal analysis to bear on problem diagnostics and recovery strategy. But the engineers admit that this is a relatively recent undertaking that meets with significant resistance from older operators and maintenance personnel at the plant.

The contrast again with Diablo Canyon could not be sharper. Formal, theory-based knowledge is the foundation for virtually all actions taken at Diablo Canyon. Indeed, acting or operating "outside of analysis" would not only run counter to all norms of the plant, but would also be a regulatory violation.

Integrated Action

The balance at Pittsburg between reliability, availability, and efficiency is a function of top-level managerial decisions. At times, a large backlog of maintenance jobs is postponed in favor of availability demands or the efficiencies to be gained from waiting until a scheduled overhaul. In one case, a control operator and several auxiliary operators on one of the generating units were upset that a cracked housing on a high pressure, hot feedwater pump was ordered temporarily "nursed" by ameliorative measures rather than replaced, because this repair would have required shutting down the generating unit during a period of peak power demand in the summer. Unit 7, as mentioned, has run far longer and at far higher outputs than it was designed for because the economics of such base-load operation are highly favorable. The plant manager and his department heads appear to believe that only at the highest authority levels of the plant can these tradeoffs in organizational goals be effectively managed.

The Pittsburg plant is governed under a single, formally specified chain of command, quite unlike the complex, negotiated order of Diablo Canyon. Here again, managerial practice seems to reflect a distinctive architecture of technical failure. (For an analysis of mismatched managerial approaches to failure, see Hirschhorn [this volume].)

THE COMPARISON OF HIGH RELIABILITY ORGANIZATIONS

The comparative framework offered here is but a rudimentary step in the analysis of contrasting approaches to achieving high reliability in managing complex, hazardous technologies. Because every organization consists of subunits that themselves constitute organizations, it must be recognized that no organization is a pure type. Even in a highly decomposable organization there are structures of integrating authority and examples of overarching analysis that come into play in the solution of critical problems. Even in the most highly integrated, holistic organization, there will be examples of individualized initiative and action taken to save the day.

But it is useful at the same time to recognize the variety of approaches that can be adopted toward the management of failure-critical systems. No single prescription can be offered on how to achieve high reliability across all technical challenges as hinted at by the papers in the second part of this volume. The character of the technical hazard itself—specifically what system states must be avoided in order to maintain safety in the face of failure—has a great deal to do with appropriate organizational structures and strategies. It is from contemplating the differences of high reliability organizations, both from conventional organizations and from one another, that we can lay the groundwork for a fuller understanding and appreciation of this remarkable organizing challenge.

REFERENCES

Downs, A. (1967). *Inside Bureaucracy*. Boston: Little, Brown.

Langer, E. J. (1989). *Mindfulness*. Reading, MA: Addison-Wesley.

LaPorte, T. R., and P. Consolini (1991). "Working in practice but not in theory: Theoretical challenges of high reliability organizations." *Journal of Public Administration Research and Theory*, 1, 19–47.

Majone, G. (1978). "Technology assessment in a dialectic key." *Public Administration Review*, 38, (January/February), 50–55.

Mayntz, R., and Hughes, T. P., eds. (1988). *The Development of Large Technical Systems*. Boulder, CO: Westview Press.

Perrow, C. (1984). *Normal Accidents*. New York: Basic Books.

Roberts, K. H., Rousseau, D. M., La Porte, T. R. (in press). "The culture of high reliability: Quantitative and qualitative assessment aboard nuclear powered aircraft carriers." *Journal of High Technology Management Research*.

Simon, H. A. (1962). The architecture of complexity. *Proceedings of the American Philosophical Society*, 106 (December), 467–482.

Strauss, A., Schatzman, L., Ehrlich, D., Bucher, R. and Sabsin, M. (1963). The hospital and its negotiated order. In Friedson, E., ed., *The Hospital in Modern Society*. New York: Macmillan, 147–169.

Thompson, J. D. (1966). *Organizations in Action*. New York: McGraw-Hill.

Turner, B. A. (1978). *Man-Made Disasters*. London: Wykeham.

Weick, K. E. (1988). "Enacted sense making in crisis situations." *Journal of Management Studies*, 25, 305–317.

4

Organizational Effectiveness as a Theoretical Foundation for Research on Reliability-Enhancing Organizations

W. E. DOUGLAS CREED
University of California, Berkeley

SUZANNE K. STOUT
University of Texas, Dallas

KARLENE H. ROBERTS
University of California, Berkeley

W. E. Douglas Creed is a doctoral candidate in organizational behavior and industrial relations at the Walter A. Haas School of Business, University of California, Berkeley. His research interests include career expectations and job changing, business ethics, network organizations, and organizational learning. He holds an M.B.A., also from Berkeley, and an M.A. (religion) and B.A. (English) from Yale University.

Suzanne K. Stout is Assistant Professor at the University of Texas at Dallas. She received her B.A. in physics from the University of Texas, an M.B.A. from Southern Methodist University, and a Ph.D. from Stanford University. Professor Stout's research interests focus on organizational learning and interorganizational relationships, collective action problems and strategic choice, nonprofit governance, and decision processes in reliability-seeking organizations.

For biographical information about Karlene H. Roberts, see page 1.

A mong the criticisms often leveled against the Berkeley group's recent research in high reliability organizations (HROs) has been its heavy reliance on qualitative observation, the relative absence of testable hypotheses, the apparent lack of generalization to other kinds of organizations, and perhaps most seriously, the absence of an explicit theoretical foundation for this stream of inquiry.[1] This essay has two goals aimed at remedying some of these problems. The first is to consider what past thinking on organizational effectiveness may have to say about research on reliability. The second is to make explicit the fundamental perspectives of the Berkeley group's current HRO research. Adopting the metaphor of the mapping of construct space (Cameron and Whetten, 1983), we suggest that reliability is a conceptual sector of effectiveness construct space. In meeting these two goals, we hope to identify ways in which this research has uncovered something new while also suggesting ways in which it can benefit existing organizational research.

THE BERKELEY GROUP'S RESEARCH

Writings stemming from the Berkeley group's research reflect an enthusiasm triggered by inductive field research. They also demonstrate the problems of interpretation resulting from the group's self-imposed care in its in-depth field observations, observations sufficiently complex as to make differences in interpretation inevitable. One consequence is that the group is divided between those who believe with a nearly evangelical fervor that HROs are indeed distinctive and reliable (e.g., La Porte and Consolini, 1991; Roberts, 1990; Rochlin, this volume) and those who believe HROs fall at one end of a continuum of reliability on which all organizations could be situated (Roberts, Stout, and Halpern, in press; Schulman, this volume). Consider also the seemingly unending debate regarding how to capture most precisely in a name and acronym the nature of the beast; are they reliability-seeking organizations, reliability-enhancing organizations, high reliability organizations, error-intolerant organizations, or perfection-demanding organizations? Alluded to in papers by La Porte and Consolini (1991), Roberts (1990), and Schulman (this volume), this debate has reached the level of self-parody in Rochlin's (this volume) *definitional prologue* when he uses TLA to refer to three-letter acronyms, suggesting that such naming is inappropriate because an acronym implicitly suggests an "accepted, relatively invariant, static descriptor" that cannot grasp the dynamism of these organizations.

Arguably, this fervent debate regarding the distinctiveness and reliability of certain organizations using complex and potentially hazardous technologies represents an implicit and poorly acknowledged theoretical perspective. Namely, inquiry into the nature of HROs represents a type of organizational

---

[1] In contrast to these criticisms, see Roberts, Rousseau, and La Porte (in press); and Roberts, Stout, and Halpern (in press).

effectiveness research that draws heavily on notions of organizational culture. Some researchers have recently come to acknowledge this implicit perspective (Roberts, Rousseau and La Porte, in press). In addition, Weick (1987) explicitly identifies organizational culture as an important factor in reliable operations. However, to the extent that some researchers persist in claiming that HROs are unique, they fail to recognize that reliability is really one of many concepts that fall under the rubric of organizational effectiveness. HROs seek to operate effectively using their own distinctive criteria, much as McDonald's makes good food and clean bathrooms its endeavor. A claim for HRO's utter distinctiveness artificially isolates the HRO research from much of organizational research. It is the Berkeley group's focus on the distinctiveness of the criteria, a distinctiveness rooted in the undeniable hazards of these organizations' technologies, that leads to the erroneous claim that they are a breed apart. On the other hand, the view that HROs are at one end of a continuum allows the HRO findings to inform an ongoing effort to understand organizational attributes that lead to effective performance.

ORGANIZATIONAL EFFECTIVENESS AND THE IDENTIFICATION OF CRITERIA

Past attempts to understand organizational effectiveness have considered nearly all possible areas of organizational inquiry—dominant coalitions, value preferences, access to resources, efficiency, job satisfaction, goal setting, decision making, interpretation systems, person–situation interaction, and so on—until the rubric of effectiveness is tantamount to the organizational behavior analogue of Milo's "anxiety closet" in the comic strip *Bloom County*. It contains everything one is concerned about, but dare one open the door yet again? Cameron describes the situation as follows:

> Effectiveness is both apex and abyss in organization behavior research. It is
> an apex in the sense that all conceptualizations and theories of organizations
> are aimed, ultimately, at identifying effective performance. It is the funda-
> mental dependent variable in organizational investigations, and judgments
> of effectiveness and ineffectiveness are an inherent part of the activities of
> theoreticians, researchers, and practitioners in organizations. It is an abyss
> in the sense that no valid theories of organizational effectiveness exist in
> organizational behavior, and no list of criteria has ever been formulated that
> is either necessary or sufficient for evaluating the construct (1984, p. 236).

In the last two decades, researchers and theorists have struggled with the frustrating quest for a broadly applicable theory of organizational effectiveness. Due to the manifest vagueness of the construct and the essentially idiosyncratic nature of organizational effectiveness, one common theme of late has been the call for in-depth studies of individual organizations, as opposed to continuing the quest for a single unifying model. The usefulness of these recent insights for research into HROs stems primarily from the repeated call for the explicit delimitation of the inquiry and for the acknowledgment of assumptions underlying any particular effectiveness research. The identification of criteria for assessing organizational effectiveness (Campbell, 1977; Cameron and Whetten, 1983; Cameron, 1984), along with explicit consideration of the processes involved in generating and meeting these criteria (Steers, 1975; Pennings and Goodman, 1977; Seashore, 1983; Zammuto, 1984), are especially important aspects of the delimitation advocated in the past two decades.

In a review of seventeen multivariate models of organizational effectiveness, Steers (1975) finds widespread inconsistency in the evaluative criteria, questionable construct validity, and a push for generalizability that obscures the multiplicity of criteria, functional specializations, and environmental differences. He (1976) proposes viewing effectiveness in terms of process rather than focusing on criteria or static end states.

Campbell (1977) advocates the forging of an idiosyncratic model of effectiveness, founded on an explicit model or theory, adopted in collaboration with organizational participants. The uniqueness of such a specific model depends on knowledge of several organizational attributes: how the effectiveness information will play a role in actual decisions or actions; articulated objectives, both means and ends; conditions for goal attainment; and the relative importance of each objective.

Consideration of how political forces affect the identification of effectiveness criteria also lends credibility to the notion of idiosyncrasy. According to Seashore (1983), what distinguishes organizations is how outside interests converge to establish coherent core values and preferences and how constituents interact in the integration of disparate values. Pennings and Goodman (1977) suggest that attributes of the organization's open system determine the identification of constraints, goals, and referents. Internal and external actors each play the dual roles of determinant and constituency of effectiveness, while a dominant coalition differentially accepts or sanctions the competing and potentially incompatible positions held by the various constituencies. Seashore (1983) draws three conclusions regarding idiosyncratic political processes that affect the understanding of organizational effectiveness. First, there can be no objective measure of organizational effectiveness: "The effectiveness estimates are always plural—potentially different and equally valid estimates for each constituent or constituency population" (1983, p. 64). Second, political or social forces are the source of integration: "There are powerful social dynamics operating that have the effect of inducing some degree of compatibility in value perspectives among key constituencies" (1983, p. 64). Third, assessing effectiveness requires the explicit identification of the constituencies served by the assessment.

Taking a contingency approach to the evaluation of effectiveness, Zammuto (1984) sees value judgments as inescapable and links the identification of values to the selection of constituencies. He concludes that effectiveness is both value-based and time-specific:

The generalizations concerning values and time can be integrated in a general, extended definition of the organizational effectiveness construct: *the construct of organizational effectiveness refers to human judgments about the desirability of the outcomes of organizational performance from the vantage point of the varied constituencies directly and indirectly affected by the organization* (1984, p. 614, emphasis his).

Weick and Daft (1983) view effectiveness as "a function of the interpretation of cues about the environment. Organizational effectiveness is similar to interpretation accuracy" (1983, p. 82). Several organizational processes contribute to the effectiveness of interpretation systems, most of which fall under the rubric of detailed causal mapping (Rochlin, this volume). Perhaps the most important of these processes entails the fostering of self-correction in the interpretation system—through a sensitivity to complexity and to the tradeoffs between generality, simplicity, and accuracy—and the acceptance of the tension between interpretational disagreement and operational coordination. These processes very likely contribute to the collective requisite complexity (Weick, 1987) necessary for understanding the demands for and the operational processes that lead to reliability in HROs.

While a trend toward particularism in effectiveness research is clearly apparent, Cameron (1984) notes the continued absence of agreement on the antecedents and indicators of effectiveness. Goodman, Atkin, and Schoorman (1983)—decrying the absence of a single parsimonious theory of effectiveness, the abundance of "atheoretical and non-cumulative empirical studies," and the improbability of convergence on a single theory—call for a moratorium on traditional organizational effectiveness studies and the redirection of attention toward "in depth microstudies of specific organizational outcomes" (1983, pp. 164–165).

With so many divergent perspectives and strong disagreement about the direction of this research enterprise as a whole, some researchers have turned their thoughts to identifying the areas of consensus and debate as a foundation for freeing up empirical research. Cameron (1986a) discerns several areas of agreement among the plentiful disagreement regarding organizational effectiveness. First, despite confusion and ambiguity, the effectiveness construct is indisputably central to organizational behavior. Second, because no conceptualization of organizations is comprehensive, neither is any idea of organizational effectiveness—as the metaphors for organizations change, so do the models of organizational effectiveness. Third, consensus on the best indicators of organizational effectiveness is impossible because criteria are based on values and preferences, and no specific construct boundaries exist. Fourth, the usefulness of different models of organizational effectiveness in research depends on the circumstances, i.e., the purposes and constraints of the investigation. And fifth, the problems surrounding effectiveness are not so much theoretical problems as criteria problems. Cameron suggests that the greatest source of consensus could come from refocusing attention on the sources of ineffectiveness—what he describes as "the factors that *inhibit* successful organizational performances rather than on the factors that contribute to or indicate successful organizational performance" (1984, p. 245, emphasis his).

Further, Lewin and Minton (1986) suggest that despite the failure of empirical research to effect the development of a universal theory of organizational effectiveness, "the components of a contingent behavioral theory of organizational effectiveness already exist, one that incorporates the paradoxes and tradeoffs inherent in real life organizations" (1986, p. 514). Drawing on the Quinn and Rohrbaugh (1983) spatial model of organizational effectiveness, Lewin and Minton propose a "contingent multiple model theory of organizational effectiveness, [with] the criteria of stability, management of information systems, and organizational decision-making . . . at the core" (1986, p. 524). One of the directions for research that they propose concerns the "instrumentality of organizational culture in generating, improving, or maintaining organizational effectiveness" (1986, p. 526). Similarly, Weick (1987) discusses culture as a source of reliability, suggesting that culture is one means for generating in human systems the requisite complexity required by increasing complex technological systems.

Clearly, exploring the implications of these areas of disagreement and consensus regarding organizational effectiveness could be valuable for HRO research. This is especially likely to be the case if one conceives of reliability as a facet of effectiveness. To date, the link between reliability and effectiveness has not been adequately explored in the HRO research. Had it been, the possible position of HROs and reliability in a broader ranging contingent behavioral theory of the sort foreseen by Lewin and Minton, could have been truly thought-provoking.

Consideration of some of the ways in which the Berkeley HRO research reflects the pain and promise of this debate in the organizational effectiveness literature begins to reveal why. Without doubt, the HRO research has tended to entail close inductive work akin to what Campbell (1977) and Goodman and Pennings (1983) advocate as a corrective to the frustrated attempts at a unifying theory. It has involved many of the steps emphasized by Campbell (1977), the identification of organizational and sub-unit tasks, of means and ends, and an implicit judgment of the relative importance of objectives, especially to the degree that reliable operations are assumed to be paramount (Roberts, in press). The problems of construct validity (Steers, 1975) are reflected in the never-ending debate over definition and acronyms previously discussed. The seemingly overwhelming concern in HROs for the accuracy of interpretation and accountability in problem solving and organizational learning (Roberts, Stout, and Halpern, in press; Roberts, in press; Schulman, this volume) parallels what Weick and Daft (1983) describe as the effectiveness of interpretation systems.

A major finding of the HRO research to date concerns the paradoxes these organizations present. While these paradoxes are difficult to handle theoretically (La Porte and Consolini, 1991; Roberts, Stout, and Halpern, in press; Rochlin, this volume), they are not disturbing to organizational members who must deal with them daily. As Lewis and Minton argue, there is a place for these paradoxes in a contingent behavioral theory of organizational effectiveness. According to Weick and to Lewin and Minton, culture is the source of effectiveness, a construct given serious attention in the HRO work (Roberts, Rousseau, and La Porte, in press; Roberts, in press). In short, the HRO research mirrors much of the concerns raised by effectiveness researchers.

The Berkeley group's HRO research has failed, however, to be explicit about its adopted theoretical framework, implicitly a facet of a larger effectiveness framework. Nor has this research investigated adequately the open system facets of HROs and the political processes that lead to the pre-eminence of reliability as a criteria. (Meyer and Starbuck, this volume, strongly suggest they do this.) Understanding the degree to which internal and external actors both determine and are constituents of reliability-enhancing activities is essential to having a full grasp of the existing pressures on organizations to behave responsibly in the face of potential catastrophe. In one way or another, Campbell (1977), Eisenhardt (this volume), Pennings and Goodman (1977), Seashore (1983), Zammuto (1984), and Weick (1987) all note the importance of understanding the role of values, goals, time, and culture in the identification of effectiveness criteria. Not surprisingly, most see it as an undeniably political process. It is, however, in this arena where HROs may be truly distinctive, for while the political interplay of various constituencies is significant, it may not be the final determinant in raising reliability above all other values.

For example, while it is possible that reliability is a value-based and time-specific concept (Zammuto, 1984)—a perspective that requires consideration of the political forces affecting the hegemony of certain values—it is also possible that in HROs, such political processes are circumscribed. Perhaps in HROs, more than in other effectiveness-seeking organizations, it is the potential dangers of the technology, not the prevailing political and social forces, that drive concern for reliability and effectiveness and that determine that the only truly inescapable value judgment is that certain potentially hazardous technologies pose risks which must be addressed.

In light of these observations, the questions at issue do not so much concern whether it is proper to attempt to integrate HRO research with the organizational effectiveness literature, but instead they address how to integrate these two lines of inquiry in a way that is fruitful for both. Can reliability criteria manifest in HROs be more explicitly linked to organizational effectiveness? How can HRO researchers avoid the problem common to organizational effectiveness research of not matching a model to the circumstances? What are the implications for understanding reliability-enhancing processes of the idea that consensus on the sources of ineffectiveness is more easily reached than consensus on the sources of effectiveness? How do the political processes and the constraints posed by potentially hazardous technologies in HROs distinguish their selection of reliability criteria from the selection of effectiveness criteria in other types of organizations?

Two ways to address these questions are found in the writings of Cameron and Whetten (1983) and Cameron (1986a). One is to make explicit researchers' assumptions through the answering of certain questions. The other is to consider the metaphors that inform the direction of inquiry. When applied to the HRO research, the first approach solves some of the more mechanical problems of the work, while the second offers insights into the implicit nature of the theoretical framework adopted. We address the first approach here.

RELIABILITY: A CORNER OF EFFECTIVENESS CONSTRUCT SPACE

Cameron and Whetten (1983) distinguish between organizational effectiveness as an abstract construct and the plethora of what they call constituent concepts. Examples of these constituent concepts include productivity, economic efficiency, job satisfaction, and a number of other measures that proponents have purported to be part and parcel of effectiveness as a construct.

They assert that the meaning of a concept—a facet of a larger construct—is subject to complete comprehension. For example, productivity can be fully gauged by output. However, comprehension depends on a careful articulation of the investigator's specific view of the concept.

On the other hand, the full meaning of a construct remains unknown and possibly unknowable. Relative to the effectiveness construct, they write: "The total meaning of effectiveness comprises more than the concept of productivity, however, and productivity represents only one aspect of the total construct space" (p. 7). According to this view, in the full gamut of organizational effectiveness related concepts, from micro-issues like job satisfaction to macro-issues like resource acquisition, each concept captures only one aspect of effectiveness. If one thinks in terms of the metaphor of construct space, each concept represents only one sector. In the instance of HRO research, reliability should be considered such a concept/sector.

As used in much of the research discussed in this volume, the concept of reliability takes on several a priori meanings rooted in the technical and social constraints faced by the particular subject organizations. Namely, each organization uses hazardous technologies and exists in a social environment with little tolerance for environmental hazard and loss of life. Reliability in these organizations means above all the avoidance of errors that can result in catastrophic consequences for the organization, its participants, and the surrounding population and environment. This means that, at one level, reliability is equivalent to averting what Perrow describes as catastrophic "system accident[s] or normal accident[s]," and the consequences of such accidents for the various "parties" of victims he identifies.[2] However, Perrow sees such accidents as inevitable due to the interactional complexity and tight coupling inherent in hazardous technologies (Perrow, 1984, p. 62).

Second, at a more elemental level, reliability for these organizations entails reducing errors that, while less consequential in themselves, could contribute to more serious problems. Again, borrowing from Perrow, this would mean error reduction or avoidance below the system-wide level.[3] The Berkeley researchers have not approached their research with these Perrowian levels of system-wide accident or component incident explicitly in mind, however.

In order to be more explicit about the meaning of reliability, it is appropriate to attempt answers to seven questions proposed by Cameron and Whetten (1983) as a means of providing necessary circumscription for the aspect of organizational effectiveness under consideration. This mapping of the conceptual boundaries is needed so that researchers are clear about what they are measuring (Cameron and Whetten, 1983; Cameron, 1986a). Continuing with the metaphor of construct space, answering these seven questions leads to a specification of the sector in effectiveness space under consideration. These writers suggest that through accepting the notion of concept/sectors, empiricists can support the building of a cumulative if not universal theory of organizational effectiveness. The process would be much like combining the efforts of various cartographers to compile a map of the globe. What follows are answers to the Cameron and Whetten questions, based on a reading of the HRO researchers' writings and comments on their work.

1. *From whose perspective is effectiveness being judged?*

The short answer is—primarily from the perspective of experts operating within the constraints imposed by technical design—but a longer answer is warranted. The HROs considered by the Berkeley researchers can be divided into two groups. The first, comprised of nuclear power plants, is regulated by a federal agency, the Nuclear Regulatory Commission, because of the wide-

---

[2] Perrow identifies operators of the technological system as the potential first-party victims of an accident. Second-party victims would include associated parties who have no influence over the system, such as suppliers and their employees or agents. Third-party victims are innocent bystanders with no involvement with the system. Fourth-party victims are those who bear the burden of operational externalities, possibly for generations to come, e.g., fetuses exposed to radiation. Beyond this, Perrow places the environment as victim.

[3] Perrow proposes that complex technical systems be divided into a four-level hierarchy—part, unit, subsystem, and system—and that the system as a whole be viewed in terms of its place in the greater environment. In distinguishing between the seriousness of mishaps, he applies the following terms: "Incidents" are events involving "damage to or failure of parts or a unit only, even though the failure may stop the output of the system or affect it to the extent that it must be stopped;" the term "accidents" applies to analogous mishaps at the subsystem and system levels, "stopping the intended output or affecting it to the extent that it must be halted promptly;" the term "component failure accidents" applies to the coincidental failures of one or more components of the whole system, from part to subsystem, which are "linked in an anticipated sequence;" and the term "system accidents" entails the "unanticipated interaction of multiple failures" (Perrow, 1984, p. 70).

spread public perception of the hazards nuclear power generation poses. The second, naval aircraft carriers and the air traffic control system, are not regulated by outside agencies and instead are self-regulated by an internal bureaucracy. For example, the Federal Aviation Administration (FAA) both staffs and regulates air traffic control, while the Naval Inspector General and inspection teams monitor aircraft carrier performance.

There are obvious external constituencies, nonetheless. Public sentiment also affects performance standards, due first, to pressures brought to bear by media coverage both of mishaps and of adherence to regulatory standards, and second, through political processes affecting the perceived institutional legitimacy of both the organizations and the regulators. The organizations' and regulators' need for public confidence forces formal responsiveness, even though public sentiment often is not based on expert knowledge of how the systems operate. Reliability becomes an issue of organizational survival for HROs and regulators alike at both the level of avoiding catastrophe and at the level of retaining institutional legitimacy. For example, in the case of nuclear power plants, reliability becomes an issue at the time of plant relicensing. For the Nuclear Regulatory Commission it is an issue because of the dual needs to assure safe operations and to retain public confidence or avoid governmental censure. For the plant operator, survival hinges on avoiding accidents fatal to human and organizational life and on the ability to continue operation of often unpopular and costly nuclear plants that can represent substantial portions of their assets.

Yet, while these technologies are likely to be considered dangerous in almost everyone's eyes, the nature of the operational vulnerability is often invisible to the public until a mishap occurs. For this reason, it does not follow that effectiveness in general or reliability in particular are judged from a universal or even popular perspective. Instead, the focus for assessing reliability is primarily determined by organizational and industry insiders and expert regulators familiar with the technological constraints of the organization under consideration.

Institutional forces work at other levels to affect the perspectives used to assess reliability, as well. For example, since the Three-Mile Island accident, the American nuclear power industry has developed more rigorous approaches to training and has shared information about the causes of incidents, or, in the case of Three-Mile Island, accidents through the Institute of Nuclear Power Organizations (INPO). Similarities between operating standards in this and other countries provide further evidence of institutionalization; after the nuclear power plant accident at Chernobyl, an international counterpart of INPO formed. In addition, in the United States, a large percentage of the industry's managers and operators gained their professional training through a single source, service in the nuclear Navy. Arguably, the result of such factors should be an increasing degree of isomorphism in industry operating and safety procedures and in professional standards beyond what one would expect due to the influence of federal regulation. In light of these considerations, reliability in the context of nuclear power plants is assessed from the perspective of technological experts employed within both the organizations and the relevant regulators.

In the case of the FAA, widespread civilian use of commercial aviation fosters popular political pressures. So while reliability is assessed from the regulators' perspective, their assessment is subject to intense public scrutiny. Similarly, in the case of the naval aircraft carriers, the standards for assessing reliability may seem to stem primarily from experts within the organization itself. The political forces likely to play a role with technologies in use in major population areas are of less consequence for ships that carry out their hazardous operations at sea, where it is the crew and the pilots themselves who bear the immediate danger of unreliable operations. Undeniably, friends and family of naval personnel and the U.S. Congress still take note when accidental deaths occur.

In all of these instances, these collections of experts are not simply a "dominant coalition" (Cyert and March, 1963), imposing its preferred standards of effectiveness. The idea of the dominant coalition includes theoretical provisions for the inevitable shifts in power resulting from the ability of an emerging coalition to deal better with changing environmental conditions. Certainly, reliability-enhancing organizations are faced with changing environments; in the illustrations cited here, one could argue that power should shift to coalitions better able to respond to popular and regulatory concern over the risk to public safety. Yet the notion of a dominant coalition suggests a possible political fiat theoretically impermissible in a reliability-seeking organization using complex and hazardous technologies. In a sense, technological design would have veto power in any emerging coalition.

2. *On what domain of activity is the analysis focused?*

In explicating this question, Cameron and Whetten write as follows:

> Organizational domains are circumscribed by the constituencies served, the technologies employed, and the services or outputs produced (Meyer, 1975). Domains arise from the activities or primary tasks that are emphasized in the organization, from the competencies of the organization, and from the demands placed upon the organization by external forces (1983, p. 270), internal citation theirs).

Error- and accident-avoidance processes, as manifest in individual and aggregate behaviors, constitute the domain of activity in most of the Berkeley group's research. The domain is large, encompassing such processes as training and socialization, the ongoing mapping of cause and effect, the codification of procedures, decision making, sense making, and enactment (Weick, 1979; Weick and Daft, 1983).

There are several advantages to the explicit focus on error-avoiding processes. First, it solves a problem common to most of the organizational effectiveness literature—little consensus on the criteria for assessing effectiveness. The same problem arises in the reliability-seeking organizations investigated by the Berkeley group. How much activity designed to eliminate error is necessary or enough? Schulman (this volume) characterizes this as the absence of "stopping rules." He likens it to holding a pie plate full of water against the ceiling with the end of a broomstick; one does not know how much force is needed to keep the pie plate aloft, but one can not afford to relax the pressure to find out.

A focus on the sources of ineffectiveness can foster greater consensus in identifying strategies for improving organizational effectiveness: "Identifying strategies for improving organizational effectiveness is more precisely done by analyzing organizational ineffectiveness as opposed to organizational effectiveness" (Cameron, 1984, p. 279). In support of this, Cameron cites Stephens' (1976) assertion that "Not only is it difficult to achieve consensus as to those design characteristics and functions, the channels and interactions, which lead to system success, but experience has shown that in complex systems, it is much easier to describe and achieve consensus as to what constitutes a failure" (quoted in Cameron, 1984, p. 247). Error-reduction processes, as an analytical domain, avoid the problem of disagreement regarding effectiveness criteria due to the greater consensus as to what constitutes a potential source of unreliability.

A second advantage is that focusing on such processes should enable analysis more responsive to the practical concern for the elimination of ineffective or unreliable procedures and behaviors, as well as for the continuation of effective ones (Cameron, 1984). In light of these advantages, it is perhaps better to pose all of Cameron and Whetten's questions in terms of ineffectiveness, rather than effectiveness.

While the nature of these processes as they occur in HROs appears to be unusual and therefore both interesting and deserving of study, it remains to be seen whether this focus captures what is truly distinctive about HROs. Is this the proper or best domain of research? Do HROs exist only or even primarily to reduce errors? This may be true of the FAA, but it is certainly untrue of aircraft carriers and nuclear power plants. Is it correct then to assert that accident-avoidance is the best criteria to be used for assessing HROs?

While it may be appropriate to consider ineffectiveness as the non-goal of HROs rather than effectiveness as their goal, Cameron's (1984) insights regarding the greater ease of achieving consensus on sources of ineffectiveness suggest that this may be a common, albeit not commonly recognized, attribute of many organizations. With the ubiquitous difficulty in reaching consensus regarding criteria for assessing effectiveness, many organizations may in fact use the non-goal approach in an operational sense, even though the articulated goals are cast in positive terms. If this is the case, HROs are perhaps not so much unique in their near obsessive concern for error avoidance as the organizational literature is backwards in its presentation of what more conventional organizations are like.

An alternative and essentially complementary domain of inquiry could be the accommodation of technology. The foundation of this is foreshadowed in the writings concerning the organizational cultures of HROs (Roberts, Rousseau and La Porte, in press; Roberts, in press; Koch and Roberts, submitted for publication). Much of the literature on organizational culture grapples with the profusion of definitions for the construct itself and with the problem of the many elements of culture. Models using multiple dimensions often configure culture as concentric layers of processes, with accessibility and malleability increasing with distance from a core of fundamental assumptions (Rousseau, in press). Although it is common to conceive of the core as consisting of unconscious assumptions which inform all other elements of culture (e.g., participants' speech and patterns of behavior [Schein, 1985]), it does not necessarily follow that these assumptions are not directly knowable to either internal or external constituents. This appears to be especially true of HROs.

Technical complexity and the potential for disaster appear to be the inescapable facts driving the near obsession for reliability in HROs (Schulman, this volume; Rochlin, this volume). While such drive is properly understood as reflecting shared understandings, values, and behavior norms, the status of the technologies themselves as an element of culture remains unclear. Along with the need for survival, the technology's potential for disaster is among the most fundamental assumptions of HRO cultures. However, technology is not a given; it evolves in ways that do not cohere with assertions about the stability of the fundamental assumptions at the cultural core. Yet in HROs, the processes of reliability enhancement and error avoidance appear as a type of higher order cultural phenomenon, the rigorous accommodation of the undeniable assumptions, while technology is at the cultural core.

In light of this, researchers should conceive of HROs as at the end of a multidimensional continuum with the contents of the cultural core (for example, the knowledge of the potential hazards of the core technology, the accessibility of the fundamental assumptions, the rigor of the accommodation of the core assumptions) as the factors that determine an organization's position on the continuum. In addition, this perspective on HROs invites reconsideration of the nature of organizational culture. It is possible that the most knowable of the core assumptions, technology, is also the most mutable.

The implications for our understanding of the dynamics of cultural changes are many. Viewing technology as a fundamental of the cultural core and adopting accommodation of the core assumptions as a domain of inquiry can also foster a greater understanding of the distinctive political processes that affect the selection of reliability criteria. The political and social forces (Seashore, 1983) and the attributes of an organization's open system (Pennings and Goodman, 1977)—believed to be the means by which constraints, goals, and referents are identified and potentially conflicting values integrated—are more circumscribed in HROs due to the nature of the core technical assumptions.

3. *What level of analysis is being used?*

Because analysis can take place at any level of activity relevant to the organization, ranging from the behavior of the individual participant to that of the surrounding society, the choice of the appropriate level of analysis "must be made in the context of other decision guides" posed by Cameron and Whetten

(1984, p. 271). Theoretical discussions (Weick, 1987) and field research in HROs (Roberts, Stout, and Halpern, in press; Roberts, Rousseau, and La Porte, in press; Roberts, in press; Koch and Roberts, submitted for publication) suggest that individual and group behaviors—especially those related to the reduction or avoidance of errors that could contribute to Perrowian incidents and accidents—reflect strong organizational cultural norms. Error-reduction processes reflect, on the one hand, the inculcation of shared values, the codification of procedures, and the manifest behavioral adherence to these values and codes at the individual level. On the other hand, they also reflect in many cases a harsh unforgiving punishment structure (e.g., the FAA dismissal policies)[4] and the real threat of injury or death. This suggests that analysis should be at the individual level and at the level of aggregated individual behaviors that constitute error-reduction processes.

This differs from the Perrowian perspective on accident avoidance, which tends to focus on technologies because of an assumption that humans are too limited in their cognitive capacities to compensate for the increasing complexity of hazardous technologies. Weick and Daft (1983) and Weick (1987) in effect counter that a requisite complexity is possible in groups and in interpretation systems, if not at the individual level. Theoretically, behaviors should be aggregated in the following manners: (1) across interdependent individuals within an organization, which would reflect a kind of organizational consensus on how to approach error reduction; and (2) longitudinally on an individual basis, which would reflect the degree to which the individual consistently manifests reliability norms.

On the other hand, the idea that the accommodation of core cultural assumptions stands as a complementary domain of inquiry suggests that any element of organizational culture could be chosen as a level of analysis. Rousseau (1990) makes the case of multiple measures of organizational culture, chosen with a sensitivity to the elemental layer of culture under consideration. Certainly, much of the Berkeley group's research has made use of the panoply of cultural concepts, but it has not dealt with the implications of viewing technology as a fundamental element of culture.

4. *What is the purpose for assessing effectiveness?*

Investigation into the nature of HROs can have several purposes. At one level there is the interest in demonstrating that Perrowian "normal accidents" in a world of tightly coupled technical systems are not inevitable and that a purposeful concern for safety and reliability can enable the avoidance of awesome consequences. The Berkeley group's research to date seems to have been based on the assumption that certain reliability-seeking behaviors are instrumental in achieving the safe operation of hazardous technologies. By focusing on error-reduction processes, the overarching purpose of research becomes determining whether or not such purposeful efforts at accident avoidance can

---

[4] Should an air traffic controller lose the five mile separation of aircraft three times in his or her career the controller is dismissed.

be successful, and if so, determining how success is achieved. However, a focus on reliability-seeking processes does not presume that these organizations are unimpeachably reliable and that the hazards they could pose to human life and the environment are either unreal or justified. The purpose is not to give an academic imprimatur to the use of controversial technologies.

Field observation to date suggests that not only is intentional reliability possible, but also that it has several identifiable characteristics. One is a near obsession for safety that is fostered by socialization processes and supported by a strong reward structure. A second is an unending process of causal mapping linking operational events with incidents and potential mishaps, which could, at another time, be the antecedents of more serious accidents (this is especially true in the case of the nuclear power plant studied). Another is the decentralization of accountability for safety, coupled with the inculcation in individuals of a sense of responsibility. And finally there is the absence of stopping rules, which is to say, the organizations offer no code or standard by which participants can conclude that they are sufficiently vigilant (Schulman, this volume). Ongoing assessment of reliability should test the theoretical connection between such features of HRO culture and error-reduction processes and the actual reduction in dependent measures of errors.[5]

5. *What time frame is being employed?*

For the organization using hazardous technologies, the need for reliability is unending. The researcher should impose a long time frame for observations in order to assess consistency of response and the effects of changing conditions. In many instances it may be appropriate to consider the lifespan of the technology. In addition, research should consider the issues of whether short-term reliability-seeking fosters long-term reliability. For example, in considering the ongoing process of causal mapping at nuclear power plants, Rochlin (personal communication) notes the danger of an increasing rigidity over time, what he calls the "brittleness of interpretation," which could undermine reliability in the long run.

6. *What type of data are being used for judgments of effectiveness?*

In the Berkeley researchers' investigations, all of the likely dependent variables measuring the rate of errors, incidents, and accidents are recorded by the organizations themselves or by the regulators. Such measures are consistent with the notion that measures of ineffectiveness—in this case, of incidence of error or of unreliability—have the benefit of being for the most part quantifiable and agreed upon. Nuclear power plant operators must keep records of safety violations and of what are called reportable and unreportable incidents under NRC guidelines. Nuclear plant owners can choose to complement these

---

[5] Field observation by the Berkeley team suggests that HROs are exhaustive in their scrutiny concerning safety stumbling blocks. No potential problem is too insignificant to overlook in HROs. That is, there are "no stopping rules [because] reliability cannot be marginalized; these organizations cannot face the risk of a reliability decrement" (Schulman, Chapter 3). If all signals are assessed in terms of their potential threat to reliability, then HROs can provide a context for testing some of Weick and Daft's (1983) theoretical assertions regarding the effectiveness of interpretations.

required measures with measures of their own. The U.S. Navy keeps records of shipboard accidents and of incidents thought to be indicators of potential hazards but that do not themselves constitute an accident. One such measure is the "crunch rate" or the number of times any two aircraft make unintentional contact while being moved relative to the number of movements on the flight or hangar decks. Thus, in 1989, the crunch rate was 1 touch in 8000 moves. One of the FAA measures is the "loss of separation" or the breaching of a minimum five-mile distance between airborne planes. All of these dependent measures are based on an expert consensus of what constitutes a hazard or what is likely to indicate the onset of hazardous behaviors. One direction for reliability research could be the processes by which expert consensus on measures of ineffectiveness is forged or changes over time.

7. *What is the referent against which effectiveness is being judged?*

For most of the HROs considered in this volume, regulatory standards and ideals serve as the referents against which reliability and safety are judged. Cameron (1984) refers to assessment vis-a-vis standards and ideals as "normative judgment." At the same time, other referents abound. Because the dependent variable measures of reliability are recorded by the organizations themselves, historical performance can serve as the basis for what Cameron refers to as "improvement judgment." When the performance of similar organizations, as reported to regulators, are matters of public record, these also can serve as the referents. In addition, the nuclear power industry shares information across many international borders. In the case of aircraft carriers, the performance of other carriers in the fleet is available for comparison. These last examples fall under what Cameron calls "comparative judgment." Assessment vis-a-vis stated organizational goals serves as the basis for "goal-centered judgment."

Finally, members of the Berkeley research team implicitly judge the performance HROs relative to the assumed lower reliability of trial-and-error organizations (TEOs). While one might consider this another example of comparison judgment, evaluation based on this theoretical distinction seems more akin to what Cameron calls "trait judgment," which involves evaluating "an organization on the basis of static characteristics it possesses, independent of its performance on certain indicators" (1984, p. 251). Although the implicit distinction between HROs and TEOs may be valid, it seems inappropriate when the analysis is focused on dynamic processes of error reduction in organizations that have the power to effect awesome consequences. Organizations that do not have the capacity to blow people up do not sweat the details in the ways one would hope to find in what should be HROs.

In evaluating the effectiveness of an HRO's error-reduction processes in achieving outstanding safety records, normative, comparative, goal-centered, and improvement judgment or some combination of these would all have a place. Based on field observations and the suggestion that a true HRO has no stopping rules when it comes to increasing the safety of its operations, normative and improvement assessments may be the most fruitful.

BEYOND THESE ANSWERS

This chapter started with a question that seems to have plagued HRO research to date—that of the purported uniqueness of the creature. If HROs are unique, then organizational effectiveness theories should offer little insight to us. But we do not share the opinion that these reliability-seeking organizations are utterly different from other effectiveness-seeking organizations in our society today. Instead, reliability is better understood as a sector of the effectiveness construct space. HROs exist on an effectiveness continuum of organizations. At the same time, we do not contend that these HROs are in no way different from other more conventional organizations.

Theoretically, one can accommodate some slight differences between HROs and more conventional organizations by recognizing that the selection of effectiveness (or ineffectiveness) criteria is an idiosyncratic process. In fact, this process—selection of effectiveness criteria—provides one interesting way of anchoring the at-times foundering HRO research. However, the differences are too great for this easy accommodation.

If HROs are really a set of organizations that sit at the end of one dimension of effectiveness space, and effectiveness is culturally derived, then reliability may be viewed as a higher-order manifestation of core cultural assumptions. Reliability is a value oriented against "ineffectiveness" rather than toward effectiveness; as such, it enjoys no equilibrium state. There are no stopping rules (see also Rochlin, Schulman, this volume). One might find that the cultures of these organizations are likewise not in an equilibrium state, and instead are always changing and striving toward the avoidance of a non-goal.

All the HROs the Berkeley group has studied have also been technologically complex. Because technology is an important decision factor—in a sense a dominant "political" interest in HROs—we need to think about the nature of an organization's technology, the dynamics of the evolution of technology, and the implications of technological evolution for organizational effectiveness. Similarly, we need to consider the possibility that cultural evolution—that of the core values, norms, and behaviors—and technical evolution coincide. If culture and technology evolve simultaneously in HROs, then technology is not a mere cultural contingency. Rather, it is an integral part of the values and core assumptions that constitute the cultures of organizations. Similarly, the stability of the cultural core—of either organizations or societies—is not something to be taken for granted.

Finally, we need to begin a search for neighboring organizations on the reliability/effectiveness continuum. Only by finding variance in what is claimed to be the outstanding feature of these organizations—their overarching concern for reliability—can we begin to examine just how the politics of technology and the culture of reliability develop differently over time. By searching for neighbors, we may finally be able to answer the nagging question of uniqueness. We may find that HROs are oriented toward avoiding ineffectiveness to the near exclusion of trying to reach effectiveness. As we move down the reliability continuum, we may find a more balanced addressing of both effectiveness and ineffectiveness criteria. By studying this phenomena we can begin to untangle criteria for both.

REFERENCES

Cameron, S. (1984). "The effectiveness of ineffectiveness." In Barry Staw and Larry K. Cummings (eds.), *Research in Organizational Behavior.* Greenwich, CT: JAI Press, 235–285.

———— (1986a). "Effectiveness as paradox: Consensus and conflict in conceptions of organizational effectiveness." *Management Science,* 32, 539–553.

———— (1986b). "A study of organizational effectiveness and its predicators." *Management Science,* 32, 87–112.

Cameron, Kim S., and David A. Whetten (1981)." Perceptions of organizational effectiveness over organizational life cycles." *Administrative Science Quarterly,* 26, 525–544.

———— (1983). "Some conclusions about organizational effectiveness." In Kim S. Cameron and David A. Whetten, eds., *Organizational Effectiveness: A Comparison of Multiple Models.* New York: Academic Press, 261–277.

Campbell, J. P. (1977). "On the nature of organizational effectiveness." In Paul S. Goodman and Johannes M. Pennings, eds., *New Perspectives on Organizational Effectiveness.* San Francisco: Jossey-Bass, 13–55.

Cyert, R., and J. March (1963). *A Behavioral Theory of the Firm.* Englewood Cliffs, NJ: Prentice-Hall.

Goodman, P. S., R. S. Atkin, and F. D. Schoorman (1983). "On the demise of organizational effectiveness studies." In Kim S. Cameron and David A. Whetten (eds.), *Organizational Effectiveness: A Comparison of Multiple Models.* New York: Academic Press, 163–183.

Koch, B. and K. H. Roberts (submitted for publication). "Safety cultural norms as a distinctive feature of potentially hazardous organizations: Development and application of a measuring instrument."

La Porte, T. R., and P. M. Consolini (1991). Working in practice but not in theory: Theoretical challenges of high reliability organizations. *Journal of Public Administration Research and Theory,* 1, (Winter), 19–47.

Lewin, A. Y., and J. W. Minton (1986). "Determining organizational effectiveness: Another look, and an agenda for research." *Management Science,* 32, 514–538.

Pennings, J. M. and P. S. Goodman. (1977). "Toward a workable framework." In Paul S. Goodman and Johannes M. Pennings, eds., *New Perspectives on Organizational Effectiveness.* San Francisco: Jossey-Bass Publishers, 146–184.

Perrow, C. (1977). "Three types of effectiveness studies." In Paul S. Goodman and Johannes M. Pennings, eds., *New Perspectives on Organizational Effectiveness.* San Francisco: Jossey-Bass, 96–105.

———— (1984). *Normal Accidents: Living with High-Risk Technologies.* New York: Basic Books.

Pfeffer, J., and G. R. Salancik (1978). *The External Control of Organizations: A Resource Dependence Perspective.* New York: Harper & Row.

Quinn, R. E., and K. S. Cameron (1983). "Organizational life cycles and shifting criteria of effectiveness: Some preliminary evidence." *Management Science,* 29, 33–51.

Quinn, R. E., and J. Rohrbaugh (1983). "A spatial model of effectiveness criteria: Towards a competing values approach to organizational analysis." *Management Science,* 29, 363–377.

Roberts, K. H. (1990). "Some characteristics of high reliability organizations." *Organization Science, 1* (2), 160–177.

Roberts, K. H., D. M. Rousseau, and T. R. La Porte (in press). "The culture of high reliability: Quantitative and qualitative assessment aboard nuclear powered aircraft carriers." *Journal of High Technology Management Research.*

Roberts, K. H., S. K. Stout, and J. J. Halpern (in press). "Decision dynamics in two high reliability military organizations." *Management Science.*

Rousseau, D. M. (1990). "Assessing organizational culture: The case for multiple methods." In B. Schneider, (ed.), *Frontiers of Industrial and Organizational Psychology.* San Francisco: Jossey-Bass, 153–192.

Salancik, G. R. (1984). "A single value function for evaluating organizations with multiple constituencies." *Academy of Management Review,* 9, 617–625.

Schein, E. H. (1985). *Organizational Culture and Leadership.* San Francisco: Jossey-Bass.

Seashore, S. E. (1983). "A framework for an integrated model of organizational effectiveness." In Kim S. Cameron and David A. Whetten, eds., *Organizational Effectiveness: A Comparison of Multiple Models.* New York: Academic Press.

Steers, R. M. (1975). "Problems in the measurement of organizational effectiveness." *Administrative Science Quarterly, 20,* 546–558.

—— (1976). "When is an organization effective? A process approach to understanding effectiveness." *Organizational Dynamics, 5,* 50–63.

Weick, K. E. (1979). *The Social Psychology of Organizations.* Reading, MA: Addison-Wesley.

—— (1987). "Organizational culture as a source of high reliability." *California Management Review,* 29, 112–127.

Weick, K.E., and Richard L. Daft (1983). "The effectiveness of interpretation systems. In Kim S. Cameron and David A. Whetten, eds., *Organizational Effectiveness: A Comparison of Multiple Models.* New York: Academic Press.

Weick, K. E., and K. H. Roberts (in press). "Organization mind and organization reliability: The case of flight operations on an aircraft carrier deck."

Zammuto, R. F. (1984). "A comparison of multiple constituency models of organizational effectiveness. *Academy of Management Review,* 9, 606–616.

5

Differentiating Reliability Seeking Organizations from Other Organizations: Development and Validation of an Assessment Device

BARBL A. KOCH
Rutgers University, Newark, N.J.

Barbl A. Koch received her Ph.D. in management from Rutgers, The State University of New Jersey. She also holds a B.A. and an M.B.A. from Rutgers. In May of 1987 her conference paper "Conflictual decision-making," co-authored with Joel Harmon at Rutgers University, received the Best Empirical Paper award from the Eastern Academy of Management. Her dissertation is anchored in the High Reliability Research at Berkeley, which she joined after she and her family were transferred to California.

The help of Karl Aquino, Northwestern University, who performed a Lisrel analysis, is greatly appreciated. Instrument copyright © by Barbl A. Koch and Karlene H. Roberts.

*T*he research program on high reliability organizations (HROs) has focused to a large extent on exploring the particular characteristics that make these organizations as reliable as they are. As Stout, Creed, and Roberts (this volume) point out, the methodology has been primarily qualitative and has tried to discern and describe specific aspects of these organizations.

The research paradigm of triangulation (Jick, 1979), however, requires that qualitative methods be combined with quantitative methods to allow for assessment of the general validity of research findings. The question posed here is as follows: "How can we capture the essence of a reliability-seeking organization with quantitative methods?" A second, related question is, "What are the specific cultural aspects of such an organization?"

As some of the chapters in this volume clearly show, a number of characteristics seem to differentiate reliability-enhancing organizations from other organizations. Among these, as described by Rochlin and Schulman (this volume), is "perfection-demanding." Demand for perfection derives from the fact that the quality of organizational processes and outcomes is of utmost importance in order to accomplish overall reliability.

Given the complex technology typical of reliability-seeking organizations (see Stout, Creed and Roberts; Rochlin; Schulman; Weick; this volume), deterioration in performance tends to result in near-misses or accidents. It seems, therefore, that safety is a cornerstone of the overall reliability of such an organization. Hence, we set out to scrutinize what makes an organization safe and how to assess safety in quantitative terms. Essentially two factors contribute to safety in an industrial organization; one, the design of the machinery, and two, the behavior of the people who handle the machines (Maier, 1973).

Our focus is on the human part of the equation. At issue is whether and how people contribute to or detract from the safe performance of highly complex organizations. We assume that actions have something to do with how individuals do their jobs and how they think about them. This eventually led us to develop a scale that assesses cultural aspects of safety, focusing on participants' safety norms about appropriate behavior and attitudes in doing their jobs in HROs. The purpose of this chapter is to describe the rationale for such a scale, its development, and its applications.

LITERATURE REVIEW

A voluminous literature deals with safety or the avoidance of accidents. The most recent of that literature focuses on the macro aspects of major disasters, such as Three-Mile Island (Perrow, 1984), the Tenerife Air Disaster (Weick, 1990, this volume), Bhopal (Shrivastava, 1987), oil platform accidents (Bea and Moore, this volume), and similar events. A concern for the disaster potential of certain complex and dangerous technologies as they exist in our society obviously motivated these investigations. Although these studies emphasize the importance of reliability-enhancing activities in organizations, they are not directly pertinent for the purposes of developing a measurement instrument because they fail to deal with the micro aspect of how safety is achieved by employees on a day-to-day basis.

A long history of research on accident and safety issues exists, however, much of it at the micro level of analysis. This stream of research was essentially stimulated by the high number of accidents that occurred in early industrialization. Legislation to compensate injured workers became effective in 1885 in Great Britain, whereas in the United States, the first compensation laws were introduced in Maryland in 1902, in Montana in 1910, and in New York in 1911. This legislation meant that plants with higher accident levels would have to pay more in worker compensation.

Eventually, these developments engendered two streams of research on safety issues: One is in the industrial relations literature, and the other is in the psychological literature. The industrial relations literature that deals with the occupational safety and health act (OSHA) emphasizes regulatory standards protecting workers from ever-increasing health hazards on the job (e.g., Ashford, 1976; Rosner and Markowitz, 1987; Davidson, 1970; Berman, 1978; Mendeloff, 1979). None of this literature is concerned with any theoretical notions about why accidents happen, other than blaming unsafe working conditions.

In the psychological literature, these issues stimulated research based on the premise that—after the safety of machinery had been assured—the worker was mainly to blame for accidents. Thus, the main emphasis was on searching for individual differences to explain why some people had more accidents than others.

The concept of accident proneness as an individual trait (Greenwood and Woods, 1919; Newbold, 1926) has long haunted this literature. Although essentially exposed as a statistical artifact and the result of studies that did not control for extraneous variables (Kirchner, 1961; Kerr, 1957; Mintz and Blum, 1949; Hale and Hale, 1970), the concept occasionally surfaces in the present-day safety literature (e.g., Harano, Peck and McBride, 1975). Overall, accident proneness is at best a temporary condition of some workers and not a permanent trait.

Other individual differences were also identified in the psychological literature that explains the occurrence of accidents. Among them are job-related skills (Viteles, 1932), age and experience (Van Zelst, 1954; Maier, 1973; Wigglesworth, 1972), and safety training (Komaki, Barwick, and Scott, 1978; Cohen, 1977; Maier, 1973). Probably stimulated by the negative outcomes of the accident proneness research, environmental and situational influences on accidents were also scrutinized. Overall plant conditions, stress factors such as production demands (Altman, 1970; Kerr, 1957), and participation in safety decisions (Maier, 1973; Pasmore and Friedlander, 1982) were identified empirically as contributors to accidents or safety.

A shortcoming of the safety literature certainly is that it has not scrutinized job behaviors of workers and how these relate to safe performance. One exception is the study of Komaki et al. (1978), which had a narrow focus, however, in that it only examined the effect of training and motivation on safe performance.

Individual traits and dispositions, such as job-related skills, have long been recognized as extremely important in quality performance by workers. As a result, tests for job relevant skills are standard procedure in hiring. Alternatively, new hires are trained in required job skills in order to assure that the lack of such skills does not pose any hazard in the performance of their jobs. It seemed, therefore, to be more beneficial to investigate other behavioral and attitudinal aspects of safe job performance. Since reliability-seeking organizations are "perfection demanding," it seemed a good strategy to go into the field to ask organizational members in one such organization about behaviors and attitudes that helped them perform safely in their daily jobs.

Safety Measurement

Although the concept of safety is important in the literature, no single measure or concept has emerged (Osborn and Jackson, 1988, p. 925). Typically, the tallying of common types of accidents is the usual form of measurement (e.g., Georgopoulos and Tannenbaum, 1957), although some newer measures differentiate the frequency and the severity of accidents, such as is done in the regulated nuclear power industry.

Jacobs (1970) explores several problems in the measurement of safety. One main difficulty is the comparison of different types of organizations on degree of safety. Clearly, a measure is needed that is more abstract and thus can be used independently of the typical kind of accident in a given organization or industry. For example, in nuclear power plants a typical accident involves back injuries sustained from incorrectly lifting equipment. While such accidents also occur aboard aircraft carriers, so too do accidents like falling overboard.

Our review of the safety literature identified one paper-and-pencil measure in the psychological literature abstract that compared four different industries in terms of safety climate (Zohar, 1980). Two weaknesses, relative to our purposes, are apparent in Zohar's instrument. First, his (1980) measure was developed on the basis of operator jobs only. Second, the dimensions of safety Zohar derived from the literature were in no way related to individual job performance. Rather, they refer to perceptions of categories such as the importance of safety training, the status of the safety officer, the status of the safety committee, management attitudes toward safety, and so on. These limitations argue for a measure that transcends both organization idiosyncrasies and role peculiarities by focusing on individuals in relation to how they approach their jobs and what they think is important in assuring safe performance. By looking at the link between individuals and their jobs, it seems that one can eliminate the peculiarities of the job that are rooted in its specific organizational and technical context.

In their demand for perfection, reliability-seeking organizations impose behavioral requirements on their employees in terms of orientation towards safety that are much stronger than in other kinds of organizations. Thus, attitudinal and behavioral norms toward safety should be pronounced in these organizations. The development of a paper-and-pencil measure that captures these norms would enable us to emphasize particular aspects of reliability-enhancing organizations rather than to focus merely on earlier literature that was not related to reliability-seeking organizations. However, for the purposes of distinguishing reliability-seeking organizations from others, the whole spectrum of jobs has to be taken into account, instead of just single functions or roles.

The present contribution, then, not only develops a safety scale for the quantitative description of reliability-seeking organizations for purposes of triangulation with other kinds of data from this research program. In addition, it captures normative aspects of job behaviors and attitudes that directly contribute to safe performance.

DEVELOPMENT OF A SAFETY SCALE

Sample

One main distinction of the safety scale described here is that it was empirically derived, unlike the safety climate scale by Zohar (1980). Focus groups of enlisted men aboard aircraft carriers were used to derive a large pool of issues they believe to be related to the safe performance of their jobs. These issues were translated into questions in an attempt to preserve as closely as possible the men's own verbal descriptions. Three general issues were addressed by these men: Trust/Reliability, Training/Education, and Safety.

A secondary agenda was to test notions of doing things right the first time, that mistakes are not mistakes if taken care of and if they don't turn into big ones, and also to determine to what degree anyone can suspend operations or shift to other facilities or equipment if necessary.

About one hundred items were initially developed. These items were reduced to forty after they were scrutinized to find those that were similar or of questionable clarity and those that tapped more than one dimension. Each of forty items were placed on a seven-point scale and introduced with the following question: "To what extent do each of the following help you meet what is expected of you to do your job well in this organization?" For purposes of validity in the development of safety scales, a different sample of respondents from another organization, also categorized as reliability-seeking, was collected.

The safety items were given to about 550 employees in all four main departments (Operations, Maintenance, Technical Services, and Support Services) of a nuclear power plant in Central California. The sample thus included not only operational jobs as in Zohar (1980), but also clerical and administrative personnel, engineers, and trainers.

Strategy

In developing our measuring instrument, we pursued two strategies. The first strategy was to derive a long scale from the 40 items, using as many items as possible to obtain a scale that would broadly describe the safety culture of reliability-seeking organizations. The major criterion for inclusion of items was that factors are interpretable in meaningful ways and that they reflect our general observations in this kind of organization. The second strategy was to derive a shorter scale based only on items that distinguish reliability-seeking organizations from other kinds of organizations.

It was hypothesized that the short scale better differentiates reliability-seeking organizations from other organizations, whereas the long scale more generally describes the normative aspects related to a safety culture. The statistical techniques used to develop the two scales were essentially the same, with the following exception: For the shorter scale, a one-way analysis of variance was carried out to test for differences in means on each of the forty items between a high reliability sample and a non-high reliability sample. We used the power plant sample and a sample of about sixty undergraduate business students for this analysis. The results provided twenty-five items that significantly differentiated the two samples.

Data Analysis

Long scale. A principal components analysis was conducted of the forty safety items with unities in the main diagonal of the correlation matrix. The solution yielded nine factors absorbing 62.63 percent of the total variance. Eigen values ranged from 13.14 to 1.05. This solution was subjected to a Varimax rotation after which the last three factors loaded only on one item each (using factor loadings of 0.4 or higher as the cutoff); it was therefore decided to delete them.

The reduced set of thirty-seven items was subjected to another principal components analysis with Varimax rotation. This resulted in a solution very similar to the one obtained when considering only the first six factors of the forty-item solution. The difference was that one of the previous factors split into two factors, resulting in a total of seven factors absorbing 60.27 percent of the variance. Again, the factors were conceptually interpretable in a way that reflected our general observations in HROs. This solution is discussed further (see Table 5-1).

Short scale. A principal components analysis with Varimax rotation was carried out with the subset of twenty-five items that clearly differentiated the student and power plant samples for development of the short scale. This analysis yielded six factors with Eigen values greater than one and an explained variance of 58.4 percent. Eigen values ranged from 8.05 to 1.05. The rotated solution is shown in Table 5-2. This solution was also interpretable in a very satisfactory manner. In fact, it resembles the long scale in several aspects (see Table 5-2), to be discussed later.

Table 5-1
Rotated Factor Solution Based on 37 Items

	Factor Name	Number of Items	Eigen Values	Percent Explained Variance	Percent Explained by Factor	Coefficient Alpha
	LONG VERSION					
F1	Accountability/ Responsibility (7, 8, 9, 10, 14, 15, 17, 18, 19, 36, 37, 38)	12	5.18	14.00	23.2	0.90
F2	Adaptiveness/ Responsiveness (13, 27, 31, 32, 40)	5	3.63	9.81	16.3	0.82
F3	Openness/ Cooperation (24, 28, 29, 30, 34, 35)	6	3.44	9.30	15.4	0.81
F4	Hazard awareness (11, 12, 22)	3	3.16	8.54	14.2	0.88
F5	Inquisitiveness/ Search for detail (1, 2, 3, 4, 5)	5	2.93	7.92	13.2	0.74
F6	Role clarity (25, 26, 33)	3	2.17	5.86	9.7	0.76
F7	Maturity (16, 23, 39)	3	1.79	4.84	8.0	0.50
			22.30	60.27%	100.0%	

Discussion of Factors

Long scale. The most important factor is a combination of *Accountability* and *Responsibility*, which is an interesting finding within our framework of reliability-seeking organizations. As discussed in more detail in Roberts, Stout, and Halpern (in press), the concept of accountability in these organizations at the top management level translates into responsibility at the operational level.

In other words, reliability-seeking organizations such as Navy Aviation try to ensure accuracy of operations by making each person responsible for decisions in preventing accidents on the flight decks. This is a very serious responsibility that is not commensurate with level in the hierarchy. To relieve themselves of this responsibility, lower level personnel report their unique

Table 5-2
Rotated Factor Solution Based on 25 Items

		Number of Items	Eigen Values	Percent Explained Variance	Percent Explained by Factor	Coefficient Alpha
	SHORT VERSION					
	Factor Name					
F1	Accountability/ Responsibility (7, 8, 9, 10, 14, 35, 36)	7	3.34	13.36	22.9	0.83
F2	Interaction/ Communication (2, 3, 4, 5)	4	2.99	11.96	20.5	0.78
F3	Adaptability (20, 30, 31, 37, 40)	5	2.60	10.40	17.8	0.71
F4	Hazard awareness (11, 13, 22)	3	2.45	9.80	16.8	0.75
F5	Maturity (16, 23, 39)	3	1.72	6.88	11.8	0.50
F6	Training/ Socialization (1, 6, 33)	3	1.50	6.00	10.2	0.59
			14.60	58.40%	100.0%	

knowledge of events upward in the hierarchy. This factor is typically represented by items such as: "doing one's job well" (19); " 'owning' a problem until it is resolved" (36); "respecting the nature of one's job activities" (8); and "not making work for others" (10).

The second factor, *Adaptiveness/Responsiveness*, reflects the crucial ability to adapt and respond to ever-changing situations in this type of organization. Based on our qualitative data, this can be interpreted in two ways: first, as an ability to adapt to various situations as they come up, such as unexpected events; second, being able to change from low-tempo to high-tempo operations, and vice versa. Schulman (this volume) discusses extensively the necessity for adaptability at Diablo Canyon. Eisenhardt (this volume) makes a similar argument about fast-decision organizations.

Typical items contributing to this factor are "familiarity with operations beyond one's own job" (13); "learning from mistakes" (27); and "being prepared to deal with the unexpected" (32). Familiarity is at the core of Foushee and Lauber's (this volume) description of high performance flight crews.

The third factor, *Openness/Cooperation*, exemplifies an aspect of HROs that is very much a reflection of cooperative attitudes in the face of potentially very hazardous situations. Typical items loading on this factor are "challenging a directive if it might not work" (24); "supervisors who readily pitched in whenever necessary" (28); "acknowledging mistakes" (34); and "taking care of others' well-being" (35).

The fourth factor, *Hazard Awareness*, indicates the importance of anticipating dangerous situations and responding accordingly. Since reliability-seeking organizations are characterized by complexity coupled with extremely high potential hazards (Rochlin; Schulman; this volume) this factor mirrors them accurately. The items that load on this factor are "paying attention to potential danger to others/to myself" (11, 12); and "being alert to the potential for serious accidents" (22).

Factor 5, *Inquisitiveness/Search for Detail*, reflects the necessity to deal with other people to find out what is going on. Being inquisitive in combination with a concern for detail ensures quality in operations and thus results in safe performance. It is typically expressed by "attending to detail" (2); "asking questions whenever necessary" (3); and "being able to rely on others" (4). Many of the papers in this volume focus on the importance of detailed information (Foushee and Lauber; Eisenhardt; Hirschhorn).

Factor 6, *Role Clarity*, delineates the importance of where one's own responsibility ends and where someone else's starts to assure safe performance. The two major items that loaded on this factor are "having clearly defined job boundaries (25); and "understanding the job boundaries of others" (26). Other papers in the high reliability project focus on role specialization (e.g., Roberts, 1992; Roberts, Halpern and Stout, in press), and Eisenhardt (this volume) compares those findings to her findings.

Factor 7, *Maturity*, depicts an aspect that seems to take on added importance in organizations that want to assure safe operations. The importance of this factor lies in the fact that potentially hazardous organizations cannot afford to tolerate immature behavior, since it is typically self-centered with no regard for hazard. The two main items loading on this scale are "being treated like a child" (16); and "kicking back" (23).

As mentioned earlier, the short version of the safety measure was developed with the intention of differentiating reliability-seeking organizations from organizations that are not oriented that way. The discussion of the short version of the scale in the next section shows that the seven dimensions of the safety-cultural aspects of reliability-seeking organizations in the long version of the scale to a large extent also distinguish characteristics of reliability-seeking organizations when comparing them to non-reliability-seeking organizations.

Short scale. Four factors in the short version replicate factors of the long version, although based on a reduced set of items. These are F1, Accountability/Responsibility (Factor 1 in long version); F2, Interaction/Communication (Factor 5, Inquisitiveness/Search for detail in long version); F4, Hazard Awareness (Factor 4 in the long version); and F5, Maturity (Factor 7 in the long version). Thus, these four factors are descriptive of a general safety culture.

However, the dimensions of the short version of the safety scale that do not overlap with the long version are the ones that actually distinguish reliability-seeking organizations from those that are not so oriented. These are Adaptability (Factor 3) and Training/Socialization (Factor 6). These two factors are discussed in more detail below.

Factor 3, *Adaptability*, as a distinguishing safety dimension is a very interesting finding that replicates our results from the qualitative data collection. This factor contains subsets of items that appear in two subscales in the long version, Adaptability/Responsibility and Openness/Cooperation. Adaptability in the short scale depicts notions of openness in dealing with others as well as adaptability in an effort to solve problems. Our field observations support this (Rochlin; Schulman; this volume). Meyer and Starbuck (this volume) point out what can happen to an organization when it fails to adapt.

The other nonoverlapping factor, Factor 6, *Training/Socialization*, is the major aspect that distinguishes reliability-seeking organizations from garden-variety organizations, and it is of great importance in validating our efforts in developing this scale. It is supported by our findings in the field that safety values are inculcated in extensive training procedures, which encompass training in job skills as well as socialization into safety (Roberts, 1990a,b). It is also supported by the extensive safety literature, which has consistently identified training as a major factor in accident prevention (e.g., Maier, 1973).

Validation of the Safety Scales

To validate the proposed scales, various analyses were conducted. First, to examine whether the presented factor structure adequately represented the data, confirmatory factor analyses were conducted for both scales. The LISREL VI program (Joreskog and Sorbom, 1986) was used to analyze the sample co-variance matrices. To evaluate the factor model, parameter estimates were obtained for the relationships between observed indicators and their underlying constructs, as well as for relationships among the constructs themselves. The factor loadings for the long and short models are shown in Tables 5-3 and 5-4, respectively. Correlations among the underlying factors for the long and short versions are shown in Tables 5-5 and 5-6, respectively.

All the items in the model were significantly related to their underlying factors. Even after deleting two items (5 and 33) that had relatively high normalized residuals, the Chi-square statistic for the long version was still significant χ (539) = 2024.93, $p < 0.000$]. For the short version, the Chi-square statistic was also significant [χ (260) = 891.12, $p < 0.000$].

However, many of the assumptions of the Chi-square statistic are violated in practice, so a significant Chi-square value does not necessarily mean that a model should be rejected (Joreskog and Sorbom, 1986). This seems especially reasonable in the scale development reported here, since the statistic for the long version was still significant (χ (539) = 2024.93, $p < 0.000$). For the short

Table 5-3
Confirmatory Factor Analysis, LISREL

Scales	Account.	Adapt.	Open.	Hazard.	Detail.	Bound.	Mature.
			FACTOR LOADINGS, LONG MODEL				
S7	0.702						
S8	0.677						
S9	0.650						
S10	0.549						
S14	0.725						
S15	0.815						
S17	0.494						
S18	0.814						
S19	0.745						
S36	0.648						
S37	0.688						
S38	0.713						
S13		0.560					
S27		0.658					
S31		0.845					
S32		0.858					
S40		0.565					
S24			0.622				
S28			0.610				
S29			0.605				
S30			0.845				
S34			0.818				
S35			0.661				
S11				0.902			
S12				0.862			
S22				0.762			
S1					0.475		
S2					0.755		
S3					0.779		
S4					0.660		
S5					0.574		
S25						0.818	
S26						0.894	
S33						0.476	
S16							0.465
S23							0.505
S39							0.715

Table 5-4
Confirmatory Factor Analysis, LISREL

	FACTOR LOADINGS, SHORT MODEL					
Scales	*Account.*	*Interact.*	*Adapt.*	*Hazard.*	*Mature.*	*Train.*
S7	0.650					
S8	0.753					
S9	0.701					
S10	0.561					
S14	0.685					
S35	0.651					
S36	0.572					
S2		0.688				
S3		0.726				
S4		0.649				
S5		0.639				
S20			0.241			
S30			0.775			
S31			0.703			
S37			0.700			
S40			0.529			
S11				0.800		
S13				0.537		
S22				0.827		
S16					0.326	
S23					0.441	
S39					0.763	
S1						0.504
S6						0.437
S33						0.744

version, the Chi-square statistic was also significant (χ (260) = 891.12, $p < 0.000$).

Our aim was not to achieve perfect statistical model fitting at the expense of neglecting empirical notions, such as other authors have sometimes done (for example, Brown and Holmes, 1986). Brown and Holmes used the items on the Zohar (1980) safety climate scale mentioned earlier and could not replicate his factor structure. Based on purely statistical means, they developed a scale that consists of three factors that tap the three dimensions of management, workers, and risk but that do not seem to do justice to the safety concept.

Furthermore, in our LISREL analyses, the values obtained for the long version for the goodness of fit index (0.784), adjusted goodness of fit index (0.750), and Bentler and Bonnett (1980) normed fit index (0.745) showed that the model fits the data reasonably well. The statistics were again stronger for the short version: goodness of fit (0.869), adjusted goodness of fit (0.836), and Bentler and Bonnett (1980) normed fit index (0.806).

Table 5-5
Confirmatory Factor Analysis, LISREL

	FACTOR INTERCORRELATIONS LONG MODEL						
Scales	Account.	Adapt.	Open.	Hazard.	Detail.	Bound.	Mature.
1. Accountability/ Responsibility	1.000						
2. Adaptiveness/ Responsiveness	0.761	1.000					
3. Openness/ Cooperation	0.663	0.746	1.000				
4. Hazard awareness	0.472	0.600	0.498	1.000			
5. Inquisitiveness/ Search for Detail	0.688	0.584	0.513	0.438	1.000		
6. Role clarity	0.612	0.647	0.646	0.356	0.433	1.000	
7. Maturity	−0.324	−0.303	−0.232	−0.132	−0.275	−0.198	1.000

Given the difficulty in developing meaningful assessment devices that are not only based on statistical relevance but that also take theoretical considerations and empirical observations into account, these two scales seem to represent a very acceptable and useful assessment.

As a second step in the validation of these two scales, their internal validity was assessed. Cronbach alphas were computed for each of the seven subscales of the long version and each of the six subscales of the short version. Their values ranged from 0.50 to 0.90 for the long subscales and from 0.50 to

Table 5-6
Confirmatory Factor Analysis, LISREL

	FACTOR INTERCORRELATIONS SHORT MODEL					
Scales	Account.	Interact.	Adapt.	Hazard.	Mature.	Train.
1. Accountability/ Responsibility	1.000					
2. Interaction/ Communication	0.737	1.000				
3. Adaptability	0.819	0.684	1.000			
4. Hazard awareness	0.667	0.516	0.662	1.000		
5. Maturity	−0.429	−0.402	−0.459	−0.253	1.000	
6. Training/ Socialization	0.710	0.681	0.676	0.370	−0.295	1.000

0.82 for the short subscales (see Tables 5-1 and 5-2). In fact, the lowest alpha of 0.50 was computed for the maturity scale, which consists of only three items. This subscale has also been somewhat problematic in other ways. Since the three items that load on this subscale are all reversed (and are the only ones that are reversed in all of the safety items), there may have been some error in response or misinterpretation of the questions. Nevertheless, we decided to keep this factor since it is of major empirical importance.

The Cronbach alphas for the other subscales were mostly in the 0.70s for the short scale and in the 0.80s for the long scale. Thus, the reliability of the two scales overall is satisfactory.

Third, the construct validity of the Safety Scales was assessed. Factor scores of the subscales of the long and short versions were computed and correlated with other measures to derive a Multi-Trait Multi-Method matrix for convergent and discriminant validity using other related and nonrelated measures (Campbell and Fiske, 1959).

The measures used in this analysis were Organizational Commitment (Mowday and Steers, 1979), Predictability, Coordination (Georgopoulos and Mann, 1962), Routinization (Whitey, Daft, and Cooper, 1983), Hazard Perception (Mann and Hoffman, 1960, as well as newly developed questions), and Job Satisfaction (Smith, Kendall, and Hulin, 1969; Kunin, 1955).

In general, we expected that the subscales would differentially be related to the validation measures because they tap different dimensions of safety. For ease in presentation, each subscale is discussed separately in terms of our predictions and then in analyzing the MTMM matrix (see Tables 5-7 and 5-8).

Long Version

Factor 1-L, *Accountability/Responsibility,* was expected to be positively associated with commitment and cooperation, since employees who are committed to the organization are assumed to be more willing to be held accountable for cooperation. It should, however, be unrelated to predictability, routinization, and hazard.

As expected, this factor was positively and significantly correlated with Commitment and Cooperation, but somewhat unexpectedly also with Coordination. As predicted, it was not related to Predictability or Routinization. It was associated with overall job satisfaction (Kunin) and satisfaction with work, but not with the other four facets of job satisfaction. This implies (and is supported by related analyses we carried out) that satisfaction with work itself is a major aspect of overall job satisfaction. In terms of the MTMM matrix, it validates the dimension of Accountability/Responsibility because of the general finding in the literature that people are more satisfied if they are in control and are taken seriously (e.g., Greenberger, Strasser, Cummings and Dunham, 1989; Packard, 1989; Spector, 1986).

Factor 2-L, *Adaptiveness/Responsiveness,* was predicted to be positively correlated with Cooperation and Hazard Perception. It was expected to be

Table 5-7
Multi-Trait Multi-Method Matrix Correlations

	LONG SCALE					
	Commit	**Predict**	**Coord**	**Cooper**	**Routin**	**Hazard**
Factor 1	0.21***	0.00	0.18***	0.15**	−.05	−.12*
Factor 2	0.11*	0.09	0.05	0.11*	−.08	0.11*
Factor 3	0.12*	0.05	0.11*	0.16**	0.02	0.09
Factor 4	−.01	−.00	−.10	−.04	0.08	0.36***
Factor 5	0.09	0.17**	0.07	0.14**	−.00	0.04
Factor 6	0.07	0.08	0.13*	0.04	0.10	−.15**
Factor 7	0.07	0.03	0.08	0.03	0.06	−.05
	Satwork	**Satspvs**	**Satpay**	**Satprom**	**Satcowk**	**Satiskun**
Factor 1	0.24***	0.06	0.07	0.05	0.04	0.19***
Factor 2	0.08	0.12*	0.03	0.03	0.12*	0.11*
Factor 3	0.14*	0.15**	0.06	0.09	0.15**	0.15**
Factor 4	−.10	−.10	−.05	−.00	−.03	0.01
Factor 5	0.06	0.14**	−.07	0.05	0.18***	0.08
Factor 6	0.03	0.10	0.07	0.07	−.01	0.04
Factor 7	0.03	0.11*	0.05	0.08	0.06	0.04

*** = $p < 0.0001$
** = $p < 0.001$
* = $p < 0.01$

negatively correlated with Predictability and Routinization since these are divergent measures.

These predictions are supported by the results presented in the MTMM matrix. This factor is also correlated with commitment, which may be explained by the fact that committed workers are also more willing to go the extra mile. There was also a smaller but significant correlation with overall job satisfaction and with satisfaction with supervision.

Factor 3-L, *Openness/Cooperation,* was predicted to be strongly and positively related to Cooperation as the major convergent measure. Foushee and Lauber (this volume) discuss how high-performing flight crews used more commands, more observations about flight status, suggestions, statement of intent, inquiries, and acknowledgments of the others' communication than lower-performing crews. It was expected that Openness/Cooperation would also be positively correlated with commitment and with satisfaction. We also hypothesized that there should be a positive correlation with hazard perception since workers might be more ready to cooperate in the face of potential danger. For divergent measures, we expected that this factor would be unrelated to routinization and negatively related to predictability.

The results show that the expected relationship with Cooperation was borne out, but it was not as high and as significant as predicted ($r = 0.16$,

Table 5-8
Multi-Trait Multi-Method Matrix Correlations

| | **SHORT SCALE** | | | | | |
	Commit	**Predict**	**Coord**	**Cooper**	**Routin**	**Hazard**
Factor 1	0.22***	−.00	0.19***	0.14**	0.04	−.10
Factor 2	0.06	0.15*	0.07	0.14**	−.03	0.05
Factor 3	0.17***	0.17**	0.14**	0.14**	−.07	−.00
Factor 4	−.00	−.00	−.10	0.01	0.03	0.38***
Factor 5	0.08	0.03	0.07	0.07	0.05	−.05
Factor 6	0.07	0.09	0.03	0.03	0.06	−.00
	Satwork	**Satspvs**	**Satpay**	**Satprom**	**Satcowk**	**Satiskun**
Factor 1	0.17**	0.04	0.06	0.07	−.00	0.19***
Factor 2	0.09	0.11*	−.05	0.03	0.14**	0.06
Factor 3	0.22***	0.22***	0.09	0.09	0.17***	0.21***
Factor 4	−.08	−.06	−.03	−.00	−.00	0.01
Factor 5	0.03	0.12	0.07	0.08	0.09	0.03
Factor 6	−.04	0.08	0.01	0.08	0.10	0.02

*** = $p < 0.0001$
** = $p < 0.001$
* = $p < 0.01$

$p < 0.001$). One possible reason for this may be the fact that our measure of cooperation is an adaptation of the original Tjosvold (1986) measure and includes only co-workers but not supervisors, although the supervisor can be a major factor in cooperation. The correlation with Commitment was also as expected. The more important correlations with satisfaction were for satisfaction with supervision and co-workers, which underlines the cooperation aspect of this dimension. The divergent measures were as expected. The relationship with hazard was in the right direction but failed to reach the significance level of 0.01. These results are consistent with Weick's (this volume) plea for more communication among participants in organizations in which catastrophic outcomes can occur.

Factor 4-L, *Hazard Awareness*, was expected to be positively and significantly correlated with the hazard scale as its convergent measure. Further, it was predicted that it would be positively correlated with cooperation based on the same rationale as above. All the other measures should be unrelated, with the exception of work satisfaction, which we expected to be negative.

The relationship with the hazard scale (which was factor analyzed earlier) was as expected. It was very high and significant ($r = 0.36$, $p < 0.0001$). Again, there was no relationship between hazard and cooperation. Although this result is unexpected, it is consistent. The relationship between Hazard

Awareness and work satisfaction was negative as expected, but it was slightly below the 0.01 level of significance.

Factor 5-L, *Inquisitiveness/Search for Detail*, was expected to be positively correlated with cooperation as the main validating measure. It was also expected to be positively correlated with hazard and commitment as instigators for this behavior and negatively related to routinization.

The factor was highly and significantly correlated with cooperation ($r = 0.14$, $p < 0.001$) but failed to show significance for hazard and commitment, although the direction was positive. It was totally unrelated to routinization, probably indicating that this factor is not the opposite of routinization but rather an unrelated concept. Satisfaction with supervision and with co-workers was positively correlated with this dimension. This is a further indication for convergence of different measurements, since this factor represents essentially a people-oriented dimension of safety.

Factor 6-L, *Role Clarity*, was expected to be positively correlated with predictability and routinization, but otherwise unrelated.

The results in the MTMM matrix show that both relationships were positive but failed to reach the 0.01 level of significance. Role Clarity was positively and significantly correlated with coordination, however. Coordination can be seen as an aspect of clarifying job boundaries and thus supporting this dimension of safety. The other relationships were as expected, with the exception of hazard, which was significantly and negatively correlated with role clarity. This is an interesting aspect, since it seems to indicate that hazard increases uncertainty.

Factor 7-L, *Maturity*, was predicted to be positively related to commitment, but unrelated to all other measures. It was expected to be positively related to satisfaction with supervisor and overall job satisfaction.

As the results show, the correlation with commitment was in the right direction, but was not significant. Maturity was unrelated to all other measures with the exception of satisfaction with supervisor, as expected. The correlation with overall job satisfaction was positive but insignificant.

Short Version

An analysis of the MTMM Matrix of the short version of the safety scale shows similar patterns of item correlations for the factor scores that bear the same name as in the long version. Therefore, a detailed discussion of these factors is unnecessary. The two factors that are different in the short version are Adaptability and Training/Socialization.

Factor 3-S, *Adaptability*, was expected to be positively correlated with cooperation and negatively correlated with predictability and routinization. It was expected to be unrelated to job satisfaction.

The results in the MTMM matrix confirm the positive relationship between Adaptability and cooperation and the negative relationship between

Factor 3-S and routinization. It does not support the expectation that Adaptability is negatively correlated with predictability. As can be seen in the matrix, Adaptability is also significantly and positively correlated with commitment and coordination. It is also positively correlated with work satisfaction, satisfaction with supervision, co-worker satisfaction, and with overall job satisfaction.

Factor 6-S, *Training/Socialization*, was expected to be related to commitment as an outcome of the socialization process. It was predicted to be essentially unrelated to the other measures. The latter prediction is borne out by the results, but the correlation with commitment does not reach the 0.01 level of significance, though it is in the right direction.

Given the solutions to the factor analyses and the validation of their dimensions discussed above, the mean of each subscale for each person was computed.

As the last step in the validation procedure of the safety scale, the means of the subscales of the long and short versions of the newly developed measure were compared to other data. Since the safety scale's main purpose was to distinguish between reliability-seeking and other organizations, the hypothesis was advanced that the means on each subscale should be higher in reliability-seeking than in other organizations. Since we envision that there is a continuum from non-reliability-seeking organizations to reliability-seeking organizations (see Schulman, this volume, for differentiation *within* reliability-seeking organizations), we expected that an organization with very low safety requirements would show lower mean values on each of the subscales. For an organization that lies somewhere in the middle on the continuum, we expected that only some of the subscales would be significantly lower; however, we found it was difficult to make exact predictions because of the exploratory nature of the research.

To validate our scales against a non-reliability-seeking organization, we collected a new set of data of the safety scale items from 180 undergraduate students in the business school of a major university. We asked these students, "To what extent do each of the following help you meet what is expected of you to do your job well as a student at _____ ?"

One-way Analyses of Variance were carried out for the long and short versions of the scale. Each of the means was significantly ($p < 0.0001$) lower for the student sample than for our developmental sample. This finding generally confirms the validity of our scale in terms of distinguishing reliability-seeking from non-reliability-seeking organizations. However, the intention was to make the short version of the scale more distinctive than the long version based on the way the subset of twenty-five items was developed. A closer look at the data analysis suggests that this is true. Although all subscale means are significantly lower for the student data at the level of 0.0001, the differences are larger in the short version, which is also reflected in the higher F-values for the short scale, indicating that they do distinguish more significantly.

DISCUSSION

In summary, this chapter describes the development and validation of a paper-and-pencil measure so that reliability-enhancing organizations could be readily discerned from other types of organizations. The short version of the scale is particularly suited for this purpose due to the way the subset of items was selected, whereas the long version of the scale is more generally descriptive of a safety culture.

A particular feature of both scales is their relative abstractness, achieved by asking questions in terms of job attitudes and behaviors that job incumbents thought were related to safety.

The major benefit of the two safety scales, and of the short scale in particular, is seen as providing a relatively simple means of assessing the reliability of a given organization in terms of safety normativeness as its major component. Within the realm of our research program on high-reliability organizations, this provides one quantitative measure for deepening our understanding of the differences among organizations that reside along a continuum from non-reliability to high reliability. Apart from our own research interests, quality and reliability are becoming more important also to other kinds of organizations (see Olsen, 1990).

In terms of overall safety, it is evident that cultural norms can have an enormous impact on how an organization approaches safety issues. A good example is provided by an analysis of the King's Cross Underground fire in the London subway (Fennell, 1988) where thirty-one people died. This tragedy could have been avoided had the organization had a more pro-active approach to accident prevention. The report concludes that nothing less than a cultural change in terms of safety norms is required to prevent future tragedies of this kind. What this report also brings out clearly is that, since technical safeguards that could have considerably reduced the risk of an underground fire were not in place, the organization essentially relied on its employees to avert the spread of fires. But since aggressive accident prevention was not part of the cultural norms, people did not know how to react properly. The point is that people are often the last straw to rely on for preventing tragedies, be it by design, as in the London subway, or be it by unforeseen events (Perrow, 1984), which makes the assessment of cultural norms so crucial.

Limitations

The amount of explained variance of about 60 percent by each of the two scales compares well with similar instruments (e.g., Zohar, 1980). One possible explanation for unexplained variance, which is particularly true for reliability-enhancing organizations, is the notion of fluidity (see Rochlin; Schulman; Eisenhardt; Foushee and Lauber; this volume). In the present context it means that a static measure cannot be expected to capture a dynamic characteristic. The safety measure is essentially a snapshot of safety orientation as a normative cultural aspect of reliability-enhancing organizations. It does not capture the dynamic aspect of the process of reliability enhancement, nor does it encompass structural characteristics that might be related to reliability enhancement (Roberts, 1992).

Validity and Reliability

As discussed, the statistical properties of the two scales are satisfactory overall. Cronbach alphas are mostly in the 0.80s for the long version and the 0.70s for the short version. Although the Chi-square statistic yielded by the LISREL confirmatory factor analysis could not confirm a perfect fit of the data to the proposed models, other indicators, such as goodness of fit and normed fit index, closely approached the rule-of-thumb values that indicate a good fit. As noted earlier, the major strength of these two scales is in their empirical derivation, which necessitated a compromise in terms of statistical properties. An analysis of the Multi-Trait Multi-Method matrix showed that convergent as well as discriminant validity was generally achieved. In addition, we also found some interesting overall patterns. Routinization was not correlated with any factor, neither in the long nor in the short version of the scale. This is also borne out by our qualitative data (Rochlin, La Porte, and Roberts, 1987; Roberts, in press).

That neither of the two satisfaction facets, Satisfaction with Promotion and Satisfaction with Pay, was correlated with any of the factors in the long or short scale seems to indicate the serious nature of safety. In other words, pay and promotion opportunities become unimportant when an organization is seeking safety. However, satisfaction with supervision, co-workers, and work itself was related to some of the subscales, indicating the people-related nature of dimensions such as Openness/Cooperation and Inquisitiveness/Search for Detail or Adaptability and the work-related nature of dimensions such as Accountability/Responsibility.

Further Research

It is clear that a good deal of work lies ahead. The development and validation of the safety scale and Schulman's work (this volume) laid the groundwork for distinguishing among organizations that lie at different points of the reliability-seeking continuum. A next step is to apply this measure to a variety of such organizations.

An obvious further extension of our research is to relate these cultural norms to objective dependent measures, such as indicators of safety performance. For example, do individuals whose responses are high on some or all of these norms perform more safely than others? This would enable us to make predictions that would have direct implications for the management of highly complex, dangerous organizations.

REFERENCES

Altman, James W. (1970). "Behavior and accidents." *Journal of Safety Research, 2, 3,* 109–122.

Ashford, Nicholas A. (1976). *Crisis in the Workplace: Occupational Disease and Injury.* Cambridge, Mass.: MIT Press.

Bentler, P. M., and D. G. Bonnett (1980). "Significance tests and goodness-of-fit in the analysis of covariance structures." *Psychological Bulletin, 88,* 588–606.

Berman, Daniel M. (1978). *Death on the Job.* New York: Monthly Review Press.

Brown, R. L., and H. Holmes (1986). "The use of a factor-analytic procedure for assessing the validity of an employee safety climate model." *Accident Analysis and Prevention, 18,* 6, 455–470.

Campbell, D., and D. Fiske (1959). Convergent and discriminant validation by the multitrait-multimethod matrix. *Psychological Bulletin, 56,* 81–105.

Cohen, A. (1977). "Factors in successful occupational, safety programs." *Journal of Safety Research, 9,* 4, 168–178.

Davidson, R. (1970). *Peril on the Job: A Study of Hazards in the Chemical Industries.* Washington, D.C.: Public Affairs Press.

Fennell, D., (1988). "Investigation into the King's Cross Underground Fire," London: Department of Transport.

Georgopoulos, B. S., and F. C. Mann (1962). *The Community General Hospital.* New York: Macmillan.

Georgopoulos, B. S., and A. S. Tannenbaum (1957). "A study of organizational effectiveness." *American Sociological Review, 22,* 534–540.

Greenberger, D. B., S. Strasser, L. L. Cummings, and R. B. Dunham, (1989). "The impact of personal control on performance and satisfaction. *Organizational Behavior and Decision Processes, 43,* 1, 29–51.

Greenwood, M., and H. M. Woods (1919). "The incidence of industrial accidents, with special reference to multiple accidents." Industrial Fatigue Research Board Reports, No. 4 (cited in Viteles, 1932).

Hale, A. R., and M. Hale (1970). "Accidents in perspective." *Occupational Psychology, 44,* 115–121.

Harano, R. M., R. C. Peck, and R. S. N. McBride. (1975). "The prediction of accident liability through biographical data and psychometric tests." *Journal of Safety Research. 7,* 1, 16–52.

Jacobs, H. H. (1970). "Towards more effective safety measurement systems." *Journal of Safety Research, 2,* 3, 160–175.

Jick, T. D. (1979). "Mixing qualitative and quantitative methods: triangulation in action." *Administrative Science Quarterly, 24,* 602–611.

Joreskog, K. G., and D. Sorbom (1986). *LISREL VI: Analysis of Linear Structural Relationships by the Method of Maximum Likelihood.* Chicago: National Education Resources.

Kerr, W. (1957). "Complementary theories of safety psychology." *Journal of Social Psychology, 45,* 3–9.

Kirchner, W. K., II (1961). "The fallacy of accident-proneness." *Personnel, 38,* 6, 34–37.

Komaki, J., K. O. Barwick, and L. W. Scott (1978). "A behavioral approach to occupational safety: Pinpointing and reinforcing safe performance in a food manufacturing plant." *Journal of Applied Psychology, 63,* 4, 434–445.

Kunin, T. (1955). "The construction of a new type of attitude measure." *Personnel Psychology, 8,* 65–78.

Maier, N. R. F. (1973). *Psychology in Industrial Organizations.* Boston: Houghton Mifflin.

Mann, F. C. and L. R. Hoffman (1960). *Automation and the Worker: A Study of Social Change in Power Plants.* New York: Henry Holt.

Mendeloff, J. (1979). *Regulating Safety: An Economic and Political Analysis of Occupational Safety and Health Policy.* Cambridge, MA: MIT Press.

Mintz, A., and M. L. Blum (1949). "A re-examination of the accident proneness concept." *Journal of Applied Psychology, 33,* 3, 195–211.

Mowday, R., and R. M. Steers (1979). "The measurement of organizational commitment." *Journal of Vocational Behavior, 14,* 224–247.

Newbold, E. M. (1926). "A contribution to the study of the human factor in the causation of accidents." Industrial Fatigue Research Board Reports, No. 34 (cited in Viteles, 1932).

Olsen, E. (1990). "Control through chaos: Building a team that never drops the ball." *Success* (November), 40–44.

Osborn, R., and D. H. Jackson (1988). "Leaders, riverboat gamblers, or purposeful unintended consequences in the management of complex, dangerous technologies." *Academy of Management Journal, 31,* 4, 924–947.

Packard, T. (1989). "Participation in decision making, performance, and job satisfaction in a social work bureaucracy." *Administration in Social Work, 13,* 1, 59–73.

Pasmore, W., and F. Friedlander (1982). "An action-research program for increasing employee involvement in problem solving." *Administrative Science Quarterly, 27,* 343–362.

Perrow, C. (1984). *Normal Accidents: Living with High-Risk Technologies.* New York: Basic Books.

Roberts, K. H. (1990a). "Managing hazardous organizations." *California Management Review, 32,* 101–113.

——— (in press). "Some aspects of organizational cultures and strategies to manage them in high reliability organizations." *Journal of Management Issues.*

———. (1990b). "Some characteristics of high reliability organizations." *Organization Science, 1,* 160–177.

——— (1992). "Structuring to facilitate migrating decisions in reliability enhancing organizations." In L. Gomez-Mehia, and M. W. Lawless, (eds.), *Top Management and Effective Leadership in High Technology Firms, 3,* Greenwich, CT: JAI Press.

Roberts, K. H., S. K. Stout, and J. J. Halpern (in press). "Decision dynamics in two high reliability military organizations." *Management Science.*

Rochlin, G. I., T. R. La Porte, and K. H. Roberts (1987). "The self designing high reliability organization: Aircraft carrier flight operations at sea." *Naval War College Review, 40,* 76–90.

Rosner, D., and G. Markowitz, (eds.) (1987). *Dying for Work: Workers' Safety and Health in Twentieth-Century America.* Bloomington: Indiana University Press.

Shrivastava, P. (1987). *Bhopal: Anatomy of a Crisis.* Cambridge, MA: Ballinger Publishing Company.

Smith, P. C., L. M. Kendall, and C. L. Hulin (1969). *The Measurement of Satisfaction in Work and Retirement: A Strategy for the Study of Attitudes.* Chicago, IL: Rand McNally.

Spector, P. E. (1986). "Perceived control by employees: A meta-analysis of studies concerning autonomy and participation at work." *Human Relations, 39,* 11, 1005–1016.

Tjosvold, D. (1986). "Organizational test of goal linkage theory." *Journal of Occupational Behavior, 7,* 77–88.

Van Zelst, R. H. (1954). "The effect of age and experience upon accident rate." *Journal of Applied Psychology, 38,* 5.

Viteles, M. S. (1932). *Industrial Psychology.* New York: W. W. Norton.

Weick, K. E. (1990). "The vulnerable system: An analysis of the Tenerife air disaster." *Journal of Management, 16,* 571–593.

Whitey, M., R. L. Daft, and W. H. Cooper (1983). "Measures of Perrow's work unit technology: An empirical assessment and a new scale." *Academy of Management Journal, 26,* 45–63.

Wigglesworth, E. C. (1972). "A teaching model of injury causation and a guide for selecting countermeasures." *Occupational Psychology, 46,* 69–78.

Zohar, D. (1980). "Safety climate in industrial organizations: Theoretical and applied implications." *Journal of Applied Psychology, 65,* 1, 96–102.

6

Interactions Between Ideologies and Politics in Strategy Formation

ALAN D. MEYER
University of Oregon

WILLIAM H. STARBUCK
New York University

Alan D. Meyer is Professor of Management and Edwin E. and June Wolt Cone Research Scholar at the University of Oregon. His research focuses on organization design, strategy, innovation, ideology, and change. He prefers using multiple methods and collecting data by talking with informants on their own turf, in their own language. His recent research involves longitudinal studies of organizations' responses to quantum changes in the structure and boundaries of their industries. He received his B.A. in economics from the University of Washington and his doctorate in organizational behavior and industrial relations from the University of California, Berkeley. He is a Consulting Editor for the *Academy of Management Journal*.

William Starbuck is the ITT Professor of Creative Management at New York University. Earlier, he served on the faculties of Purdue University, Johns Hopkins University, Cornell University, and the University of Wisconsin–Milwaukee; he was a research fellow at the International Institute of Management, Berlin; and he held visiting positions in England, Norway, and Sweden. He has published articles on accounting, bargaining, business strategy, computer programming, computer simulation, forecasting, decision making, human-computer interaction, learning, organizational design, organizational growth and development, perception, scientific methods, and social revolutions.

S ome changes in strategy originate within organizations; others spring from their environments. Consider, for instance, these two strategic changes:

1. In the 1950s, Company A towered over sectors of the busi- ness-machine industry. This firm dominated the cash-register business so completely that its stiffest competition came from its own used machines. But Company A's top managers realized computers would revolutionize their industry, and they re- solved to protect their hard-won gains. In 1953, Company A launched a new strategy by acquiring a California computer maker. Six years later, the new subsidiary developed the first commercial transistorized computer in the world. Company A seemed well positioned to challenge IBM's slim lead in the emerging computer industry. Throughout the 1960s, Wall Street analysts touted Company A's stock as a glamour issue, and it rose to a price-earnings multiple of 63.

2. Company B's 1971 losses nearly exhausted its capital reserves. Competitors were ravaging the firm's traditional markets, and Wall Street analysts predicted that Company B was "headed for the corporate scrap heap." It needed strategic reorientation desperately, but the top managers seemed too bewildered and demoralized to set a new course. With bankruptcy looming, Company B's directors put an executive from an overseas sub- sidiary into the presidency. He immediately changed the com- pany's name, altered accounting practices, built a costly new corporate headquarters, and imitated competitors' marketing tactics. Company B lost $60 million in 1972.

When strategies shift, financial results usually become the bases for judg- ing both the new strategies and the leaders who crafted them. Consider these epilogues to the two stories above:

1. One company earned more in two years than it had in the previous seven. Mr. X, the CEO, received wide acclaim as a strategic genius. A grateful board of directors awarded him a generous bonus.

2. One company experienced record losses. The directors fired Mr. Y, the CEO, because they judged him an ineffective leader who lacked vision.

Which strategic change preceded which outcome? Which CEO was the hero, and which the goat? The answers seem obvious: The strategic genius must have spurred Company A's bold move into computers, and the ineffective leader who lacked vision must have designed the superficial changes that mag- nified Company B's losses.

But this was real life, so it happened just the other way around. The record losses came on the heels of Mr. Y's computer acquisition, and Mr. X's "superficial changes" preceded the earnings surge. What is more, "Company A" and "Company B" are really the same firm—National Cash Register.

What explains these paradoxical events? How could NCR fall so far, so fast? Why did Mr. Y's foresight draw punishment, whereas Mr. X's perfunctory actions brought reward?

This article argues that Mr. Y's strategic thrust into the computer business failed because it clashed with NCR's strong ideology and because it challenged entrenched power holders. Then, as the firm atrophied, managers channeled their attention and resources into reassuring investors. The facade fooled Wall Street for almost 15 years. Finally, the facade crumbled, performance plummeted, and the top managers got fired. When Mr. X replaced Mr. Y, he turned NCR around through political acumen and shrewd management of ideology.

These events illustrate the paper's central argument: Fundamental strategic changes often start because of environmental shifts, such as breakthroughs in technology, changes in regulatory policy, or shifts in the boundaries and structures of industries. Top managers typically respond by using rational planning to hunt for good strategic responses. Rational processes, however, are ill-suited to abrupt strategic reorientations: Rational processes focus on incremental changes that mesh with the past, and they de-emphasize political and ideological issues. Successful reorientations require effective managing of political and ideological processes.

Research on high reliability organizations has so far disregarded external and political forces, although Eisenhardt's (this volume) account of fast and slow decision makers points to environmental factors. Indeed, Creed, Stout, and Roberts (this volume) argue that enhancing reliability requires organizations to downplay political processes. However, further studies of high reliability organizations probably will show the importance of political processes.

CONCEPTS AND TERMS

Organizational ideologies are "logically integrated clusters of beliefs, theories, world views, values, goals, visions, expectations, plans, myths, stories, rituals, symbols, and terminology" (Starbuck, 1982, p. 3). Ideologies inhabit all organizations, but some ideologies grow more robust than others (Meyer, 1982a). Robust ideologies incorporate many elements that have logical links. They bind members together and explain their worlds (Beyer, 1981).

Organizational politics are processes in which people advance their individual or shared interests by amassing power and using it (Pfeffer, 1981). Political processes may reflect either selfish or altruistic motives; they may either reinforce or overturn existing power structures.

Strategic changes alter products, services, or markets. Such changes may be variations or reorientations (Normann, 1971; Tushman and Romanelli, 1985). *Variations* are incremental changes that harmonize with existing ideologies and sustain power structures. *Reorientations* are revolutionary changes that entail ideological revisions and political upheavals.

ORIGINS OF STRATEGIES AND IDEOLOGIES

New organizations undergo transitions "from no beliefs to new beliefs, from no rules to new rules, and from no culture to new culture" (Pettigrew, 1979, p. 574). When leaders with entrepreneurial visions create organizations, their visions turn into goals that become the bases of commitment of new members (Kimberly, 1979; Pettigrew, 1979; Starbuck, 1965). Environments, too, imprint structures, processes, and norms onto new organizations (Stinchcombe, 1965). Imprinted properties can persist long after the individuals and environments that fostered them have departed.

The history of NCR shows the effects of imprinting. This chapter's senior author compiled the history from forty-six articles in sixteen business periodicals. The articles were published between January 1958 and June 1991. Significant changes in NCR's strategies and environment were arrayed on a timeline. Content analyses isolated excerpts relating to ideology, strategy, politics, and performance. All direct quotations have come from one of the analyzed articles.

> In 1884, John Patterson began making a machine that recorded retail sales. But merchants displayed little interest in Patterson's "Incorruptible Cashier." Shopkeepers saw it as an expensive gadget, and clerks saw it as an insulting accusation that they had been stealing from the cash box. Patterson set about creating a market—by instructing his salesmen, "Don't talk cash registers. Don't talk machines. Talk the prospect's business."
>
> Patterson blazed the trail for modern sales techniques. He was among the first to develop sales manuals, to run company-sponsored sales training schools, to pay generous commissions, and to grant exclusive sales territories. Patterson also pioneered the practice of increasing rather than cutting marketing efforts during recessions, as well as the practice of intimidating competitors with retaliatory price cuts. This aggressive marketing cornered 95 percent of the cash-register business by 1915. It also drew antitrust lawsuits.

Strong leaders' personalities and actions supply raw materials for organizational sagas (Clark, 1972). Sagas are evocative narratives about heroic exploits in the face of adversity. They are ideological parables that express, enhance, and codify beliefs (Meyer, 1982a). Sagas help perpetuate ideologies by anchoring the present in the past and by lending meaning to the future. They blend notable events, wishes, and retrospective justifications. Sagas magnify and institutionalize founders' personal values, but they also can carry founders' personal shortcomings into the future.

> In 1912, the government indicted Patterson on three counts of violating the Sherman Antitrust Act. Convicted, he was fined $5,000 and sentenced to a

year in prison. While his case was on appeal, a disastrous flood struck Dayton, Ohio, where NCR had its headquarters. Patterson spearheaded a rescue effort, spent two-thirds of NCR's 1913 profits on flood relief, and became a national hero. Disavowing calls for a presidential pardon, he proclaimed: "I am guilty of no crime. I want no pardon." In 1915, a federal appeals court overturned his conviction.

A teetotaler and a health faddist, Patterson revered physical fitness. He insisted NCR's executives rise at 5:00 A.M. to go horseback riding. One morning, he told an inept rider, "Anybody who can't handle horses can't handle men." That was how Charles F. Kettering ended up at General Motors.

Patterson would tolerate no opposition from his subordinates. He declared, "When a man gets indispensable, let's fire him." Patterson applied this dictum to one eighteen-year veteran, and that was how Thomas J. Watson wound up at IBM.

In this capricious fashion, Patterson trained and fired many promising successors. Patterson's dominance also created an ideology that abhorred dissent. The danger in this ideology lay dormant for decades.

STRATEGIC VARIATIONS

Strategic variations exploit organizations' knowledge and stabilize their environments. Organizational ideologies accept strategic variations easily since they make only incremental changes in products, markets, or clients. Variations signal top managers' responsiveness to changing environments, but they also validate existing ideologies and structures because prevailing values support the variations. Thus, variations let top managers finesse the fundamental tension between their organizations' needs for stability and change.

Top managers can program their organizations to produce variations, freeing the top managers themselves to attend to other matters: Sales forces automatically gather information on established customers' changing tastes; research departments extend technologies linearly; and planning groups methodically predict the actions of familiar competitors.

As variations embellish strategies, they support ideologies and reinforce power structures. Strategic variations embody their proponents' perceptions and ensure that the proponents' expertise will remain relevant in the future. In this sense, strategies are artifacts of bygone power struggles as well as blueprints for future actions.

NCR's founder died in 1922. Having triumphed over NCR's rivals in the marketplace and having quelled dissent within the firm, Patterson left a legacy of harmonious beliefs that bound people together and expressed the outlook many shared. Organizational folklore carried Patterson's values forward, and his loyal disciples shared control. This structure could accommodate only minor variations in strategy.

Patterson's successors supported and elaborated NCR's strategy, for they accepted its tenets: Profitability and growth come from marketing prowess, product quality, and total control of manufacturing. They cautiously expanded NCR's product line to serve the financial industry. Onto the core structure, they grafted adding-machine and accounting-machine divisions that had their own direct sales and service departments. Within each division, engineers refined products carefully, and managers pursued vertical integration with diligence. NCR was machining its own screws, building electric motors designed by its own engineers, and employing skilled cabinetmakers to assemble cash-register drawers. As time passed, the new divisions succeeded in their respective markets, divisions serving overseas markets appeared, and NCR unreflectively evolved a rigid product structure. Affluence bred complacency.

IDEOLOGICAL GROWTH AND MUTATION

Left undisturbed, organizational ideologies tend to grow in size as they attract new elements, and they tend to become more tightly integrated as logical links among the elements proliferate. Believers reinforce and reproduce ideology through socialization and selective recruitment. As logical links multiply, believers come to view the beliefs, values, sagas, and other ideological elements as inextricable. Each part takes its meaning from the whole (Clark, 1972). Eventually, ideologies develop auras of objectivity: No longer are they subjective doctrines of fallible people; instead, they become objective realities of the external world. Similarly, strategies lose the feeling of free choice and become ironclad demands of environments.

Although ideologies and strategies resist change, they never reach long-run equilibria. Organizations invariably contain groups with divergent interests and multiple ideologies that are partly inconsistent. Since strategies are simplistic expressions of organizations' relations with their environments, even stable strategies interact with changes in technologies, industries, and societies to produce new effects. Over time, these effects subtly alter even robust ideologies and clear strategies.

Schulman's (this volume) analysis of the Diablo Canyon Power Plant illustrates the endless changes. The papers by Eisenhardt (this volume) and Foushee and Lauber (this volume) imply that high reliability organizations react and change more rapidly than other organizations. These papers also argue that rapid reactions are critical for high performance by such organizations. However, observations of individual workers, such as these authors made, may give an impression of greater reaction speed than do observations at an organizational level.

> Traditional midwestern values percolated into NCR's headquarters. Visionary leaders were banished, and the surviving leaders embraced the past. Dissent stilled, and NCR came to look more and more as its ideology said it should look.
>   Profits accumulated, but harmony and complacency were insidiously undermining NCR's ideology. People forgot that success had come from

solving customers' problems; they came to believe that success was due to the elegant designs of their unrivaled products. Fiscal conservatism and a stolid sales mentality gradually replaced an entrepreneurial spirit and an aggressive marketing ethic.

Ideologies become most durable and potent when visible practices ratify them (Clark, 1972; Meyer, 1982a). When commonplace acts link symbolically to shared values, they gain uncommon meanings. Organizational language, for instance, often expresses ideology. Language both reflects experience and shapes future actions. It encapsulates shared ideas and deletes from conscious experience the events with no names. Thus, ideological language helps construct an apparent reality that fits its assumptions.

Because organizations establish programs to repeat their successes, they want stable environments, and so they try to choose strategic variations that will halt social and technological changes (Starbuck, 1983). Large, powerful organizations are most successful in this effort: They can force their immediate environments to adapt to their strategies and to accept their ideologies for long periods.

But the environmental stability seen by people in such organizations is partly illusory. Their misperceptions accumulate, and the longer organizations succeed in imposing their strategies on their environments, the more they undermine their own adaptive abilities.

When humans get no sensory stimulation for some time, their brains begin hallucinating. Similarly, when organizations systematically drain the variety out of their environments, they experience "self-imposed sensory deprivation" (Pondy and Mitroff, 1979, p. 23). Then organizations' ideologies can begin inspiring collective fantasies: "We are thriving in stable, benevolent environments." Such fantasies shield strategies from danger signals.

> NCR spun such a tight cocoon around its Dayton operations that employees elsewhere were called "outsiders." Observers remarked on the friendliness and loyalty of NCR employees. The president during the 1950s and 1960s had been born less than one mile from NCR's headquarters; he began working for NCR as a file clerk in 1933, and he never worked for another firm. Most executives lived in a suburb overlooking the plant, and each morning they met on street corners to walk to work together. It was traditional for more than 100 managers and executives to eat lunch together daily at a long table.

Top managers are especially likely to misperceive and fantasize. Like all humans, they see successes as resulting from their own actions, and they blame failures on environmental events. However, stronger biases probably afflict top managers than other organization members. Having fashioned their organizations' strategies, or at least having come to believe they designed the strategies, top managers are especially liable to discount evidence that the strategies have outlasted their usefulness. In addition, top managers often operate with less accurate and up-to-date information than their subordinates. Their firsthand experience in making products, selling, or applying technology is usually obsolete; and people relaying secondhand information often omit messages that might displease them.

> When asked in 1958 about technological change, NCR's president retorted, "I've been hearing about 'saturation of the market' ever since 1912. Make no mistake—mechnical bookkeeping is still going to be around for quite a while." But of course! One of NCR's cash registers, after all, retained the same design it had back in 1921.
>
> NCR shunned research and development. For nearly 20 years, the general manager repeatedly asked the president for permission to develop and market adding and accounting machines. The president saw no reason to diversify. Then, when he finally did agree, NCR had lost its position of undisputed leadership in the business-machine industry. His successor echoed this note of caution: "There are sound arguments for perfecting your product before you take the plunge."
>
> Within competitors that did research, however, engineers were fomenting an electronic revolution.

ENVISIONING STRATEGIC REORIENTATIONS

Visualizing reorientations is hard because strategists must imagine sweeping changes that would redefine organizations' domains in fundamental ways. People lack experience outside their domains, so proposed reorientations arouse confusion and uncertainty (Starbuck, 1983). Reorientations often look utterly irrational when managers consider them within current frames of reference (Greenwood and Hinings, 1988; Watzlawick et al., 1974). Reorientations also impugn top managers' wisdom (Argyris and Schön, 1978). Moreover, reorientations redistribute power—taking from those having ties to the past, and giving to those having promise for the future. Thus, managers oppose reorientations to avoid uncertainty, protect their reputations, and maintain power. Nevertheless, organizations' environments make strategic reorientations necessary.

> By 1953, the business press had developed an infatuation with electronic data processing (EDP). Also about that time, business writers and industry analysts began describing NCR as "stodgy, hidebound, and tradition-encrusted." NCR's top managers saw that computers might someday transform the business-machine industry. But that would not happen just yet. "After all," said the president, "our customers in banks and stores have little interest in the newfangled electronic equipment—NCR's mechanical products are cheaper and more reliable. No one knows more about merchants than NCR."

When the need for reorientation grows so strong as to be undeniable, managers may resort to facades (Nystrom and Starbuck, 1984). Facades can safeguard cherished ideologies while creating the illusion of adapting to environmental change.

Indeed, efforts to embellish organizations with veneers of technological elegance have fueled the computer revolution on both the supply side and the demand side. By making computers, NCR and other business-machine firms could manifest their modernity; by buying and installing computers, customers could manifest theirs. Ironically, the computer's rise as the ultimate symbol of rationality spawned a market in high-tech imagery. The reflexive self-sealing of this symbolic rationality is quite remarkable.

> In 1953, NCR bought a California computer maker. One insider likened the acquisition to a "pint of plasma," but NCR reacted as though a mismatched organ had been transplanted into the corporate body. In 1959, the California subsidiary developed the first commercial solid-state computer in the world. NCR's managers saw this development not as an opportunity but as a threat. They warned that corporate earnings would sag if the computer-leasing business grew too rapidly, and NCR's conservative accounting practices made their fears seem prudent.

This "threat" may have been yet another facade. Expanding the computer business would have reallocated power from Dayton to California. Managers in California proposed using standard methods of accounting for leases, arguing that these methods would measure leasing profits more objectively. The managers in Dayton vetoed this proposal. Thus, losses counterfeited by accounting practices may have been ploys in political intrigue.

> NCR's product-oriented sales managers also realized that the computers jeopardized their power, and they responded more candidly. "Don't waste your time on computers," they told their sales staff, "sell posting machines." That is just what the staff did, and so they sold only 30 computers. Reflecting upon the large losses that resulted, NCR's chairman remarked thoughtfully, "Anyone who wants to get into EDP without a steady and profitable line of allied products to support his investment has two strikes against him."

Thus do robust, logically integrated ideologies cause superstitious learning (March and Olsen, 1976). This form of learning stems from "a failure to act, rather than a failure while acting" (Weick, 1979, p. 149). Avoiding tests that could discredit shared beliefs, organizations think they see constraints in their environments. Because organizations avoid acting where they expect to fail, they rarely succeed where they expect to fail (Starbuck, 1983). Ideologies that are already robust grow stronger and even more impractical.

> In 1968, nearly four years after IBM unveiled its third-generation computer, NCR introduced a competing model. NCR's chairman admitted: "We're getting in a little late—as we have on other products. But we never mind being a little late. We learn a lot by others' mistakes—and if all the

prospects for anything are going to be sold in the first two years, it's a damn poor business to go into, anyway." This time, NCR extensively planned and amply funded the new product's marketing. "We had to resist the temptation to release it prematurely," explained one executive. But IBM had gained such momentum that it benefited nearly as much from NCR's lavish promotional campaign as NCR did. "NCR's late entry is opportune," the chairman reassured stockholders. "Our timing is perfect."

The chairman was either whistling in the dark or lying. Rumors about an imminent fourth-generation computer were already circulating, and NCR's ambivalent third-generation offering would eventually siphon off $150 million in capital reserves.

The market failure of NCR's third-generation computer illustrates the inability of rational planning alone to ensure intended results (Grinyer and Norburn, 1975; Starbuck et al., 1978). By detailing plans, planners often build monuments to irrationality. Plans rest on unreliable predictions about future events; and plans develop through social interactions that muster commitment by allaying misgivings, constructing justifications, and affirming planners' wisdom (Meyer, 1984). While plans are taking shape, corrective actions remain untaken.

NCR's reticence about electronics also affected its main businesses: cash registers, adding machines, and accounting machines. While competitors were switching to electronics, NCR clung to the past and perfected its mechanical technology. "We would go to them and describe exactly the kind of computerized systems we needed," recalled one mass retailer. "Their people would listen politely and then tell us what a great machine the Class V cash register was."

Eisenhardt (this volume) might call NCR a slow decision maker. Slow decision makers run the risk of becoming late entrants into markets. However, this risk may be invisible because robust ideologies create commitment and goodwill that instill false confidence (Meyer, 1982a). Signals of impending danger are disregarded, and bad results lose their ability to instigate changes. Indeed, danger signals may even bolster commitment to flawed strategies (Staw, 1980).

NCR towered over its industry, and its strong world-wide marketing organization concealed the effects of encroaching obsolescence.

"The company is making more profit because of computers than it would if it didn't have any," asserted NCR's financial vice-president. "I can say it, but I can't prove it." Investors demanded no proof, however, for NCR had erected an exquisite and stylish facade of computerization. Wall Street analysts touted NCR as a glamour stock, and early in 1970 it reached a price-earnings multiple of 63.

INITIATING STRATEGIC REORIENTATIONS

Reorientations interrupt tranquil interludes when logical links multiply, programmed actions accumulate, and searches for new strategies dwindle. Organizations may drift complacently into crises as programs become less effective and environmental changes go unnoticed.

When crises finally hit, organizations often react in ways that make the crises worse (Starbuck et al., 1978). Because crises call for responses that are not in repertoires, instinctive responses usually worsen them. But the managers who fashioned the outmoded responses defend them to retain power. Thus, replacing top leaders is often essential in turnarounds.

> Late in 1970, the computer revolution overtook NCR. The facade started crumbling. NCR began losing its traditional markets, and profits turned into deficits.
>
> Within two years, Wall Street analysts were predicting that NCR could not possibly survive in the computer age. NCR needed a strategic reorientation desperately, but top managers' beliefs had petrified. They were unable to see, let alone effect, a change in course. In 1971, bankruptcy loomed, investors revolted, and NCR's directors finally had to intervene.
>
> They appointed a new president, William Anderson. He had headed NCR's Japanese subsidiary, the largest and most profitable overseas division. Never having worked at the home office, he was free of the Dayton mentality.

People must abandon old ideologies before they can invent and pursue new strategies. Consequently, strategic reorientations fail unless ideological changes precede them. Even at the best of times, this is a tall order. Efforts to change beliefs and values are always difficult because these elements live in people's brains. Moreover, reorientations are threatening, and research shows people generally think and behave more rigidly when threatened (Staw et al., 1981; Meyer, 1982b). Stress and anxiety lead people to cling tighter than ever to current beliefs and expectations. When crisis looms, how can a leader—particularly a new one—overturn a cherished ideology before the organization succumbs?

The answer lies in the leader's control of symbols, sagas, rituals, and language.

It may seem that advising leaders to manipulate symbols while bankruptcy looms is akin to advocating witchcraft. Urging them to formulate sagas while resources dwindle may sound like administering last rites. Still, great effects may have subtle causes, and dramatic efforts may have trivial effects. Commands and plans and injections of funds may produce almost nothing if ideological changes do not lay the groundwork. Ideological changes alone may instigate profound reorientations without anyone issuing orders, drawing up new plans, or investing large amounts of new money.

When William Anderson leapfrogged over dozens of senior executives into the NCR presidency, a new saga quickly sprang up about his exploits. Born in China, Anderson had attended school in Shanghai. He survived a Japanese World War II prison camp, where he had befriended an NCR employee. His friend persuaded him to join NCR after the war, and he had transformed its beleaguered Japanese subsidiary into a corporate showcase.

Anderson was a "perfectionist" with a "computer brain" and sometimes he uttered eastern proverbs in Chinese pidgin English. The business press announced that he had "restored pride in the company and confidence in the future" and was "leading NCR out of the wilderness."

Most of Anderson's inaugural acts were symbolic ones designed to discredit NCR's prevailing ideology. "Complacency and apathy—these are NCR's greatest sins," he declared in a videotaped address to employees. "Until we see a return to profitability, something akin to martial law will be in effect in Dayton."

At that time, manufacturers were the most promising market for electronic business machines. It was hard for a company with "cash register" in its name to sell to manufacturers, so Anderson renamed the firm "NCR Corporation."

The old yellow-brick headquarters memorialized NCR's past—the walls bore oil portraits of former presidents and bronze plaques honoring salesmen from 1900. Anderson razed the old corporate headquarters and built a new one.

Accounting offers some of the most potent symbols available to leaders (Boland and Pondy, 1983). Accounting categories create meanings by focusing attention, defining what is important, and interpreting events. However, the power in accounting stems partly from its subtlety: Accounting data seem literal, precise, and value-free. Shrewd leaders can exploit the myth that fixed principles, standards, and practices dictate accounting and auditing decisions (Boland, 1982).

Anderson's first major appointment was a new financial vice-president—the Price Waterhouse partner who had supervised the auditing of NCR's financial reports. A few weeks later, despite NCR's tenuous financial condition, the new vice-president advised Anderson to take a financial bath. He did, inflating the 1972 deficit by writing off $135 million of mechanical cash-register inventories.

This financial legerdemain had four important effects: (1) It signaled the obsolescence of NCR's old strategy; (2) it pinned the blame for NCR's predicament on Anderson's predecessor; (3) it underscored the gravity of the crisis to Wall Street investors, Dayton civic leaders, and NCR employees alike; and (4) it guaranteed that NCR's financial performance would improve in 1973.

Each of these effects helped Anderson consolidate power.

COMPLETING STRATEGIC REORIENTATIONS

Crises legitimate unorthodox acts, and they destabilize power structures. They offer opportunities to infuse organizations with energy and to camouflage wanted changes as responses to crises (Meyer, 1982b). Research shows that mandating new behaviors is a powerful method of altering beliefs. As behavioral changes grow familiar, beliefs adapt to the behaviors (Salancik, 1977).

> Having gathered power, Anderson upended NCR's most tradition-bound sector: the marketing organization. He launched crash programs to teach sales staff how to speed up customers' paperwork by stringing together computers, data terminals, and other business machines. Salesmen either became technical consultants or lost their jobs.
>
> In 1973, Anderson proclaimed, "In the future, we will not make anything that cannot be linked to a computer." He went on to replace two-thirds of NCR's corporate officers, to close antiquated factories, and to furlough highly paid mechanical craftsmen. Anderson introduced an array of new electronic products, capitalized on a strike to eliminate 10,000 jobs, shifted production out of Dayton, and hired low-paid assemblers to staff the new plants.
>
> The results were impressive: NCR earned more in two years than it had in the previous seven. Sales grew, but earnings grew faster—partly because new accounting practices magnified them, and partly because demand persisted for the "obsolete" machines NCR had written off. Through luck, cunning, or both, Anderson scored again: The income from mechanical cash registers fueled the firm's recovery from the very problems that writing them off had induced!
>
> Thus, did William Anderson complete the strategic reorientation his predecessor had begun twenty years earlier by buying a computer company. Observers credited Anderson with rescuing NCR from disaster single-handedly. The business press hailed him as an "intellectual giant" and a "strategic genius."

Anderson deserves much credit for the turnaround, but these particular accolades appear unjustified. His insights were not profound; his strategies were not especially innovative. Every industry insider knew that NCR needed to start making electronic products that could link to computers.

Anderson's actions look prosaic and superficial: He changed the firm's name, cooked the books, pruned the dead wood, and imitated competitors' marketing. Even the vaunted strategic reorientation looks more symbolic than substantive. Electronic cash registers, terminals, and other products for traditional markets continued to generate most of NCR's profits.

But these looks deceive: The longer people postpone corrective action, the more prosaic it appears when it is finally taken. The greater the need for strategic reorientation, the more powerful the symbols necessary to create one.

Anderson's success testifies to his shrewd management of ideology, political acumen, and impeccable timing. His ideological actions look astute: He inspired a new saga, revived core beliefs, and transformed NCR's ideology from a relic into a template for the future. He anticipated and blocked political resistance. He magnified the crisis before attempting radical actions.

> Anderson planted two new values in NCR's ideology—eagerness to compete and tolerance of dissent. "If we go outside and stand toe-to-toe with the smartest people in the industry, that'll make us better manufacturers."
> In 1981, NCR moved into the competitive semiconductor market; and in mid-1983, it was the first computer maker to venture into the long-distance telephone business. As computing moved from mainframes to desktops, NCR was the first to commit itself completely to networks of inexpensive PCs. "We're on the brink of a major crossover between micros and mainframes," predicted Anderson's successor, Charles Exley. In 1988, Exley gambled on an even riskier strategy: He converted NCR's entire computer line from proprietary to open systems architecture. "We're a 106-year old, $6 billion startup," declared NCR's chief scientist.

WHEN INDUSTRIES COLLIDE

Violent upheavals sometimes recreate industries' boundaries, overwhelm organizations' adaptive abilities, and bewilder top managers. Organization theory and research offer little guidance to managers facing these conditions. One reason is that industries in flux make unappealing research settings. Like earthquake victims, researchers take cover, wait for the dust to settle, and then return to poke cautiously through the debris. Another reason is that many researchers implicitly assume organization–environment systems are moving toward equilibria (Meyer, Goes, and Brooks, 1993). They assume that most organizations are making incremental changes to fine-tune their alignments with their environments. When sweeping changes are overturning an existing order, however, equilibrium is impossible.

NCR's history encompasses two industry-wide discontinuities, and in both instances, NCR responded too slowly.

The first discontinuity was the "electronic revolution" that erased the boundary separating the business-machine and computer industries. This revolution arose from a technological innovation—the use of transistors in computers.

In this case, NCR's slow response forced the firm to undergo an abrupt reorientation rather than a smooth adaptation. Even though an NCR subsidiary had pioneered this innovation, NCR's top managers ignored its implications because they saw an impenetrable boundary between the computer and business-machine industries. That is, they ignored its implications until competitors began selling electronic cash registers! At that point, saving NCR required a leadership succession, an ideological revival, and a strategic reorientation.

A second industry-wide discontinuity jolted NCR in 1990, triggered by two environmental changes: (1) Federal deregulation of telecommunications, and (2) the digitalizing of words, images, sounds, and virtually all other forms of information. The computer and telecommunications industries merged rapidly. As the boundary separating them eroded, well-known corporate actors began to play new roles: Kindly Ma Bell emerged as an aggressive corporate raider, while self-reliant NCR turned into a weak victim under assault.

In this case, NCR's slow response cost the firm its autonomy.

> After resisting for five months, NCR surrendered and was absorbed by AT&T. AT&T's chairman predicted: "A significant presence in computers is going to be a prerequisite for telecommunications leadership in the 1990s." The merged firm would "link people, organizations, and their information in a seamless . . . global computer network . . . as accessible and easy to use as the telephone network is today."

Exley's move into open-architecure computing seemed sure to improve NCR's fit with its environment, but NCR was perhaps adapting too well to its current environment. NCR devoted so much attention to open architecture that it neglected a sweeping environmental change—the collapse of the boundary between the computer and telecommunications industries.

NCR emphasized fine-tuning within familiar domains while neglecting the wider context. This nearsightedness proved dangerous in 1972 and deadly in 1990. Similarly, high reliability organizations run a risk of focusing so sharply on maximizing the reliability of their current operations that they fail to learn more important lessons.

"MAY YOU LIVE IN AN INTERESTING TIME"

Sweeping changes have been happening in airline transportation (Pearce, 1985), business machines, computers, electric power (Russo, 1991), financial services (Haveman, 1992; Pant, 1991), healthcare (Meyer et al., 1990), pharmaceuticals, and telecommunications. NCR's history teaches several lessons for managers in such industries:

1. *Distinct industries and discrete technologies are ephemeral.* NCR's story shows that "industry" means an arbitrary and temporary grouping of firms, and that technologies overlap. NCR discovered how to dominate parts of the business-machine industry, and then this industry integrated with the computer industry. NCR learned how to make computers, and then this industry integrated with the telecommunications industry. Current divisions of industries and technologies make unreliable maps for the future.

2. *Coherence can pay off between reorientations.* NCR's founder laid out a clear strategy, structured the organization to support the strategy, and instilled matching beliefs and values. The beliefs and values grew into a strong ideology. Strategy, structure, and ideology formed a coherent configuration that succeeded for more than 80 years. However, that success took place in a placid industry—business machines. By contrast, the computer industry has

been so turbulent throughout its existence that coherence has repeatedly proven dangerous.

3. *Success and failure have the same roots.* The same properties that produced NCR's success promoted rigidity and complacency. Hard-won gains created resistance to change, and a winning strategy and a strong ideology made ingrained responses hard to abandon. Probably the opposite would have been true for a firm that succeeded through experimentation and persistent change: Such a firm would be inclined to continue experimenting and changing after the need had passed. Those actions and processes that enable firms to succeed also and simultaneously lay the foundations for failure (Miller, 1990).

4. *Ideologies can stabilize organizations.* Ideologies often escape notice: Insiders take them for granted, and outsiders seldom observe them. Yet they are powerful. Because robust ideologies inspire commitment and elicit cooperation, they can replace elaborate structures and formal controls (Meyer, 1982a). NCR's ideology was an internal gyroscope that promoted self-control by members and that kept the structure aligned with the strategy.

5. *Ideologies can also change organizations.* NCR's turnaround in 1973 shows how careful management of ideology may allow organizations to cut free of tradition, precedent, and past practice. Language, symbols, and rituals that invest events with meaning are among leaders' most powerful tools.

6. *Industry revolutions confound organizations.* Revolutions plunge people into strange worlds filled with misleading signals and unknown causal relations. NCR's history shows that the triggers of revolutions can appear so unimportant, and the onsets can be so sudden, that managers have to act before they understand what is happening. Moreover, revolutions evoke strategic reorientations that overturn organizations' power structures and raise questions about who ought to be leading.

7. *Managing reorientations takes good timing.* Like stand-up comedy, turning organizations around requires timing. William Anderson realized that changes in ideologies and politics should precede changes in strategy and behavior. If he had waited three years to write off the mechanical cash registers instead of doing so immediately, NCR's recovery would have been less spectacular. Had Anderson launched his presidency by acting rationally (closing Dayton factories and firing 10,000 workers) instead of symbolically (razing the old headquarters and changing the firm's name), NCR's people and Dayton's civic leaders would have risen in vehement opposition.

8. *Managing reorientations takes political acumen.* Just ask Mikhail Gorbachev.

REFERENCES

Argyris, C., and D. A. Schön (1978). *Organizational Learning.* Reading, MA: Addison-Wesley.

Beyer, J. M. (1981). "Ideologies, values and decision making in organizations." In P. C.

Nystrom and W. H. Starbuck (eds.), *Handbook of Organizational Design, 2.* New York: Oxford University Press, 166–202.

Boland, R. J., Jr. (1982). "Myth and technology in the American accounting profession." *Journal of Management Studies, 19*; 109–127.

Boland, R. J., Jr., and L. R. Pondy (1983). "Accounting in organizations: A union of natural and rational perspectives." *Accounting, Organizations and Society, 8,* 223–234.

Clark, B. R. (1972). "The organizational saga in higher education." *Administrative Science Quarterly, 25,* 300–316.

Greenwood, R., and C. R. Hinings (1988). "Organizational design types, tracks, and the dynamics of strategic change." *Organization Studies, 9,* 293–316.

Grinyer, P. H., and D. Norburn (1975). "Planning for existing markets: Perceptions of executives and financial performance." *Journal of the Royal Statistical Society, Series A, 138,* 70–97.

Haveman, H. A. (1992). "Between a rock and a hard place: Organizational change and performance under conditions of fundamental environmental transformation." *Administrative Science Quarterly, 37,* 48–75.

Kimberly, J. R. (1979). "Issues in the creation of organizations: Initiation, innovation, and institutionalization." *Academy of Management Journal, 22,* 437–457.

March, J. G., and J. P. Olsen (1976). *Ambiguity and Choice in Organizations.* Bergen, Norway: Universitetsförlaget.

Meyer, A. D. (1982a). "How ideologies supplant formal structures and shape responses to environments." *Journal of Management Studies, 19,* 45–61.

——— (1982b). "Adapting to environmental jolts." *Administrative Science Quarterly, 27,* 515–537.

——— (1984). "Mingling decision making metaphors." *Academy of Management Review, 9,* 6–17.

Meyer, A. D., G. R. Brooks, and J. B. Goes (1990). "Environmental jolts and industry revolutions: Organizational responses to discontinuous change." *Strategic Management Journal, 11* (Summer), 93–110.

Meyer, A. D., J. B. Goes, and G. R. Brooks (1993). "Organizations reacting to hyperturbulence." In G. Huber and W. Glick, (eds.), *Organizational Change and Redesign: Ideas and Insights for Improving Managerial Performance.* New York: Oxford University Press.

Miller, D. (1990). *The Icarus Paradox.* New York: HarperCollins.

Normann, R. (1971). "Organizational innovativeness: Product variation and reorientation." *Administrative Science Quarterly, 16,* 203–215.

Nystrom, P. C., and W. H. Starbuck (1984). "Organizational facades." *Proceedings of the 44th Annual Meeting of the Academy of Management,* 182–185.

Pant, P. N. (1991). *Strategies, Environments, Effectiveness: Savings and Loan Associations, 1978–1989.* New York University: Doctoral dissertation.

Pearce, J. (1985). "Braniff International Corporation." In J. Pearce and R. Robinson, (eds.), *Strategic Management.* Second Edition. Homewood, IL: Irwin.

Pettigrew, A. M. (1979). "On studying organizational cultures." *Administrative Science Quarterly, 24,* 570–581.

Pfeffer, J. (1981). *Power in Organizations.* Marshfield, MA: Pitman.

Pondy, L. R., and I. I. Mitroff (1979). "Beyond open system models of organization." *Research in Organizational Behavior, 1,* 2–39.

Russo, M. V. (1991). "The multidivisional structure as an enabling device: A longitudinal study of discretionary cash as a strategic resource." *Academy of Management Journal, 34,* 718–733.

Salancik, G. R. (1977). "Commitment and the control of organizational behavior and belief." In B. M. Staw and G. R. Salancik (eds.), *New Directions in Organizational Behavior.* Chicago: St. Clair.

Starbuck, W. H. (1965). "Organizational growth and development." In J. G. March (ed.), *Handbook of Organizations:* 451–533. Chicago: Rand McNally.

———— (1982). "Congealing oil: Inventing ideologies to justify acting ideologies out." *Journal of Management Studies, 19,* 3–27.

———— (1983). "Organizations as action generators." *American Sociological Review, 48,* 91–102.

Starbuck, W. H., F. Greve, and B. L. T. Hedberg (1978). "Responding to crises." *Journal of Business Administration, 9,* 111–137.

Staw, B. M. (1980). "Rationality and justification in organizational life." *Research in Organizational Behavior, 2,* 45–80.

Staw, B. M., L. E. Sandelands, and J. E. Dutton (1981). "Threat-rigidity effects in organizational behavior: A multi-level analysis." *Administrative Science Quarterly, 26,* 501–524.

Stinchcombe, A. L. (1965). "Social structure and organizations." In J. G. March (ed.), *Handbook of Organizations.* Chicago: Rand McNally.

Tushman, M. L. and E. Romanelli (1985). "Organizational evolution: A metamorphosis model of convergence and reorientation." In *Research in Organizational Behavior, 7.* Greenwich, CT: JAI Press.

Watzlawick, P., J. H. Weakland, and R. Fisch (1974). *Change.* New York: Norton.

Weick, K. E. (1979). *The Social Psychology of Organizing.* Reading, MA: Addison-Wesley.

7

High Reliability Organizations Meet High Velocity Environments: Common Dilemmas in Nuclear Power Plants, Aircraft Carriers, and Microcomputer Firms

KATHLEEN M. EISENHARDT
Stanford University

Kathleen M. Eisenhardt is Associate Professor of Organization and Strategy in the Department of Industrial Engineering and Engineering Management at Stanford University. She holds degrees in mechanical engineering and computer science. Her Ph.D. in Organizational Behavior is from Stanford University's Graduate School of Business. Dr. Eisenhardt's research interests include strategic decision making and the management of technology-based firms. She has published numerous articles in both academic and managerial outlets and was the recent recipient of the Pacific Telesis Foundation Award. Dr. Eisenhardt's current research includes a study of the strategic issues facing U.S. semiconductor ventures and an examination of strategic decision making in the microcomputer industry.

O rganizational researchers have long been interested in the effectiveness of organizations. Typically, that interest has translated into studies of profitability, growth, cost, and efficiency, as well as more individual-level outcomes such as satisfaction and employee well-being. However, a recent stream of research (e.g., Perrow, 1984; Shrivastava, 1986; Weick, 1987; Roberts, 1990), some of which is discussed in this volume, examines effectiveness along a different dimension, reliability. This research probes the ways organizational members perform—time and time again—with little or no deviation in outcomes.

This emerging perspective on organizational reliability proceeds from the observation that certain technologies have characteristics that make them unusually hazardous (Perrow, 1984). Given the potential for enormous negative consequences, it is essential that organizations that use these high-risk technologies operate them in a reliable fashion (Roberts, 1990). The emphasis here is on repeatable and safe, though not necessarily peak, performance.

The operation of high risk technologies carries several difficult challenges. One is that they are particularly difficult to operate because of the inability to learn about them using trial-and-error learning (Weick, 1987). Thus, it is difficult for operators to have firsthand information about how to handle crisis situations. The other challenge is lack of time. Errors in high risk technologies characteristically propagate very rapidly (Perrow, 1984). As a result, operators must keep pace. Thus, high risk technologies place operators in situations in which they must make wise choices with little experience or information and compressed time.

The research on high reliability organizations has been done in settings in which technological features are paramount. However, an alternative perspective is to focus on environments and environmental challenges similar to those posed by high risk technologies. That is, environments may present the same need for reliable performance when there is little firsthand experience and limited time. One such environment is termed "high velocity" (Bourgeois & Eisenhardt, 1988). High velocity environments are those "in which there is a rapid and discontinuous change in demand, competitors, technology and/or regulation, such that information is often inaccurate, unavailable or obsolete" (Bourgeois and Eisenhardt, 1988, p. 816). Like high risk technologies, these environments put a premium on fast and accurate choice processes in the context of limited information and experience.

The purposes of this chapter are twofold. One is to describe the characteristics of fast decision-making organizations in high velocity environments. Specifically, the focus is on the strategic decision-making processes at the heart of accurate choices in the context of limited information and demands for speed.

Special thanks go to Jay Bourgeois for his efforts in design and data collection in the microcomputer industry study. I also benefited from the expert help of research assistants, Theresa Lant, Mike Boehm, Anita Callahan, Dave Ellison, and Paul McCright. Related articles appeared in the *Academy of Management Journal*, 1989, and the *California Management Review*, 1990. This research was supported by National Science Foundation, Grant #SES-8813329.

The second is to compare some of the salient features of fast decision organizations with those of high reliability organizations. Obviously, high reliability organizations are not identical with fast decision organizations. For example, the demands on nuclear power plant operators clearly differ from those borne by senior executives in fast-paced industries. Prevention of errors is key in potentially high risk technologies. High reliability researchers have thus far concerned themselves with operational decisions and operating personnel. In contrast, speed is the critical issue in high-velocity environments. Decisions are strategic, and the decision makers are executives. Nonetheless, there are sufficient similarities between the two kinds of organizations to make their comparison potentially helpful in improving our understanding of high reliability organizations.

This chapter begins with a background review of the research on high risk technologies and high reliability organizations. It continues with a discussion of the research design and central findings related to a study of fast decision processes. The chapter concludes with a discussion of the insights forthcoming from a comparison of fast decision making with high reliability organizations.

BACKGROUND

High Risk Technologies

Technology research has a long tradition within organizational studies. However, scholars have only recently begun to examine technology from the perspective of potential hazard. Perrow's (1984) work is perhaps the best example of literature that explores the dimensions of potentially hazardous technologies. He examines a variety of disasters, including the Three-Mile Island mishap and collisions between supertankers. Each of these involves the failure of a hazardous technology.

Perrow defines these so-called "high risk" technologies as those in which accidents are both likely to happen and likely to be catastrophic when they occur. He argues that two central facets characterize high risk technologies. One is complexity. High complexity occurs in technologies that serve multiple functions or that interact in numerous subtle and unpredictable ways. The ramifications of interventions and other changes in such high risk technologies are thus enormously difficult to predict. Unanticipated and occasionally disastrous consequences are often the result.

According to Perrow, the second characteristic of high risk technologies is tight coupling. Tight coupling refers to the brittleness of connections between and among subsystems. Typically, tightly coupled systems have limited slack and an invariant sequencing of processes (i.e., step A must precede step B). In addition, tightly coupled systems are usually time sensitive such that they can whirl rapidly out of control under failure conditions.

The organizational implication of high risk technologies is that their users must place a premium on reliable operation, given the potentially catastrophic consequences. Yet, this reliability must also occur in situations in which there is little experience with crises and great time pressure.

High Reliability Organizations

Weick (1987) takes on this reliability issue with his emphasis on learning when reliability is paramount. He notes that a major learning strategy, trial-and-error, is inappropriate for high reliability organizations because error cannot be tolerated. Thus, organizational members must find other ways to learn and to compensate for limited experience. This problem is exacerbated by the complexity of high risk technology. Typically, these technologies are difficult to understand and are "susceptible to accidents that result from unforseen consequences of misunderstood interventions" (Weick, 1987, p. 112).

Weick stresses the importance of requisite variety in high reliability organizations. As he observes, "This is a problem of 'requisite variety' because the variety that exists in the system to be managed exceeds the variety in the individuals who must regulate it" (1987, p. 112). The implication is that organizational structures and processes must match the complexity of the technology.

The challenges to creating high reliability organizations are also exacerbated by the dynamism of the technology (Weick, 1987). Dynamism refers to the potential for frequent change within the technology. The implication of dynamism is that users of high risk technology must be constantly vigilant and constantly changing to maintain the same reliable outcomes. What makes this vigilance so difficult is that the system changes are often invisible. That is, operators often observe nothing happening. For example, nuclear power plant operators spend most of their time doing nothing more than observing apparently stationary systems (see Schulman, this volume, for another perspective).

Finally and most importantly, Weick (1987) argues that strong culture is essential in high reliability organizations. Culture allows organizational members to benefit from the accumulated experience within the organization (Roberts, Rousseau and La Porte, in press). This is particularly important in high reliability organizations because most members have very little firsthand experience with managing crises. At the same time, culture also allows latitude for interpretation and improvisation as new situations are encountered.

The Berkeley researchers are conducting probably the most extensive research program on high reliability organizations, attempting to differentiate reliable organizations from other potentially hazardous organizations. They define high reliability organizations as those potentially hazardous organizations that have operated nearly error free for very long periods of time (Roberts, 1990). As Roberts explains, "One can identify this subset by answering the question, 'how many times could this organization have failed, resulting in catastrophic consequences, that it did not?' If the answer is on the order of tens of thousands of times the organization is 'high reliability' " (1990, p. 160).

The key in these organizations is the capacity to react appropriately to unexpected sequences of events triggered by complex technology. People do this, in part, by constant training during which all possible disaster scenarios are presented to operators. The idea is that such training allows operators to learn both the capabilities and parameters of the technology and appropriate responses to unexpected events (Roberts, 1990).

A second way of coping with complex technology is through specialization. Very explicitly defined jobs ensure that all facets of the technology are covered. As with Weick's argument, the notion here is that the complexity of the organization or the collective complexity of the assembled participants must match the complexity of the technology.

Consistent with Perrow's (1984) dimensions of high risk technologies, the other key in these organizations is coping with the brittleness of the technology. Imagery of brittleness evokes the notion that various internal and external pressures could shatter the organization. It puts a premium on time-sensitive actions because the organization must react rapidly to prevent or reduce these pressures.

High reliability organizations handle this brittleness in ways that are similar to the handling of complexity. These include breaking down jobs into specialized roles and the extensive use of rehearsal training. However, of principal importance is the use of redundancy such that breakdowns in technology can be handled quickly either through backup of identical processes or through rerouting to different parts of the system (Roberts, 1990).

HIGH VELOCITY RESEARCH

High Velocity Environments

High velocity environments are characterized by "rapid and discontinuous change in demand, competitors, technology and/or regulation such that information is often inaccurate, unavailable or obsolete" (Bourgeois and Eisenhardt, 1988, p. 816). Decision making is difficult in these environments because change is so frequent and dramatic and because it is hard to predict its significance as it occurs. The implication is that it is particularly easy to make poor strategic choices. The traditional prescription for avoiding strategic errors is to wait and see how events unfold or to imitate others (Bourgeois and Eisenhardt, 1988). However, in high velocity environments, "wait-and-see" and "me-too" strategies often result in failure as competitive positions shift and windows of opportunity close. The decision-making dilemma in such environments comes from the fact that it is easy to make mistakes by deciding too soon and equally ineffective to delay choices or to imitate others.

The microcomputer industry is a prototypical example of a high velocity setting. The industry was launched in the mid-1970s by electronic hobbyists experimenting with the newly developed microprocessor. The first computers were sold by mail to do-it-yourself amateur hobbyists. In 1976, Commodore became the first major corporation to enter the industry. The following year the "two Steves," Wozniak and Jobs, launched Apple.

By 1980, the microcomputer industry had transformed from an experimenting and emergent industry to one experiencing rapid growth. Perhaps most striking was the start-up fever of the early 1980s. Motivated by new capital gains tax laws and the lure of rapid growth, venture capitalists fueled the dreams of numerous computer entrepreneurs. Many companies entered the industry between 1977 and 1982. In addition, many established computer firms joined the melee. Digital Equipment, Hewlett Packard, Burroughs, and Texas Instruments all became players in the turbulent industry. But the most successful was the industry giant, IBM. Entering in 1981, IBM permanently changed the direction of the industry. The world's dominant computer firm set the enormously important norm of open architecture, which permitted software writers and peripheral hardware designers wide access throughout the industry to key computer designs.

Between 1981 and 1986 sales of multi-user computers more than doubled. The personal computer became an office place fixture and common home appliance. Technological turbulence was unrelenting. Winchester disk drives, UNIX operating systems, RISC computer architecture, 1 meg RAM, and 32 bit microprocessors were just a few technological advances of the time. Technical change was mirrored by marketplace change. Firms like Osborne and Fortune rocketed onto the scene and died equally rapid deaths.

This rate of change persisted through the 1980s and into the early 1990s. The competitive landscape continues to shift as newcomers such as Sun and Microsoft become important players, while oldtimers, especially the mainframe segment, struggle. It was against this backdrop of immense opportunity and "high velocity" pace that my colleague, Jay Bourgeois, and I conducted a research program on strategic choice processes within the industry.

Research Setting

The impetus for the research was our interest in better understanding strategic and organizational processes in fast-moving and hotly competitive environments. We were struck by the fact that the extant literature dwells on very large bureaucracies operating in stable environments. Further, these organizations are often non-profit and consequently are not faced with the high performance pressures of the competitive marketplace.

The research design was an in-depth multiple case study. Such a design permits the use of replication logic—that is, a series of cases is treated as a series of experiments in which each case is used to confirm or disconfirm the inferences drawn from the others (Yin, 1984). We also used an embedded design—that is, multiple levels of analysis. Specifically, the study focused on the strategic decision, top management team, and firm levels of analysis. This is a complex but more realistic research design than is a single-level design.

Twelve functionally organized and privately held microcomputer firms participated in the study. A subset of eight firms was used to develop the ideas relating to the speed and quality of choices. Presentations of these ideas appear in the academic (Eisenhardt, 1989a) and managerial (Eisenhardt, 1990) presses. This chapter focuses specifically on the ideas for fast decision making in the context of one of the most successful firms in the study and the industry, Zap Computers. In a later section, these ideas are related to high reliability organizations.

There were four data sources: (1) initial chief executive officer (CEO) interviews; (2) semi-structured interviews with each member of the firm's top management team; (3) questionnaires completed by each team member; and (4) secondary data sources.

Members of the research team interviewed every member of each of the eight top management teams. These included the CEO plus his or her direct reports—typically the heads of the major functional areas such as sales, engineering, manufacturing, and finance. Team sizes ranged between five and nine executives. The interviews consisted of two parts. The first part included questions about the firm's overall strategy and the decision-making climate. In the second part, each executive related the story of how one or sometimes two recent strategy decisions were made.

Each executive also completed a questionnaire about interactions within the top management team. Secondary data included industry reports, journal articles, and firm documents. Data on financial performance, top management team demographics, and office location were also obtained.

Analysis

Given the limited prior research on decision making in high velocity settings, the logic of the research is inductive. The data were analyzed using various techniques for cross-case, inductive comparison, such as pair wise comparisons and assessments of the presence or absence of constructs described by Eisenhardt (1989b). Hypotheses were further shaped by comparison with existing literature in a variety of fields. These types of analyses serve to sharpen the development of constructs and hypotheses. The result was a framework describing fast decision-making processes. Overall, this framework addresses the problem of how senior executives make rapid, yet high quality decisions in high velocity environments. Such decision making is the result of processes that accelerate cognitive processing, maintain group harmony, and create confidence—conditions just the opposite of those discussed by Hirschhorn (this volume).

FAST DECISION-MAKING ORGANIZATIONS

Real-Time Information

How do organizations make fast decisions? One strategy is simply to skimp on the amount of information considered. For example, executives can examine only limited data sources, develop only one or at most two options, or gather ideas from only a few people. This method is probably fast and, in fact, some executives in the larger study did exactly this. The obvious problem is that such skimping seriously compromises the quality of choice. Further, lack of confidence, which may be triggered by the use of such limited information, may actually slow down the decision process for some decision makers. This kind of strategy may well have driven the kind of behavior discussed by Meyer and Starbuck (this volume).

What do successful, fast decision makers actually do? They do just the opposite of slashing information. In fact, they often use more information than their slow decision-making counterparts. What differentiates the two is the type of information. Fast decision makers look at real-time information, that is, information about current operations or the current environment which is reported with little or no time lag. In contrast, slow decision makers spend their time focusing on planning and projected information.

Fast decision makers get real-time information several ways. One way is through frequent operations meetings. Two to three such meetings per week are not at all unusual. The meetings are often intense and are considered a "must" on executives' calendars. These meetings cover activities throughout the corporation, typically through status reports from each functional head. The reports are laced with questions and comments from all participants. The subjects of the meetings are usually not limited to internal operations. Rather, external data on topics such as competitor moves and technological developments are shared.

A second source of real-time information is widely disseminated, operational measures of performance. Fast decision makers typically examine a wide variety of operating measures on a daily, weekly, or monthly basis. Popular measures include bookings, backlog, margins, engineering milestones, cash, scrap, and work-in-process. Of notably little interest is profitability, which is a more historical and manipulable measure of performance. The senior finance executive in fast decision-making firms is particularly important because of his or her role as the chief provider of data. This person usually develops the information that tracks the "pulse" of the firm.

Zap Computers, a very successful microcomputer firm, provides an outstanding example of the use of real-time information. Its executives claim to measure "everything." While they obviously exaggerate, they do come close. For example, the CEO listed exact targets for gross margin and expenses for research and development, sales and administration. Bookings are tracked daily and engineering schedules are reviewed weekly. The vice-president of finance is charged with making the weekly churn of the financial model for the firm. Monthly, the entire executive team pours over a wide array of quantitative measures, including revenue per employee, gross margin, backlog, cash, scrap, and inventory indicators.

Face-to-face communication is also essential at Zap. Members of the top management team meet frequently in regularly scheduled "don't miss" meetings. Five-foot-high partitions are the only barriers separating the vice-presidents of finance, marketing, and sales. The CEO has a private office but it is unprotected by an administrative assistant and is just steps away from the others. Everyone on the top management team also relies extensively on the electronic mail.

Why does the constant perusal of real-time information accelerate decision making? One reason may be that such information permits early identification of problems so that action can be taken before the problems become too substantial. Another reason is more subtle. Constant review of real-time information gives the top management team the opportunity to practice working together as a group. The frequent review of real-time information may help senior executives develop the social routines and patterns of trust necessary to respond quickly and reliably in crisis situations.

Multiple, Simultaneous Alternatives

Another myth of fast decision making is that cutting the number of alternatives accelerates choice. Executives in some firms in the microcomputer study do this, but very often such tactics are associated with slower choice processes. These executives often wind up analyzing a single alternative, but in great depth. By contrast, executives in fast decision-making firms develop multiple alternatives, but limit the amount of analysis of each.

One focal decision at Zap provides an illustration of this analysis. Zap executives were faced with a need for quick infusion of cash. The impending cash shortfall was discovered in the financial modeling reports prepared by the vice-president of finance. The team's initial reaction was to question the results of the model by seeking additional advice from the firm's outside financial advisors. As the vice-president of finance related, "We were suspicious of the in-house model, so the banks and investment bankers wrote new models. They all came up with the same answer—that is, cash problems on the horizon." This was in May.

By early summer, the CEO focused on the decision, and several alternatives for raising additional cash were shaped. An initial public offering (IPO), bank loans, and new venture equity were active options. The bank loan and venture capital were well-known options within the firm, but the IPO was new and controversial. A final option, a strategic alliance, was broached during conversation among senior executives on an airplane flight. The CEO explained the rationale for an alliance as follows: "The idea is to talk to ten or twelve corporate investors who make strategic sense. My motivation for this is that the structure of the industry is going to change dramatically. If we can be seen to be in partnership with some very strong players—and this partnership is not just financial, of course we also have some technological reasons to be in the partnership with them—then we'll float to the top of the shake-out."

Thus, Zap executives formulated four key alternatives within about six weeks of their initial recognition of the problem. They also elaborated several sub-options and began to forge implementation plans for several of the alternatives.

Admittedly, multiple, simultaneous alternatives are complex, but most fast decision teams prefer to have multiple options on the table. By contrast, slow decision teams usually have few alternatives and look for a new one only when the old one is no longer feasible.

Why are multiple, simultaneous alternatives fast? One reason is that they accelerate the analysis of options. Comparative logic results in quick yet accurate analysis because it is easier for individuals to ascertain strengths, weaknesses, and preferences when alternatives are compared. Multiple alternatives are also fast because they bolster confidence. Decision makers feel they are well informed and have not overlooked a vastly superior option. Finally, multiple alternatives are fast because they give decision makers fall-back positions. In effect, there is built-in redundancy. If the first choice becomes unavailable, decision makers can quickly switch to a second. By contrast, when a single alternative fails, decision makers are forced to begin anew the search process.

Counselors and the Two-Tier Process

Another myth of fast decision making is that centralization accelerates the process. However, as with skimping on information and alternatives, centralization in the context of high velocity environments again fails to deal with the need for a high quality choice. Further, it ignores the potential for procrastination that can stem from the isolation of the centralized decision maker. In contrast, fast decision makers pool the advice of all members of the team. At the same time they also focus on gaining the advice of particularly experienced executives, termed "counselors." These counselors usually operate in the background, acting as confidential sounding boards for the CEO.

The two-tier advice process is evident in the focal decision on cash described earlier at Zap. The CEO sought advice from all the team members. However, he obtained more extensive advice from the vice-president of sales, whom he considered to be the most in touch with the market and industry, and from his vice-president of engineering, whom he considered to be the best manager.

This strategic decision illustrates the dynamics of the counselor role further. The vice-president of engineering played a particularly strong role in shaping the strategic alliance option. He and the CEO structured the option while on a business trip. They then continued to shape the option and target candidates for partnership at later meetings. The CEO then relied on both counselor executives to sound out the advantages of the IPO versus the alliance. The vice-president of sales, who previously worked for a firm that missed the IPO window, favored going public as quickly as possible. As the CEO related, "He [the vice-president of sales] saw what happened there [at the previous employer of the vice-president of sales] and was nervous. He would like to be liquid." On the other hand, the vice-president of engineering expressed reservations about the IPO primarily because it would limit the firm's ability to attract star research and development recruits. As one executive summarized, "Jim [the vice-president of engineering] would rather be private in the long run."

An important feature of the counselor role is its informal nature. Plane trips and after-hour socializing provide frequent opportunities for the decision makers to test ideas. Often advice from different counselors conflicts, and sometimes their recommendations are not heeded. But what seems most useful is the ability of counselors to aid in shaping issues and identifying key decision factors. They help other decision makers think through pertinent issues.

Finally, counselors in fast decision-making firms also have a specific demographic profile. They are usually the oldest and most experienced executives on the top management team. They often have long-standing relationships with the CEO and they are usually on a career plateau. For example, Zap's counselors were ten to twenty years older than most team members. The vice-president of engineering had worked as a senior general manager at a major computer firm for about fifteen years. He was known as a skilled project administrator and had years of experience competing with IBM, the Goliath of the industry. The CEO regarded him as the best manager on the top management team. The other counselor, the vice-president of sales, was a rare individual because he had been in the microcomputer industry since its inception. He had held senior management positions at two other major microcomputer firms and was regarded as "the person most knowledgeable about the market" on the top management team.

In contrast, the slow decision teams usually do not have an executive who serves as a counselor. There was one exception, but the counselor in this case did not fit the profile observed at Zap. This person was the youngest member of the team and had only limited operating experience and tenure within the industry. While he was acknowledged as "bright," he clearly lacked the experience of the counselors in the fast decision firms.

Why is two-tier advice fast? One reason is that the counselor provides a quick sounding board for ideas formulated at the broader level of the full top management team. This feedback, in turn, accelerates the shaping and evaluation of alternatives. This is particularly true because such counselors are typically very experienced. Second, counselors accelerate decision making because they provide high quality advice, which shortens the decision process. Their experience is often the most extensive on the team. So, counselors combine speed and quality. Perhaps most importantly, counselors give decision makers confidence. The process of simply discussing complex and ambiguous high stake issues gives a decision maker confidence even when the counselor disagrees.

Conflict Resolution

Another myth concerning fast decision making is that limited debate accelerates choice processes. Debate means conflict, and conflict can drag out decision making as executives bicker over differences of opinions. Moreover, the more powerful the combatants, the longer the conflict is likely to last. So a traditional argument is that suppressing conflict weakens choice processes.

The flaw is in thinking that quelling conflict among dedicated senior executives is possible. These people are likely to bridle at attempts to muzzle them. In addition, the lack of voice may undermine their motivation and certainly deprives the decision process of critical information and advice. Thus, suppression of conflict might hasten choice, but at the expense of the quality of the decision, and the motivation and cohesiveness of the top management team.

The microcomputer firm research found that the level of conflict does not influence the pace of the decision process. Decisions made in high conflict situations can be fast or slow. Instead, what is important is conflict resolution. Fast decision makers actively deal with conflict, resolving it on their own. In contrast, slow decision makers have much more difficulty resolving conflict. They tend to wait for consensus to emerge. It sometimes does occur. But, given the controversial nature of most strategic decisions, it often does not. As one executive said, "We found that operating by consensus essentially gave everyone veto power. There was no structure. Nothing was accomplished."

Fast decision-making teams use a simple, two-step process to deal with conflict. First, all members of the top management team discuss the issue at hand and attempt to reach consensus. If consensus occurs, then the choice is made. If it does not emerge, as is often the case in strategic choices, the CEO and often the most relevant senior manager make the choice. This process is termed "consensus with qualification" by one of the executives.

The Zap strategic decision process provides a good example of consensus with qualification. As described earlier, the decision at Zap concerned how the firm should raise cash. By about mid-summer (six to eight weeks into the decision process), Zap executives had formulated several options for dealing with the cash shortfall. However, they could not agree among themselves as to the best choice. The debate centered on the IPO and alliance options.

The CEO outlined several key issues surrounding the IPO alternative. He described the situation as follows:

> What drives what we do in this case is IBM. It impacts timing and (stock) valuation. We're expecting them to have a product announcement for a high resolution graphics (microcomputer) in January. There are two points of view on this. One is that we should go public now—prior to product introduction—so that it won't have a depressing effect on our stock price. The other is that we should wait until IBM shows its machine, and once the public (customers) sees how lousy it is, then we should go public. So the first factor is IBM. The second factor is liquidity—liquidating people's holdings in the firm. Liquidity is good for each individual's net worth but it is also bad. There is a question of whether people will sell their stock, get rich, and just leave. The third item is the "war chest syndrome." We need a deep war chest to weather a variety of things: IBM moves into the mar-

ketplace, losing people, losing cash. When you've got a big war chest, it's easy for you to go out and borrow more money. It's when you don't have any money that it's hard to come up with more or go public.

Others emphasized different factors. For example, the vice-president of finance was concerned with problems of public ownership. Wall Street punishes volatility, and so public firms are under more pressure to smooth their earnings than are private firms. The vice-president of research and development explained, "To go public we need to keep our lines (growth rates) more even." Another noted the lack of flexibility that accompanies public ownership. Several were also concerned with the attractiveness of the firm to key research and development recruits. Going public would diminish the attractiveness of the firm to new employees because ground floor equity positions would no longer be available.

Some, notably the CEO, favored a strategic alliance. The argument for this was that alliances would raise cash and increase the legitimization of the firm. Zap's power and image would be enhanced if it were seen as having established and powerful firms as allies.

Others opposed the alliance option. Some feared a loss of control to the alliance partner, especially if that firm were large and powerful. Others were concerned that an alliance would delay the IPO even further. Others expressed severe reservations about alliances with foreign firms. As one person described it, "I'm not as excited about getting a lot of large companies to invest in us. I don't want Japanese management, for example. I've made my thoughts known. I think it's a risky gamble to be involved with certain companies. There are others I would like to have be a part. From a marketing standpoint I would prefer going public. It would involve more press. We wouldn't be thought of as somebody's little sister."

After a series of meetings, Zap executives were unable to reach consensus. At that point, the CEO intervened and selected the alliance option. He reasoned that the legitimization that a key alliance partner could bring to Zap was of paramount importance. He further believed that Zap would gain more money in the long run with an alliance followed later by an IPO. He argued, "I would like to liquidate later and get more." The vice-president of engineering described this consensus with qualification in more general terms. He claimed, "Most of the time we reach consensus, but if not Randy [the CEO] makes the choice."

Why is consensus with qualification fast? It is fast because it involves actively coping with conflict, rather than waiting for outside events like deadlines to force choice. In contrast, slow decision teams often hope that opponents will leave the team, but that may not happen. Slow decision makers may wait for others to agree. Sometimes others do eventually capitulate, but this can take a long time. Sometimes they wait for deadlines, but these do not always come. In contrast, fast decision makers are willing to choose, even when conflict in their ranks is extensive.

Consensus with qualification is also fast because it is popular. Most executives want a voice in the decision-making process but are willing to leave the actual choice to others. This is particularly true when the choice is outside their own area. As one Zap vice-president claimed, "I'm just happy to bring it up." The upshot is that executives like consensus with qualification, and so time consuming politicking is reduced.

Integrating Strategic Decisions and Tactics

The final characteristic distinguishing fast and slow decision makers involves decision integration. Slow teams tend to treat each decision in isolation. In contrast, fast teams tend to see decisions as related and attempt to integrate them more directly. This integration involves weaving together decisions in a fluid pattern that can change over time. The strategic decision process at Zap illustrates this type of integration.

As described previously, the Zap CEO chose to pursue a strategic alliance. Once this was decided, he worked to convince the company's board of the merits of an alliance. He also laid out a calendar of events and continued negotiations with several prospective partners. An alliance with the first-choice partner unexpectedly fell through because of financing problems and concerns about conflicts of interest between board members and the potential alliance partner. Zap executives rapidly closed an alliance agreement with a second partner. The deal was signed in October and the money was in by November.

While pursuing this strategy, Zap executives simultaneously continued to develop plans for an IPO and for bank loans. In particular, they structured the reassessment of the decision to go public on a quarterly basis, awaiting specific profit numbers and market conditions. In other words, Zap executives programmed the IPO to happen based upon the occurrence of key contingencies and triggers. If the triggers were encountered, each senior executive had a list of tasks to complete such that Zap would go public very quickly. Thus, at the end of the decision period, Zap executives had made a short-run decision to form a strategic alliance, but they had also integrated that decision with longer-term plans for an IPO and with various tactical plans. By contrast, some of the slow decision makers made decisions that took a very long time and yet poorly integrated them with other decisions in the firm.

Why is decision integration fast? One reason is that it helps executives assess the viability of their options more quickly. Tying the focal decision to other decisions and tactical plans helps decision makers to anticipate future problems and to gain both speed and quality in the decision process. Second, decision integration helps decision makers cope with the anxiety of high stakes choices. The development of concrete ties to other choices and tactical plans such as engineering milestones, personnel assignments, or budget allocations gives decision makers an important sense of coherence and control. These, in turn, produce the confidence to act. This picture is just the opposite of that produced by the case study of a nuclear reactor discussed by Hirschhorn (this volume). He elucidates controlling processes designed to stifle problem solving, the use of good judgment, and the ability to react to rapidly changing conditions.

COMMON THEMES

On the surface, the description of fast decision organizations is different from that of high reliability organizations. Their settings are different as are their decisions and decision makers. Even the high reliability vocabulary of *requisite variety*, *redundancy*, and *training* does not cover the same issues as the fast decision-making vocabulary of *real-time information*, *counselors*, and *consensus with qualification*. But closer inspection of underlying ideas suggests a number of common themes.

One common theme is task specialization. As Roberts (1990) observes, such specialization separates activities whose mingling could be catastrophic. For example, aircraft carrier decks are typically divided into three distinct areas. Personnel are assigned to only one area and can perform only specialized jobs. Further, uniforms are color-coded so that supervisors can readily keep track of deck activities. Such specialization also helps ensure that individuals have appropriate expertise, which in turn facilitates reliability.

Weick (1987) also argues that specialization is critical in high reliability organizations. He notes that requisite variety, necessary to manage complex and unpredictable technology, is enhanced by the assignment of personnel to relatively fixed, organizational roles. Weick uses the example of a nuclear power plant control room to illustrate his point. He states, "The lead person on the team is the shift foreman whose responsibility is to maintain the 'big picture' and not to get into details. There is a shift technical advisor who has engineering expertise and a senior control room operator who is the most senior person in the control room. Under the senior operator are the control room operator and the assistant control room operator, the latter being the person who has the newest operating license and who most recently has worked outside the control room." (p. 116) Schulman (this volume) alludes to similar job specialization among air traffic control operators. The result of such specialized jobs is explicit attention to all areas. Specific individuals are assigned to particular areas such that all essential duties are performed and no critical information is overlooked or lost.

Fast decision organizations are also marked by specialization. For example, the practice of consensus with qualification assigns particular responsibilities to various functional areas (Eisenhardt, 1989a). The leaders of those areas then have more influence on decisions in their own domains. Indeed, the power pattern in high velocity organizations is such that functional heads are invariably the high power individuals in their own functional areas (Bourgeois and Eisenhardt, 1988). By contrast, power tends to be concentrated in the hands of autocratic CEOs or other decision makers who are very powerful outside their own formal areas of responsibility in slow decision firms (Bourgeois and Eisenhardt, 1988). Further, fast decision organizations often have specialized roles within their decision-making processes. For example, as described earlier, counselors often emerge in fast decision teams.

In sum, specialization is an important characteristic in both high reliability and fast decision organizations. Both segment tasks into clearly defined jobs. Such specialization mitigates the chances of commingling operations and ensures that information and responsibilities do not fall through the cracks. The performance of such specialists is likely to be both reliable and rapid.

A second common theme is the importance of rich real-time information in both types of organization. Flow of information is evidenced in several ways. The Berkeley researchers describe the number of both direct and indirect communication channels connecting various locations in high reliability organizations. They use aircraft carriers to illustrate the point. For example, Roberts observes, "The ship's control tower, responsible for all activity on the flight deck and hangar deck, uses more than twenty communication devices to contact critical parts of the ship, ranging from radios to sound powered phones. The landing signal officer (LSO) on the flight deck is connected to the airboss (a commander) in the tower in five different ways. There is a regular telephone, a sound powered 'hot' line (akin to two tin cans and a string), a radio, and a public address system. These are supplemented by tower capability to call the deck 'foul' which is the final way to communicate with the LSO" (pp. 165–166). Thus, there are multiple, real-time channels between individuals and multiple individuals connected with one another. The result is a dense web of communication.

Weick (1987; this volume) also emphasizes the need for communicating rich information. He stresses the importance of frequent, face-to-face contact. Such contact creates networks of rich, dense talk needed to maintain a match with the complexity of the technology. It builds trust and teamwork and provides greater information, all of which are helpful in managing and avoiding crises in high-risk technologies. These arguments are consistent with Schulman's discussion (this volume) of the Diablo Canyon Nuclear Power Plant as a holistic organization.

Fast decision organizations also place similar emphasis on rich, dense communication networks (Eisenhardt, 1988). As described earlier, fast decision makers keep a continual eye on real-time information—that is, on what is new in the environment and operations. The advantages are both early warning and development of management's intuition. As in high reliability organizations, much of this communication is face-to-face, so esprit de corps is enhanced, as are the depth and range of what is communicated.

Overall, both high reliability organizations and fast decision organizations rely on dense and thick webs of communication on operating matters. Such webs are fast because they give early warning. They are reliable because they allow sophisticated intuition to develop and because they cultivate a sense of trust and teamwork essential in managing and avoiding crises.

A final common theme is the dynamic balance between centralization and decentralization. Roberts (1992) describes how the Navy attempts to push responsibility down to the lowest possible level. For example, even the lowest level participant can abort landings on aircraft carriers (Roberts, Stout, and Halpern, in press). Accountability goes with this responsibility. The idea is that individuals own problems until they explicitly pass them on to others. On the other hand, senior officers step into decision-making situations and recentralize the process. This occurs particularly when their training and expertise provide advantages in crises.

In a similar fashion, Weick (1987) identifies the importance of simultaneously maintaining centralization and decentralization in high reliability organizations. While emphasis is more on culture than is the Berkeley group's bureaucratic conception, the underlying idea of maintaining a tension between centralization and decentralization is apparent in both. Weick argues that culture allows organizational members to benefit from the experience of others in the organization. This is the centralizing feature of culture. Yet simultaneously, culture gives organizational participants latitude for interpretation and improvisation in the face of novel situations.

In citing the example of the culture of the Forest Service ranger cadre, Weick describes the situation as follows: "Whenever you have what appears to be successful decentralization, if you look more closely, you will discover that it was always preceded by a period of intense centralization where a set of core values were hammered out and socialized into people before the people were turned loose to go their own 'independent' and 'autonomous' ways" (1987, p. 124). He also points out that stories are particularly important because of the concise way in which they convey appropriate actions and values within the organization.

The same theme of simultaneous centralization and decentralization is also apparent in fast decision organizations (Eisenhardt, 1989a). The two-tier advice process is one example. The advice process is decentralized in the sense that all can contribute. It is centralized in that key decision makers rely on a smaller cadre of counselors. These counselors both provide advice and serve as sounding boards. An even clearer example is the consensus-with-qualification process that fast decision makers use to resolve conflict. As described earlier, this is a two-step process. The first step is decentralized in that everyone attempts to reach consensus. The second step is centralized. If consensus cannot be reached, the leader and possibly the other executives most affected by the decision make the choice.

Overall, high reliability and fast decision making organizations exhibit a dynamic balancing between centralization and decentralization. Centralization provides coordinating values and permits the best use of the experience in the organization. Thus it is reliable. In addition, it is fast because it provides a way to move beyond a conflict deadlock. On the other hand, decentralization allows sensing and action to occur where problems occur. Thus it is likely to lead to faster response because hierarchy is circumvented. The response is likely to be reliable because those at the source of the problem make the choices.

In summary, both high reliability and fast decision organizations are organizations of specialists, linked together in dense and real-time communication networks and balanced in dynamic patterns of centralized and decentralized responsibility. These characteristics, plus redundancy and training, as noted by the Berkeley group, lead to successful coping with demands for reliability and speed in settings with incomplete or ambiguous information.

CONCLUSION

One purpose of this chapter was to describe fast decision organizations, using a premier microcomputer firm of the 1980s as an example. The resulting description emphasized a set of practices by which firms achieve fast, yet high quality decision making: real-time information use, multiple alternatives, a two-tier advice process, consensus with qualification, integration of strategy and tactics.

The second purpose was to compare salient features of fast decision organizations with those of high reliability organizations. At first glance, nuclear power plants, aircraft carriers, and the air traffic control system have little in common with the executive suite of microcomputer firms. The former are challenged by problems of high risk technologies, while the latter face high velocity environments. Indeed, people who operate high risk technologies probably overweigh concerns with safety and error-free operations (see Schulman, this volume). There is a culture of reliability (Weick, 1987, Roberts, Rousseau and La Porte, in press). In contrast, individuals in high velocity environments can very often tolerate some errors if such errors can be detected and corrected very quickly. Theirs is a culture of speed. Yet demands for rapid pace and high quality in contexts of limited, changing information are the same for both types of organizations.

The result of the comparison of the two types of organizations is a set of common themes—specialization, extensive rich and real-time information, and dynamic balancing of centralization and decentralization. These themes, plus concerns for reliability and training, characterize both high reliability and fast decision organizations.

Finally, these organizational similarities also have a broad message for the study of organizations. They indicate that we will gain a more complex view of organizations if we define effectiveness to mean reliability and speed, not just survival and profit.

REFERENCES

Bourgeois, L., and K. Eisenhardt (1988). "Strategic decision processes in high velocity environments: Four cases in the microcomputer industry." *Management Science*, 34, 816–835.

Eisenhardt, K. (1990). "Speed and strategic choice: How managers accelerate decision making." *California Management Review*, 32, 39–54.

————— (1989a). "Making fast strategic decisions in high-velocity environments." *Academy of Management Journal, 31*, 9–41.

————— (1989b). "Building theories from case study research." *Academy of Management Review, 14*, 532–550.

Perrow, C. (1984). *Normal Accidents*. New York: Basic Books.

Roberts, K. H. (1990). "Some characteristics of high reliability organizations." *Organization Science, 1*, 1–17.

————— (1992). "Structuring to facilitate migrating decisions in reliability enhancing organizations." In L. Gomez-Mejia and M. W. Lawless, (eds.), *Top Management and Effective Leadership in High Technology Firms, 3*. Greenwich, CT: JAI Press.

Roberts, K. H., D. Rousseau, and T. La Porte (in press). "The culture of high reliability: Quantitative and qualitative assessment aboard nuclear powered aircraft carriers." *Journal of High Technology Management Research*.

Roberts, K. H., S. K. Stout, and J. Halpern in press. "Decision dynamics in two high reliability military organizations." *Management Science*.

Shrivastava, P. (1987). *Bhopal: Anatomy of a Crisis*. Cambridge, MA: Ballinger.

Weick, K. (1987). "Organizational culture as a source of high reliability." *California Management Review, 2*, 112–127.

Yin, R. (1984). *Case Study Research: Design and Methods*. Beverly Hills, CA: Sage Publications.

8

Hierarchy Versus Bureaucracy: The Case of a Nuclear Reactor

LARRY HIRSCHHORN
Center for Applied Research
Philadelphia, Pa.

Larry Hirschhorn is with the Center for Applied Research. He consults to industry and government on issues of organization design and process. He is also on the faculty of the William Alanson White Institute's program on organizational development and consultation. His most recently published book is entitled *Managing in the New Team Environment: Skills, Tools and Methods,* 1991. He is also the author of *Beyond Mechanization: Work and Technology in a Post-Industrial Age.*

*I*t is common to assume that bureaucratic and hierarchical organizations are ineffective and unresponsive. In particular, people concerned with risky tasks and high-risk settings suggest that such organizations do not enable employees to respond flexibly to unpredictable situations. Facing the challenge of landing an airplane on an aircraft carrier, controlling a complex nuclear reactor, or launching a satellite, employees need to respond to and control an unpredictable flow of events.

This argument lacks sophistication and subtlety. Based on the examination of a case of a nuclear power reactor, this paper argues that we need to distinguish between hierarchy and bureaucracy. Working in hierarchies, people can respond flexibly to their task demands. But when organizational leaders cannot or will not manage the inherent risks of the enterprise, they paradoxically undermine the hierarchy and create a dysfunctional bureaucracy in its place. Diffusing responsibility and reducing the leader's apparent accountability, the bureaucracy burdens employees while making it difficult for them to work. Bureaucracies, in effect, deform the hierarchical structure. We need to construct hierarchies in which authority is widely delegated, while the chain of command is preserved and secured. We return to this argument later.

This chapter is divided into four sections. Using the case of a nuclear power plant called Ocean Reactor, the first section shows how organizational rules and procedures complicate employees' work and create irrational organizational processes. The second section shows how the plant's bureaucratic structure reinforces the impact of procedures by diffusing accountability and creating an unworkable system of checks and balances. The third section examines the distinction between hierarchy and bureaucracy, and the last suggests how an effective hierarchy and an appropriate set of procedures can authorize workers to accomplish their tasks while assuring that leaders manage the overall risk of the enterprise.

THE LIMITS OF PROCEDURES

Ocean Reactor, built in the 1970s and owned by a small utility, supplied a significant amount of electricity to its utility customers and contributed significantly to its profits. But its managers faced growing problems in managing the reactor efficiently. The number of unplanned outages grew; it took workers increasingly long periods of time to shut down and start up the reactor, and maintenance work increased. My colleagues and I were asked to assess the organizational issues faced by reactor and utility managers and to suggest changes in structure, roles, or responsibilities that might improve the reactor's performance.

This case represents a composite picture of two nuclear power plants. This was done to protect the confidentiality of the plants and their employees. There are a limited number of nuclear power plants in the United States and the community of managers and employees leading them, working in them, and regulating them is small. The themes and issues developed here were common to both plants.

Interviews suggested that reactor managers and workers faced the problem of using an increasingly complex set of procedures to guide their work. Before Three-Mile Island, workers in most reactors could exercise considerable discretion in accomplishing their tasks. They had to follow emergency operating procedures strictly but could follow broad guidelines for other work such as bringing a pump on line, testing equipment, or replacing a valve. As one supervisor at Ocean Reactor noted, "Procedures in the past were simply step lists and you could go out of sequence in implementing them." After Three-Mile Island, the Nuclear Regulatory Commission (NRC) encouraged utility managers to develop a detailed and comprehensive set of work procedures. If workers complied with these procedures—so the NRC reasoned—employees could prevent accidents. Indeed, in the decade after Three-Mile Island, Ocean Reactor managers developed over 500 operating and 600 test performance procedures, and hundreds of maintenance procedures.

This system of procedures proved increasingly burdensome for operating and maintaining the reactor. Top management developed an operating philosophy they called "verbatim compliance." Workers and supervisors had to comply with the "letter of the law" and implement procedures without deviating from them in any detail. This philosophy, combined with the procedures, posed great difficulties. Because they cover thousands of work steps, articulated procedures are incomplete, contradictory, and inaccurate. For example, design modifications make certain procedures inaccurate, while abnormal operating circumstances render others incomplete or inaccurate.

Describing the problem of both consistency and completeness, one supervisor noted that during a particular incident, maintenance workers needed to lift wires to repair a motor but discovered that the written procedures did not specify how to perform this step. To complete their work, the mechanics lifted the wire, but now technicians assigned to test the motor before it was put back on line faced a new situation. The testing procedures did not cover the situation in which maintenance workers lifted the wires! Similarly, one supervisor stated that when top management rewrote a plant administrative order—a broad policy statement that shapes and "covers" many other procedures—lower-level managers and supervisors had to rewrite two hundred other test procedures unexpectedly.

Since a procedure writer cannot anticipate all situations and conditions that shape an operator's or mechanic's work, he or she is likely to commit many errors of omission. While accurate, the procedures are often incomplete. As one supervisor suggested, "If you write the instructions for repairing valve lifters, a good mechanic will understand the steps. No procedures, however well written, can substitute for technical knowledge. We are in fact very weak on errors of omission."

Fear and Uncertainty

These dilemmas of consistency, completeness, and accuracy made it hard for operators, mechanics, and their supervisors to understand management's philosophy of verbatim compliance with procedures. If a procedure is wrong, incomplete, or contradicts another, what should the mechanic or operator do? This dilemma created a climate of uncertainty or fear. Uncertain of their authority, workers did not know if they would be chastised if they followed a bad procedure or corrected it. As one high-level manager noted, "People think procedures cover every possible circumstance. They don't. A million things could go wrong. We've made operators afraid." This ambiguity creates a double bind. As another supervisor suggested, "Responsibility for success or failure in implementing a procedure is on the operator right now. If he violates a procedure, even if he's right, he's wrong. If he doesn't violate a procedure and it's wrong, he's wrong."

These dilemmas burden operators, mechanics, and technicians. These people have a good deal of responsibility. As licensed professionals, they can be personally fined for errors but are uncertain of their authority. What freedom of action do they have? What are they responsible for? This gap between responsibility and authority means that operators and their supervisors feel accountable for events and actions they can neither influence nor control. Thus, for example, one health physics technician, responsible for assuring the safety of mechanics working near or around sources of radiation, noted that even when someone else made an error, "If it leads to excessive exposure I will be fined for their mistake." In effect, people feel personally exposed to being fined or punished. The organization as a whole neither supports nor protects them. By relying on procedures and a philosophy of verbatim compliance, top management takes authority away from employees while creating a climate in which they feel personally vulnerable and exposed.

The system of procedures is not fully inflexible. Operators, mechanics, and technicians can request a temporary procedure revision (TPR) to correct a procedure they deem inappropriate. But this process proves cumbersome, making it difficult for workers to complete their assignments on time. As one senior operator described it, "The sign off for a TPR goes to the supervisor, then to the shift technical advisor, and then to the operations managers. This process can take as long as two hours." Indeed, under the pressure of deadlines, first-level supervisors often discourage the use of the TPR. As one manager noted, "If every minor change requires going through a number of reviews, then operators and technicians can never get anything done. The guy will always do what the boss wants, not what the boss says."

Finally, senior managers at the reactor do not always respond effectively to a TPR. A TPR means that a procedure has to be re-examined and, if necessary, changed, but it takes the TPR management committee a long time to review them and create revised protocols. Anticipating lengthy reviews, operators, supervisors, and managers often collude to subvert the official standing of a particular procedure. When filling out a TPR, the operator can note in the appropriate space that he is not changing the "intent" of the procedure. This reduces the time supervisors spend in reviewing it and the time management spends later in addressing its overall viability. As operators and managers define a growing number of procedural deviations as minimal, the gap between the actual work system and the official procedural system grows.

This picture is in stark contrast to the picture Eisenhardt (this volume) paints of fast strategic decision making. The contrast itself offers insight into why her organizations are successful and why Ocean Reactor is less successful. Eisenhardt (this volume), Roberts (1990), and Weick (1987) all explicitly make the point that one requirement for safe operation of potentially catastrophic technologies and for appropriate responses to volatile environments is to develop thickly articulated communication networks.

The Balancing Act

While working with procedures that are inaccurate, that contradict one another, and that are incomplete, workers and supervisors developed a covert work system through which employees created an effective balance between the philosophy of verbatim compliance, normal production pressures, and the unpredictable contingencies of operating and maintaining a nuclear reactor. This means that Ocean Reactor works reasonably well. Even though unscheduled outages grew, it had a good safety record (emergency operating procedures were accurate and followed to the tee), and is profitable. By drawing electricity from other utilities when necessary, the utility supplied its customers with power reliably. But the balancing act that made Ocean Reactor reasonably successful exacted a psycho-social price. People at all levels felt personally exposed and at risk. Feeling that they were likely candidates for punishment, they worked covertly rather than openly, "doing what the boss wants, not what he says." They subverted formal management processes to meet management's expectations.

Indeed, the balance between procedural compliance, production goals, and the reactors' inherent unpredictability may prove unstable. As one manager indicated, "The next major accident in the nuclear industry (after TMI) will be caused by operators following procedures." The very system created to contain and control risk may actually create danger. As Figure 8-1 shows, to get their work done, operators subvert the procedural system. Managers covertly support them, leading workers to doubt management's capacity to exercise leadership and authority in running the reactor. Feeling unprotected, workers hang back and either follow bad procedures unthinkingly or correct them carelessly. As one technician stated, "Workers don't use all of their intelligence and skills here." Consequently, they paradoxically create new dangers by either overtly complying with or covertly undermining a system of procedures designed to limit risk in the first place.

This diagnosis supports the Berkeley group's research in high reliability organizations. They highlight that reliable organizations do not develop punishing work environments. In fact, Schulman (this volume) discusses the mandate of trust and credibility that is nurtured and renewed on a daily basis at Diablo Canyon Nuclear Power Plant.

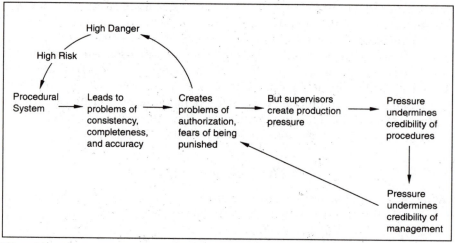

Figure 8-1
The Vicious Circle of a System of Procedures

THE ORGANIZATIONAL STRUCTURE

These dilemmas of authority and accountability are reproduced in the organization's structure and management process. As the simplified diagram in Figure 8-2 shows, the organization is divided into three parts—an operations group responsible for producing power, a maintenance group, and a central services group responsible for writing procedures and enforcing health–physics regulations. The Chief Operating Officer ostensibly oversees and integrates the work of these three divisions but in fact is preoccupied with broader business and regulatory issues and does not keep track of daily operations. People look to the operations manager as the reactor's unofficial plant manager since he is accountable for power production. But, unlike a true general manager, he does not formally supervise the other two managers and is not authorized to resolve conflicts among these three divisions. Schulman (this volume) discusses a very different use of structure in both his nuclear and fossil power producing plants.

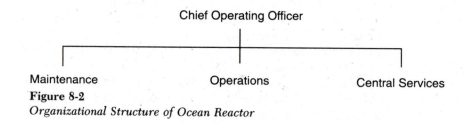

Figure 8-2
Organizational Structure of Ocean Reactor

Checks and Balances

Managers indicated that their organizational processes are based on the principle of *checks and balances*. This is a suggestive term. Used to characterize the U.S. federal government, it describes a system in which no branch or division has power over the others. Instead, each constrains or checks the other, assuring that power and authority are never concentrated in one branch. *Checks and balances* is thus a quintessential *political* principle implemented to prevent tyranny. In this sense, it is inherently an antihierarchical principle. When implemented, it prevents any one manager from representing the interests and goals of the organization as a whole.

The Berkeley group uses this notion in a different way in discussing high reliability organizations. They argue that checks and balances provides redundancy so that important organizational processes do not fall between the cracks (Roberts, 1990).

This case suggests that checks and balances can provoke a great deal of mistrust and suspicion between the divisions and defensive behavior on the part of each. Authorized to constrain one another, each divisional manager assumes the others are irresponsible and have to be "checked." Operations has to prevent maintenance from tying up the reactor; safety workers must prevent maintenance from overexposing workers to radiation. Operations has to prevent safety workers from delaying maintenance. Rather than supporting one another, each division manager is asked to prevent others from doing damage.

A health physics supervisor described a typical pattern. Health physics workers, feeling their role is to check the "irresponsible" behavior of maintenance supervisors, are conservative in estimating the length of time a worker can spend in an area exposed to radiation. Maintenance supervisors, often pressed by operations supervisors to complete their work, then resent this perhaps unnecessary constraint. They, in turn, subvert the goals of the health physics group by simply putting more workers on the job than is customary, thus limiting each worker's exposure but increasing the total number of workers exposed to health hazards. This behavior in turn proves to the health physics manager that indeed maintenance supervisors have to be carefully monitored!

Similarly, one supervisor from central services described how a "test and performance" technician determined that a recently repaired component could not be put back into operation because it failed a performance test. But the senior watch supervisor, though required to complete a report on the test failure, refused to do so because it would delay refueling. Since the component only barely failed, he ordered another test for the next morning. Such incidents only reinforced the test and performance technicians' beliefs that they have to be tough on operations to protect the integrity of the equipment.

Because the system of checks and balances actually increases interdivisional conflict, people throughout the organization feel that they are working in an overly politicized system. As one manager noted, "We work here along turf lines; we need a team concept;" and as a second also said, "There is no structure here for conflict resolution." Finally, as a third similarly noted, "We alienate the team concept here; a good baseball team does not have checks and balances."

These statements are provocative. *They suggest that people experience a well-functioning hierarchy as the precondition for team work.* In a hierarchy, the general manager contains the potential conflicts between divisions by representing the interests and goals of the entire organization. The work of containing and integrating then enables people from different divisions to work together without stumbling into core conflicts over priorities. The hierarchy enables top management to represent the whole organization to its members. Buttressed with such a conception of the whole, people are free to exercise their initiative in working across divisions and groups. No longer consumed by the politics of their organization, they can focus on the task.

Indeed, Creed, Stout, and Roberts (this volume) point out that in well-running high reliability organizations, political issues are minimized. Technological imperatives rather than personal gain, loss, and frustration need to drive system activities.

One manager described the origins and implications of a checks and balance system beautifully: "Our work in the fossil stations was totally different. The plant manager made clear that there was a prime directive (in force). Everything was treated on a plant-wide basis. Basically, your role was to make the plant manager look good. If I was a supervisor and didn't identify a components problem by Friday afternoon, then I got yelled at for spending overtime dollars. Here at Ocean Reactor we yell at maintenance people for working overtime."

This statement highlights three interrelated issues. First, in a well-functioning hierarchy there is a chain of command and thus a source for a "prime directive." Second, in complex production systems people integrate psychologically the many different goals and objectives they experience daily by identifying with the person of the "commander." The commander comes to represent the organization as a whole. This is a principle of leadership. Third, when these conditions are absent, managers at all levels avoid acknowledging their accountability for their actions and instead blame the workers. Feeling unauthorized, management no longer takes responsibility for the risks of guiding and leading the enterprise. There is consequently a felt vacuum of authority throughout the organization.

I had a vivid personal experience of this climate when I was consulting the operations manager. I met with him and with other members of the management group as they assessed the dilemmas they faced in managing with and through a set of procedures. As they reached the end of their deliberations, it was unclear who had the authority to end the meeting. The operations manager tried to sum up the discussion several times but was interrupted by the central services and maintenance manager. They would not let him close the meeting. Curiously, though I had helped other management groups navigate through such quandaries in the past, this time I felt stuck. I then realized that since my client could not find the authority to take his role as the meeting's convener, I also could not find the authority to consult the group. Just as the organizational structure took authority from its employees, it had taken authority from me. My co-consultant appeared similarly stymied and spoke up in a loud voice, saying, "Now who is responsible for doing what here?" Most strikingly, at that moment the Chief Operating Officer appeared and stood hugging the door frame of the conference room as if to communicate that he would observe the group's difficulties but would take no steps to join the group and wrestle with its dilemmas. I felt stuck, unauthorized, and unsupported by the organization's top management.

Procedures and Checks and Balances

We can now see how this system of checks and balances and the system of procedures reinforce one another. Facing risk and danger, management deploys a system of checks and balances. While ostensibly designed to secure the organization's goals, this system takes authority from employees and burdens line workers with responsibilities they cannot possibly fulfill. The system of procedures then promises to compensate for this process by investing authority in *rules rather than roles*. But since such a system is incomplete, inconsistent, and inaccurate, managers and workers must take initiative and exercise their intelligence to compensate for inappropriate procedures. But since they work within a system of checks and balances, they take initiative warily and are reluctant to stick their necks out.

There has been no major incident or accident at Ocean Reactor. While the organization burdens rather than supports its employees, the workers and supervisors are nonetheless personally committed to the plant's and the community's safety. While many are angry at the organization, they nonetheless identify with their profession as nuclear power plant operators and technicians and with their maintenance craft. Consequently, they can still perform successfully despite the political disorganization around them. They "decathect" the organization and find their own personal reasons to work rationally, carefully, and effectively. They nonetheless work in a difficult climate, and, as one manager noted, the "next accident" can happen as a result of an operator following procedures.

HIERARCHY VERSUS BUREAUCRACY

Let us return to the themes of hierarchy and bureaucracy mentioned in the beginning of this paper. Let me suggest the following hypotheses drawn from them. In a well-functioning hierarchy, the leader absorbs the primary risks of managing the enterprise and then delegates authority and accountability to others to accomplish the more delimited but still complicated and important tasks. The leader in his or her role represents the organization as a whole and integrates the actions of its different divisions. This structure and process facilitate team work. By contrast, when hierarchy is poorly defined or weakened, leaders who do not take up their leadership roles fully, who do not manage the risks of the enterprise fully, cannot delegate authority to others. Instead, they rely on both a "technical" fix and on disorganizing politics. They try to use technically developed procedures or rules as substitutes for roles, and they employ the political principle of checks and balances to orchestrate interdivisional relationships. The principle of checks and balances replaces the principle of unity of command; rules replace roles; and politics ultimately drives out team work.

I suggest that the latter option best describes our intuitive understanding of bureaucracy. Consider Figure 8-3. In Weber's ideal-typical bureaucracy (Gerth and Mills, 1946), a system of procedures can accurately describe the organization's tasks. In this sense, it is "means-centered." People focus on the rules and not on the purposes or ends of their work. In Mannheim's (1940, p. 53) terms, bureaucracy promotes functional or instrumental rather than substantive rationality. Since in this ideal-typical state the rules are complete and consistent, authority is vested in the rules, and people need only to follow their "orders." While this ideal-type bureaucracy exists nowhere, we can hypothesize that in low-risk settings organizational routines are stable over long periods of time and employees, working by the rules, can completely describe the organization's tasks. By contrast, in high-risk settings no set of rules can completely describe the organization's tasks. Consequently, if the organization is means-centered, people are unable to accomplish their tasks and leaders will come to use the principle of checks and balances to orchestrate and coordinate work. Such bureaucracy is ultimately dysfunctional.

On the other hand, hierarchies are goal- or "ends-centered." By delegating authority to their subordinates, leaders ask them to accomplish the *purpose*

	Low Risk	High Risk
Means Centered	Ideal type bureaucracy	Dysfunctional bureaucracy
Ends Centered	Hierarchy with low delegation	Hierarchy with high delegation

Figure 8-3
Four Ideal Types of Organizations

of the roles—that is, the substance of their authorization—with a range of means at their disposal. As Figure 8-3 suggests, because tasks are predictable in low-risk settings, the level and depth of delegation in a hierarchy is limited. Leaders can effectively monopolize the bulk of the authority. But in high-risk settings, the level of depth of delegation is extensive. Leaders then take up the risk of integrating the unpredictable actions of subordinates with the contingent events in the environment of the enterprise.

Moreover, as Figure 8-3 and our argument suggest, bureaucracy in high-risk settings can be usefully interpreted as a *regressed form of hierarchy*. Facing high risks and unwilling to manage them, leaders avoid their responsibility for guiding the enterprise. Instead, they abdicate to a system of checks and balances and a system of procedures.[1] Figure 8-3 suggests that hierarchical organizations face a branch point. As they move from low- to high-risk settings, and this process characterizes organizations in a wide range of settings today, leaders can either extend and deepen the quality of their delegations to subordinates, or they can regress to bureaucracy by building systems that diffuse accountability and politicize decision making.

This argument is consistent with the standards for effective organizational performance discussed by Schulman; Eisenhardt; Creed, Stout, and Roberts (all this volume). Eisenhardt discusses both her own and some of the Berkeley group's observations of successive use of centralization and decentralization in order to carry out organizational activities in a timely manner.

THE EFFECTIVE ORGANIZATION: A MODEL

Confusion over the meaning of the terms *hierarchy, bureaucracy,* and *teams* makes it difficult to construct useful models of organizations that are well adapted to functioning in high-risk settings. As this argument suggests, bureaucracies diffuse authority, hierarchies support team processes, and by supporting meaningful delegation, hierarchies help leaders and followers collaborate. If these conclusions sound paradoxical, it is because we fail to understand the dynamics and interrelationships of hierarchies, bureaucracies, and teams.

A four-part model of effective organization for high-risk settings is proposed:

1. The organization is hierarchical in structure. Because the level of risk is high, organization members need to feel there is unity of command and a single role through which conflicts, divisions, and tensions

---

[1] Of course, the NRC played a role here. By using procedures to regulate the industry, they helped set into motion the organizational processes described here. However, the NRC did not mandate any particular organizational form. I believe that facing pressures from the NRC, utility managers in many settings abdicated responsibility for managing risk. Instead, they left it up to the NRC on the one side and to their own employees on the other.

within the organization can ultimately be integrated. Unity of command helps people contain their own anxiety, frees them up to use their initiative and skills in their work, and helps them identify psychologically with the organization's leaders and with the enterprise as a whole.

2. Delegation is broad and deep. While leaders are ultimately accountable for the organization's performance, a leader delegates substantial authority to his or her subordinates. This frees subordinates to use their tools and skills creatively in accomplishing their sanctioned ends. Delegation, while supporting the chain of command, is also a vehicle for sharing the leadership in the organization.

3. Management develops two classes of procedures. The first class, *guiding procedures,* is broad in scope and applies to a wide range of circumstances. Employees implement these procedures in the spirit of strict compliance since in fact the procedures are statements of policy or philosophy. Employees strictly apply the organization's policies. The second class, *detailed procedures,* applies to specific situations. Employees are free to vary the precise steps they take in implementing a procedure *as long as they fulfill its intentions.* Indeed, since employees presumably understand management's basic policies, they can change a detailed procedure while assuring themselves that it supports management's overall priorities. *By applying policy strictly, they can change specific procedures safely and creatively.* To use a legal analogy, the first class of procedures represents the organization's "constitution," the second its "common law." The latter evolves while always staying within the bounds established by the former.

4. Emergency procedures integrate the two classes. They represent both management policy and detailed procedures, which must be followed strictly to the "letter of the law."

This model cannot promise to create a conflict-free organization nor an organization without risk. No model can. But it aligns roles, risks, and procedures in a more effective and hopeful way. People are authorized to vary procedures but do so within the bounds set by the leaders' formal policy. Moreover, leaders can assess the viability of their policies only as it is tested by the employees in the workplace. Thus, they come to depend on employee initiative and curiosity to test and renew the organization's policies and philosophy. Top and bottom are joined in a learning process, as the evolution of "common law" slowly reshapes the meaning of the organization's "constitution."

As we begin to open up organizations and reduce leaders' monopoly over decisions, we must also learn to respect the enduring strengths of hierarchical form. Deriving from the military and the contingencies of battle, it remains a powerful social invention for managing risk. Just as we can modernize the military, so can we modernize hierarchy. We need more open hierarchies: organizations in which delegation is deep and leaders and followers can learn together.

REFERENCES

Gerth, H., and C. W. Mills, (eds.), (1946). *From Max Weber.* New York: Oxford University Press.

Mannheim, K. (1940). *Man and Society in an Age of Reconstruction.* London: Routledge and Kegan Paul.

Roberts, K. H. (1990). "Some characteristics of high reliability organizations." *Organization Science, 1,* 1–17

Weick, K. (1987). "Organizational culture as a source of high reliability." *California Management Review, 2,* 112–127.

9

The Effects of Flight Crew Fatigue on Performance: A Full-Mission Simulation Study

H. CLAYTON FOUSHEE, JR.
Federal Aviation Administration

JOHN K. LAUBER
National Transportation Safety Board

H. Clayton Foushee, Jr., is Managing Director, Flight Procedures Training and Standards, at Northwest Airlines. At the time this chapter was written, he was Chief Scientific and Technical Advisor for Human Factors for the Federal Aviation Administration (FAA), served as scientific and technical advisor to the FAA Administrator and Executive Board, and was the agency focal point on human performance issues. He is heading a joint effort of the FAA and the National Aeronautics and Space Administration (NASA), with Department of Defense assistance, to implement a comprehensive National Plan for Aviation Human Factors. Prior to his FAA appointment, Dr. Foushee was Principal Scientist of the Crew Research and Space Human Factors Branch of the NASA-Ames Research Center, where he headed a research program on team and organizational factors in both aviation and space. Dr. Foushee holds a B.A. degree in Psychology from Duke University and a Ph.D. degree in Social Psychology from the University of Texas.

John K. Lauber became a member of the National Transportation Safety Board in November 1985.

Dr. Lauber is a research psychologist who began his career at the U.S. Naval Training Devices Center in 1969. He came to the Safety Board from the National Aeronautics and Space Administration where he directed the Aeronautical Human Factors Research Office at NASA's Ames Research Center. He has worked extensively with airlines, cockpit crews, and affiliated organizations throughout the world on safety issues that involve human factors.

Dr. Lauber was president of the Association of Aviation Psychologists and chairman of the Aerospace Medical Association's Aviation Safety Committee. He served as assistant technical director of President Reagan's task force on airliner crew size, and also as a member of the Institute of Medicine panel at the National Academy of Sciences that reviewed scientific evidence relating to the mandatory retirement of airline pilots at age 60. He has been the Board Member on scene at several major accident investigations, including the mid-air collision at Cerritos, California, and the crash of Northwest 255 at Detroit, Michigan.

*D*espite impressive advances in aircraft technology over the past several decades and an overall decline in the accident rate since the introduction of turbine-powered aircraft, flight crew performance problems continue to dominate the statistics. Many hypotheses concerning the persistence of operator performance problems exist, and pilot fatigue has traditionally received a considerable amount of attention. This interest has stimulated a large volume of laboratory research, but much of this work is difficult to generalize to the operational world, and the issues surrounding its applicability have prompted considerable disagreement regarding the extent and operational significance of fatigue-related performance decrements.

Aside from research focusing on cockpit design and engineering issues, relatively few pilot performance studies have been carried out in actual operational environments (see Graeber, Foushee, and Lauber, 1984, for a more comprehensive discussion). Field research is very difficult to do because of an almost complete lack of experimental control over operational events. Moreover, flight safety considerations prohibit the examination of many variables in the in-flight environment. Thus, fatigue studies have generally been confined to laboratory or part-task research environments, often using tasks that are not relevant to the task of flying a complex transport aircraft.

Because of these limitations, it is difficult to summarize the implications of the fatigue-performance literature for air transport operations (see Holding, 1983; Gagne, 1953; Bartlett, 1943; McFarland, 1953; Chiles, 1955; Brown, 1967; Dureman and Bowden, 1972). Even studies that utilize tasks with some face-validity to piloting an aircraft (e.g., Bartlett, 1943) are crude simulations, and the primary performance criteria are relatively simple monitoring or vigilance tasks that do not comprise the entire performance spectrum.

Only one study measured performance in flight simulators using experience pilots (Klein, Bruner, Holtmann, Rehme, Stolze, Steinhoff, and Wegman, 1970). In this study, subjects were tested periodically after exposure to successive trips eastward and westward across eight time zones. Performance was measured by percent deviation from preset flight parameters and exhibited significant deficits depending on such factors as time of testing, direction of flight, and number of days in the new time zone. While this is one of the few studies to demonstrate a potentially operationally significant effect of circadian dysrhythmia of performance, it left many questions unanswered. The simulator tests lasted only 12 minutes, and were limited to manual control skills, and therefore did not evaluate any of the higher-level cognitive skills required on the flight deck. Furthermore, the study examined only single-pilot operations. In multipilot operations, a number of other factors affect flight safety and efficiency.

Pilots who are highly proficient in manual control skills continue to be involved in incidents and accidents. The vast majority involve failure of information transfer and inadequate crew coordination and decision making. Yet no studies have examined the possible effects of fatigue on higher-level decision-making skills and those skills related to effective teamwork and coordination.

The objective of this study was to assess whether any behavioral or performance changes are associated with typical short-haul duty cycles, but more importantly, whether these behavioral and performance changes (if any) are operationally significant. Operational significance is defined as performance that has a major bearing on flight safety and efficiency. Unlike the majority of previous research efforts, this study sought to measure performance on a realistic group performance task that induced high motivation and arousal.

METHOD

Subjects participated in this study either before or just after they had completed a three-day, high-density (short flight segments with numerous takeoffs and landings), short-haul trip. The "target trips" in this study consisted of high-density, short-haul airline operations averaging eight hours of on-duty time per day and five takeoffs and landings, with at least one day (usually the last) averaging close to eight takeoffs and landings and thirteen hours on duty.

There were two experimental conditions. Subjects in the "Post-Duty" condition flew a full-mission, line-oriented simulation as if it were the last segment of a three-day trip, while subjects in the "Pre-Duty" condition flew the same simulation after a minimum of two days off duty (usually three), as if it were the first segment of a trip. Twenty volunteer crews participated in the study (forty pilots). One Post-Duty crew was eliminated when it was learned that the captain had been informed by another subject about the operational events associated with the scenario. This left eleven crews in the Pre-Duty condition and nine in the Post-Duty condition.

Subjects and Recruitment

All subjects were recruited from the ranks of active line pilots in one domicile of a major U.S. air carrier. The decision to use pilots from one airline was necessitated by differences in standard operating procedures and aircraft configurations across air carriers. Thus, for experimental control purposes and because of the need to maintain the highest possible degree of realism, the scenario was designed to simulate precisely a single airline operation. All subjects currently flew the transport aircraft simulated.

Experimental Equipment

The simulator utilized in this study has a six-degree-of-freedom motion platform and four-window computer-generated visual system manufactured by CAE, Inc., of Canada. It was equipped with the special effects and aircraft performance data required to meet Federal Aviation Administration (FAA) Phase II certification, and successfully completed the certification process.

Experimental Procedure

When each crew arrived at the simulation facility, it was met by the principal investigator who briefed members on the purpose of the investigation. The importance of operational realism was emphasized, and pilots were urged to treat the simulation as if it were an actual flight. They were informed that they would have access to all resources they would normally have during operations, including complete air traffic control (ATC) services, dispatch, access to maintenance, and Automatic Terminal Information Service (ATIS, weather and airport formation). However, no details were provided to flight crews other than the flight's origin and destination. Subjects were asked to treat the flight as a "captain's segment," with the captain flying the aircraft and the first officer performing support duties. This was done for experimental control purposes and to assure consistent performance evaluation opportunities at both crew positions. The flight dispatcher provided crews with the same information and paperwork they would have normally received prior to a trip. This information included the route of flight, weather information for the vicinity of the flight, fuel information, weight and balance information, number of passengers, and so on. All information was provided on standard company forms.

Following receipt of these materials, crews did normal pre-flight planning. When it appeared that crews were nearing completing of pre-flight checks and as departure time approached, the simulator operator extinguished the rear cargo door light, prompting most flight crews to realize that the aircraft was loaded and ready. Shortly thereafter, the captain was called over the interphone by ground personnel and was informed that the aircraft was ready.

At this point, or shortly thereafter, the co-pilot radioed for a clearance to push back from the gate. Push back was simulated by activating the simulator motion platform at the appropriate moment, which produced a small jolt quite similar to that associated with the tug beginning to push the aircraft backward. The recording of performance data began at push back. Taxi and ground operations were accomplished in accordance with standard operating procedures, as was the remainder of the simulated flight. After landing, pilots were escorted back to the flight dispatch area where they completed rating forms and were extensively debriefed by the principal investigator.

Simulation Scenario

Crews were scheduled to fly a segment from Greensboro, North Carolina (GSO), to Richmond, Virginia (RIC). The weather along the flight route was characterized by a frontal system passing through the area that had low ceilings and visibilities. The segment included the departure airport, which was still acceptable for takeoff but was nearing the legal landing minimums (Runway Visual Range (RVR) 1600 feet, ¼ mile). The airplane was relatively heavy (gross weight 104,000 pounds), and the takeoff was "runway-limited" because the longer runway at the departure airport was closed (aircraft were unable to take off at the maximum gross weight because of inadequate runway length).

Since weight was critical, the aircraft was dispatched with a minimum, but legal amount of fuel (13,200 pounds). Because of this factor and the poor weather, which increased the probability of diversion, crews should have been concerned about the amount of fuel, and as in actual flight operations, captains had the option of requesting additional fuel from the flight dispatcher. This, of course, would increase aircraft weight above the runway-length imposed limit. Therefore, if more fuel was requested, which was a prudent course of action under the circumstances, the crew was informed that baggage had to be off-loaded to meet the runway limitations. The dispatcher was instructed to explain the implications of extra fuel to flight crews and to be reluctant to provide the extra fuel, as is sometimes the case in reality. However, if the captain persisted, the dispatcher would agree to add 5000 extra pounds of fuel. Eighteen out of the twenty crews asked for and received this extra amount.

After the crew pre-flighted the aircraft and received clearance to push back and taxi, ATC issued a special weather observation to all aircraft in the vicinity indicating that the visibility had deteriorated to RVR 1600, ⅛ mile, in rain and fog. The operational implications of this were that takeoff was still legal, but that landing was not. This meant that crews were legally required to obtain a takeoff alternate in case mechanical problems forced a quick return for landing. If a takeoff alternate was requested, Roanoke, Virginia (ROA), was provided by dispatch since it had the best weather within a relatively short distance from GSO. ROA was also given as the regular alternate landing site for RIC. (As will be seen later, ROA was selected intentionally because of certain characteristics and because it was the site where all flight crews were ultimately forced to land.)

As in all of the operational events programmed into the simulation, some crews recognized the implications and acted appropriately, and some did not. Once airborne, a relatively low workload, routine flight segment allowed crews to relax so that their behavior would more closely approximate actual flight behavior. This procedure is effective in both training and research applications of full-mission simulation (cf. Lauber and Foushee, 1981).

Two minor events were inserted in the low workload segment to probe crew vigilance. These were icing conditions (to determine how attentive crews were to environmental conditions) and unexpected rain and moderate turbulence along the route of flight. The aircraft was dispatched with radar inoperative, and "vigilant" crews would have checked with ATC for ground-based radar advisories or pilot reports in order to assure sufficient separation from potential severe weather. Crew awareness of such events was included in both observer rating dimensions and in the error analyses.

The "high workload" phase of flight began when crews started their approach to RIC. Weather information for the arrival indicated that the weather was poor (RVR 1200) and required a complicated Category II instrument approach. Further, there was a substantial cross-wind on the active runway, and this cross-wind was near the legal limit. As crews continued their approaches and contacted the tower for landing clearance, they were advised by the RIC Control Tower that the winds had increased to thirteen knots from 230 degrees, which was three knots over the legal limit of a ten-knot cross-wind component for a Category II approach. Some crews recognized this and executed the mandatory missed approach, and some did not. All crews, whether they realized that landing was illegal or not, were eventually forced to execute a missed approach because those who continued the approach to RIC were unable to establish visual contact with the ground at the decision height of 103 feet above the surface.

During the missed approach, crews experienced a "System A" hydraulic failure. The implications of this malfunction are complex: (1) landing gear and flaps have to be operated manually; (2) the aircraft has reduced braking, which means increased stopping distances; (3) the aircraft must be operated with a fifteen degree of flap approach, instead of the normal thirty or forty degrees of flap extension requiring higher approach speeds; (4) once the landing gear is extended manually, it cannot be raised again (having substantial implications for fuel consumption and subsequent possible missed approaches); and (5) nose wheel steering is inoperative (which means the aircraft has to be towed off the runway).

Crews were now faced with a number of complicated decisions and procedures. They had to decide where to land, since the original destination did not have legal landing conditions, and in some cases there was only a limited amount of fuel (remember the beginning of the scenario and the original dispatch with minimum fuel). They had to diagnose the System A failure, realize its implications, and secure the failed system. Since higher approach speeds and reduced braking effectiveness are consequences of the System A failure, the most desirable alternate landing site was one with a relatively long runway.

The operational problems induced by the hydraulic failure were more severe than they normally would have been because of poor weather in the general vicinity. Airports that should have been considered as alternates included Tri-Cities, TN (TRI); Dulles International (IAD); Washington National (DCA); Raleigh/Durham, NC (RDU); Charlotte, NC (CTL); and Greensboro, NC (GSO), but all had visibilities of ¼ miles or less, and some were closed due to weather conditions. The only reasonable alternate was an airport (ROA) with acceptable weather, but with a relatively short runway (runway 33, 5800 feet long) that was wet, sloping downhill, and adjacent to mountainous terrain. ROA had a 1000-foot ceiling, five miles visibility, and winds from 360 degrees at ten knots. That the ROA weather was relatively good was not surprising to most flight crews, who were familiar with the fact that ROA frequently has favorable conditions when other airports are marginal. Although the relatively short runway and mountainous terrain posed a dilemma for many flight crews, it was the best choice compared to the other alternatives.

Another feature of the scenario was that the manual gear and flap extension procedures were time-consuming and required a fair amount of pre-planning. The flight time from RIC to ROA was relatively short (approximately 30 minutes), so time had to be apportioned carefully. In short, this simulation required a high level of crew coordination for effective performance—it provided a good test of high-level decision making and crew performance. Some of the features of this scenario are similar to those seen in past incidents and accidents.

Fatigue Measures

Immediately after the simulation, subjects reported their sleep–wake schedules for each of the four previous nights. They rated the quality of their previous night's sleep on four dimensions: difficulty falling asleep, deepness of sleep, difficulty arising, and how restful the sleep was. In addition, subjects completed a twenty-six-item mood adjective checklist (Moses, Lubin, Naitoh, and Johnson, 1974) and estimated their level of fatigue by placing a mark on a 10-centimeter line representing a continuum from most alert to most drowsy (Wever, 1979).

Crew Performance Measures

A variety of measures was used to assess both individual and crew performance parameters since the primary objective was to determine whether or not any observed performance changes were operationally significant. Crew performance measures included expert observer ratings, subjective assessments of workload, aircraft handling data, error analyses (both real-time and videotape), and crew communication patterns. Each is discussed in detail below.

Observer Ratings. Two types of ratings were obtained. The first was partitioned by phase of flight (e.g., pre-flight, taxi/takeoff, climb, cruise, approach/missed approach, emergency procedure/hydraulic failure, cruise to alternate, and approach/landing). Within each section, expert observers rated both the captain and the first officer on each dimension. Each dimension was scored on a five-point Likert scale.[1] Many dimensions were common to each phase of flight (for example, crew coordination/communications, aircraft handling, planning/situation awareness, procedures, overall performance, etc.). However, some were relevant only to specific flight phases or situations (such as thunderstorm awareness, stress management, takeoff alternate, and the like).

The second rating was more general and completed by the expert observer for both captains and first officers immediately after the simulation. It consisted of nine categories (overall knowledge of aircraft and procedures, technical proficiency, "smoothness," crew coordination and internal communication, external communication, motivation, command ability [for captains], vigilance, and overall performance). These ratings were also made on five-point Likert scales and were intended to assess the expert observer's overall impression of performance throughout the simulation.

Subjective Workload.   Pilot perceptions of workload were assessed via a technique developed by Hart and co-workers (e.g., Hart, Battiste, and Lester, 1984). It consists of ten workload-related dimensions: task difficulty; time pressure, performance, mental effort, amount of attention required, complexity, busy-ness, motivation, fatigue, and overall workload. Each dimension was scaled on a seven-point Likert scale.

Aircraft Handling Data.   These data were recorded directly from the simulator computer. Twelve parameters related to aircraft configuration and handling were sampled every 15 seconds. These included airspeed, altitude, vertical speed, magnetic heading, engine power setting, glide slope deviation, localizer deviation, gear position, flap position, navigational frequencies, and elapsed time. All measures were time-synchronized with the videotaped records so that other performance parameters could be examined along with aircraft configuration. These measures were utilized primarily for analyses of the final approach at ROA and for cross-checking during the error analyses.

Error Analyses.   Error analyses were undertaken using two independent sources of data. First, the expert observer kept a record of all errors observed during the course of the simulation. The second source was the videotape records. Two independent "blind" observers reviewed the tapes for operational errors. Reliability analyses revealed 81 percent agreement between both sources of error information, yielding a high level of confidence in these data.

Since the operational significance of performance differences was of primary importance, an attempt was made to categorize errors according to level of severity. A three-level classification was utilized—Type I errors were defined as minor, with a low probability of serious flight safety consequences; Type II errors were defined as of moderate severity, with a stronger potential for flight safety consequences; and Type III errors were classified as operationally significant errors, having a direct negative impact upon flight safety.

---

[1]Scale anchors ranged from 1 = below average performance to 5 = above average performance.

Examples of Type I errors include missed clearances that were quickly corrected, checklists that were not run according to standard operating procedures (missing an item, or accomplished from memory), and altitude deviations of less than 200 feet. Type II errors included the failure to notify the company or ATC of an abnormal situation, altitude deviations between 200 and 400 feet, failure to use ice protection, going over or under speed for current configuration, delayed recognition or handling of the hydraulic failure, and failure to run a required checklist. Type III errors included failure even to recognize that the hydraulic failure had taken place, speed brakes and thrust reversers deployed prior to touchdown, no consideration of landing alternates other than the company-recommended ROA, missing the cross-wind or takeoff and landing restrictions, improper handling of abnormal procedures, and altitude deviations of more than 400 feet.

Flight Crew Communication Patterns

Since past research shows the interaction of flight crew members to be a significant predictor of flight crew performance (e.g., Foushee and Manos, 1981), extensive analyses of communications data were undertaken in this investigation. The findings are consistent with the importance placed on communication by many other authors in this volume (see Rochlin; Schulman; Eisenhardt; Weick; among others). The procedure used to analyze within-cockpit communication patterns was adapted from the Foushee and Manos (1981) procedure that was in turn derived from the work of Bales (1950). Each statement or phrase was coded into one of eighteen categories of communication: command, observation, suggestion, statement of intent, inquiry, agreement, disagreement, acknowledgment, answer supplying information, response uncertainty, tension release, frustration/anger/derisive remark, embarrassment, repeats, checklist, non-task related, non-codable, or ATC communications. Coders worked independently.

Two coders were trained extensively in the coding procedures by the principal investigator, and maintained a 71 percent level of agreement throughout the coding process.

RESULTS

Fatigue Data

Captains in the Pre-Duty condition had significantly more sleep for three nights before the experimental runs than did those in the Post-Duty condition, as might have been expected. Despite differences in the amount of sleep, no significant differences in sleep quality were reported by captains. Differences between pre- and post-duty conditions on the amount of sleep prior to the experiment for first officers were not as robust, but in the same direction. No sleep quality differences were reported for first officers.

On measures of subjective fatigue, no significant differences were evident for captains or first officers on the ten-centimeter line measure of alertness. However, on the seven-point bipolar scale for fresh versus tired, captains and first officers in the Post-Duty condition indicated that they were significantly more tired than captains in the Pre-Duty condition. Analyses of the mood data tended to confirm that Post-Duty subjects experienced more fatigue at the time of the simulation. Post-Duty subjects tended to report significantly more negative mood. However, differences on the positive and activation mood indices were not statistically significant.

Taken together, these data indicate that Post-Duty crew members experienced significantly more fatigue than Pre-Duty crew members. They reported less sleep, more "tiredness," and more negative mood states than Pre-Duty crew members. Though no attempt was made to control for the off-duty activities of Pre-Duty crew members (they may have been engaged in fatigue-inducing activity during this off-duty time), it may safely be assumed that these fatigue differences between conditions are associated with the duty cycle.

Crew Performance Measures

Observer Ratings. In the pre-flight segment of the simulation, Post-Duty captains were rated better in crew coordination and marginally better in overall performance ($t = -2.81$, $p < .02$; and $t = -1.81$, $p < .09$, respectively). Differences were in the same direction for first officers, but were not statistically significant. The lack of significant results for first officers on these measures probably reflects the fact that captains are primarily responsible for coordinating pre-flight activities.

No significant differences were evident for either captains or first officers in the taxi–takeoff segment. The same pattern was evident during the relatively uneventful climb segment, though there was a slight trend for better rated performance by Post-Duty crew members. The only significant measure was for first officer ATC procedures, with Post-Duty first officers rated higher on this measure ($t = -2.10$, $p < .05$).

Both coordination and procedures were rated better in captains in the Post-Duty condition during the cruise segment ($t = -1.99$, $p < .07$; and $t = -2.22$, $p < .04$, respectively). These differences appear to reflect better handling of the vigilance measures programmed into this flight phase (icing conditions and moderate turbulence). Mean differences on overall performance for captains in this segment suggest a slight edge for Post-Duty captains, but this difference is not statistically significant. Post-Duty first officers were also rated better on the coordination measure during the cruise segment ($t = -2.58$, $p < .02$). They were rated as having performed better on the planning dimension in this segment, as well ($t = -2.02$, $p < .06$).

For the approach segment into RIC, Post-Duty captains were rated better on the approach planning measure ($t = -2.01$, $p < .06$). The coordination rating was marginally significant, with Post-Duty captains again exhibiting better performance ($t = -1.85$, $p = .08$). First officers in the Post-Duty condition were also rated better on the planning measure ($t = -2.07$, $p < .06$).

For the missed approach and emergency procedure segment involving the System A hydraulic failure, Post-Duty captains were again rated better on planning and procedure measures ($t = -2.19$, $p < .05$; and $t = -2.10$, $p < .05$, respectively). The planning rating was also higher for first officers in the Post-Duty condition ($t = -2.23$, $p < .03$). Differences between groups in this flight phase on the planning and procedures measures are particularly significant because they were designed to tap performance during a critically high workload period of the simulation scenario (dealing with the implications of the hydraulic failure). None of the other ratings for cruise to the alternate airport and landing were statistically significant, although in several cases the means were in the same direction (higher ratings for crew members in the Post-Duty condition).

Taken as a whole, it is particularly meaningful that all of the reliable differences on this rating were in the same direction. Post-Duty condition subjects performed better in several phases of flight. In fact, for all ratings, there were no cases in which the pattern was reversed.

Overall Ratings. None of the overall ratings assessed at the end of the simulation approached statistical significance.

Subjective Workload Ratings. Captains in the Pre-Duty condition felt they exerted significantly more mental effort than did captains in the Post-Duty condition ($t = 2.16$, $p < .05$). The workload rating measure also asked how tired subjects were, and as previously discussed, Post-Duty captains reported that they were significantly more tired. For first officers, only the fatigue measure was significant.

Aircraft Handling Data. Since the focus of the investigation was on operational significance, analyses of aircraft handling data were confined to the particular flight segment in which these parameters were expected to be critically important, the last few minutes of final approach to ROA. This was also the part of the scenario in which a number of high workload procedures (e.g., manual gear and flap operation) might conspire to compromise normal aircraft handling performance. As we have seen in other papers in this volume, as complexity of operations increases so does the possibility of serious error.

The four measures of stability used during this segment were airspeed, vertical speed, localizer, and glide slope deviation. Absolute values were obtained for each measure during the last two minutes and thirty seconds prior to touchdown at ROA—yielding ten samples of each of the four parameters for all experimental runs. Due to computer problems, complete data were available for only fifteen of the twenty experimental runs (nine in the Pre-Duty condition and six in the Post-Duty condition). To derive an overall index of aircraft stability (the parameters are intercorrelated), an average for each of the four parameters was computed for each experimental run, and these values were converted to z-scores. The z-scores for each of the four parameters were then summed, yielding an overall index of aircraft stability. Comparison of the stability index revealed that approaches flown by Pre-Duty crews were significantly more unstable than those flown by Post-Duty crews ($t = 2.35$, $p < .05$).

Given the aircraft weight and fifteen-degree flap setting, the correct reference speed in the landing configuration was 135 knots. Following widespread practice, crews added ten knots to this reference speed to compensate for the ten-knot head wind. Thus, target speed for final approach was 145 knots. Post-Duty crews were closer to the correct target speed.

Precise tracking of the Instrument Landing System (ILS) glide slope at ROA results in a vertical descent rate of approximately 800 feet per minute at the speed used for this approach. Again, Post-Duty crews were very close to this value (803.17 feet/minute), while Pre-Duty crews averaged a higher vertical sink rate (858.89 feet/minute). Pre-Duty crews also averaged larger localizer and glide slope deviations than Post-Duty crews.

None of the three categories of error (Types I, II, III) or total errors were significantly different between Pre- and Post-Duty crews. However, mean differences were in the same direction as previous results, particularly on Type III (operationally significant) and total errors. Mean Type III errors for Pre-Duty crews were 4.3 versus 2.33 for Post-Duty crews. Pre-Duty crews averaged 9.2 total errors versus 7.0 for Post-Duty crews.

In an effort to understand better this somewhat counter-intuitive overall pattern of findings (tired crews apparently performing better than rested crews), other analyses were performed. Post-Duty crews had typically flown the entire trip together, while Pre-Duty crews were typically composed of individuals who may not have flown together recently. At the end of a trip, a pilot is more aware of the capabilities and tendencies of other crew members than at the beginning of a trip. It was felt that this "crew familiarity" factor may have had some impact on the results.

Additional analyses addressed the familiarity factor. One of the Post-Duty crews did not fly their last trip together prior to simulator evaluation, while two of the Pre-Duty crews had flown together the last time on duty. Thus, all of the data were re-analyzed based on who had flown together the last time on duty and who had not.

Several significant differences apparently attributable to this crew familiarity factor emerged. The difference between Type I (minor) errors was not significant; however, for Type II (moderate) errors, crews that had not flown together averaged significantly more errors (4.78) than did crews that had flown together (2.20) on the last duty cycle ($t = 2.20$, $p < .04$). The same pattern was evident for Type III (major) and total errors.

In summary, significantly better performance by Post-Duty crew members was suggested by differences on several key crew performance measures. While many comparisons were nonsignificant, there were no reversals of this general pattern.

Crew Communication Analyses

Extensive analyses of crew communications were undertaken since these variables are perhaps the best reflection of how the crews coordinate their activities. It was expected that these measures would facilitate interpretation of the performance differences, as has been suggested in the past (e.g., Foushee, 1984).

Two types of analyses were performed. First, a 2 × 2 (Pre- vs. Post-Duty × captain vs. first officer) between-subjects analysis of variance (ANOVA) was performed for each communication category as well as for total communication. The second type of analysis was designed to look at communication variables as they were affected at different phases of flight. Thus a 2 × 2 × 3 (Pre- vs. Post-Duty × captain vs. first officer × phase of flight) mixed-design ANOVA was also performed for each category. The three-factor phase of flight parameter was a within-subjects variable and was broken down in the following manner: (1) the ten-minute period immediately after takeoff that was routine; (2) the ten-minute period beginning after the decision to execute a missed approach at RIC; and (3) the ten-minute period immediately prior to touchdown at ROA. Thus, one relatively low workload period and two relatively high workload periods were included in these analyses.

Since the familiarity variable appeared to be strongly related to crew performance, the same analyses were conducted incorporating this factor. Both the 2 × 2 between subjects ANOVAs and the 2 × 2 × 3 mixed-design ANOVAs were identical, except that the Flown Together–Not Flown Together variable was substituted for the Pre Post-Duty variable.

Commands. A significant main effect for the Pre Post-Duty variable ($F(1,32) = 4.07$, $p = .05$), indicated that Post-Duty crew members, in general, exchanged more commands, and this was true of both captains and first officers in this condition. Not surprisingly, captains utilized this form of communication more often than did first officers [$F(1,32) = 107.34$, $p < .001$]. It is suggested elsewhere (Foushee and Manos, 1981) that commands have a coordinating effect on crew performance because of their strong influence on subordinate crew member actions. Commands were much more predominant during high workload phases of flight [$F(2,64) = 37$, $p < .01$].

It is also interesting to note that first officers who had recent operating experience with their captains were more likely to use command-type statements. Increased familiarity may raise the probability that subordinate crew members are more assertive when circumstances call for such behavior. The same pattern appeared for the familiarity factor. In short, performance appeared to be facilitated by the more prevalent use of commands by captains in the Post-Duty condition, particularly during high workload phases of flight.

Observations. The analyses revealed a significant main effect on observations about flight status for crew position [$F(1,32) = 14.84$, $p < .001$]. First officers utilized this category of communications more frequently than captains. This is logical in light of the support role assigned to first officers in flight duties. The main effect for phase of flight was significant [$F(2,64) = 13.23$, $p < .001$], indicating more observations during high workload periods. The interaction of crew position and flight segment was also significant [$F(2,64) = 3.23$, $p < .05$], and is due to the more prevalent use of these communications by first officers during high workload phases.

Suggestions. The main effect of crew position was again significant for suggestions [$F(1,32) = 26.97$, $p < .001$]. This likely reflects the captain's role in directing subordinate behavior; however, suggestions are a "softer" means of providing directions than commands. The crew position by crew familiarity interaction approached statistical significance [$F(1,32)$, $p < .09$]. Captains who had flown with the same first officer tended to offer more suggestions than those who had not. This may imply a somewhat less "directive" style among captains who are relatively familiar with other crew members on the flight deck.

Statement of Intent. This category was also presumed to reflect the amount of overall coordination. Such communications are generally utilized to inform others of the actions that the speaker is about to undertake, and thus serve to keep other crew members informed. Again, the main effect for crew position was significant [$F(1,34) = 9.6$, $p < .004$]. First officers utilized this form of communication more frequently than captains, but the crew familiarity main effect was also marginally significant [$F(1,34) = 3.58$, $p < .07$]. Statements of intent were relatively more prevalent among crew members who had flown together. Coordination deficiencies observed in the Pre-Duty or Not Flown Together conditions may occur because of lack of statements of intent in those situations. Lack of statements of intent may be responsible for the performance differences previously discussed.

Inquiries. These are information-seeking behaviors designed to elicit assistance from other crew members. Captains sought more information than first officers [$F(1,34 = 3.87$, $p < .06$], but this type of information-seeking behavior was far more prevalent during high workload phases of flight [$F(1,32) = 9.81$, $p < .001$]. Neither the fatigue nor the crew familiarity variable were associated with differences on this measure.

Agreement and Disagreement. There were no differences on the agreement variable, but it occurred infrequently. On instances of verbal communication reflecting the disagreement of one crew member with the actions, intended actions, or statements of another, significant two-way interactions were associated with crew position on both the familiarity and the fatigue variables. In both cases, first officers were largely responsible for this effect. First officers in the Post-Duty condition were far more likely to disagree with the actions of captains [$F(1,34) = 6.20$, $p < .02$]. The same was true for first officers who had flown with the same captain previously; only the effect was stronger [$F(1,34) = 11.37$, $p < .002$]. It has been suggested that first officers, due to the role structure of the flight deck, are often hesitant to question or correct the actions of captains and that this reluctance has been a factor in a substantial number of incidents and accidents (Cooper, White, and Lauber, 1979; Foushee and Manos, 1981; and Foushee, 1984). This result suggests that crew member familiarity may mediate against this hesitancy and raises the possibility that subordinate crew members accustomed to working with a particular captain will be more assertive when the circumstance call for such behavior.

Acknowledgments. Past research demonstrates that acknowledgments of other communications are often associated with fewer crew performance errors, and that this tends to reinforce the interaction process (e.g., Foushee and Manos, 1981). The same is true in the present investigation. Acknowledgments were significantly more prevalent in crews that had flown together [$F(1,33) = 8.33$, $p < .007$] than those that had not. Acknowledgments were also seen more frequently in high workload segments of flight [$F(2,64) = 3.35$, $p < .05$], suggesting that they play an even more important role in the communications process during critical phases of flight.

Answer Supplying Information. Responses to requests for information were prevalent among first officers ($F(1,34) = 3.99$, $p < .06$), and this is not surprising since by definition, these behaviors are usually responses to commands, inquiries, or observations that are more likely to come from the captain. These differences were significant for first officers in the Post-Duty condition [$F(1,34) = 3.84$, $p < .06$], and first officers who had recent operating experience with their captains [$F(1,34) = 3.38$, $p < .07$]. These results again imply that more overall information exchange occurred in crews with recent operating experience together.

Response Uncertainty. No differences were evident as a function of any of the independent variables on this measure.

Tension Release. This category was operationalized as a reflection of non-task related behavior and typically consisted of laughter or humorous remarks. A significant main effect for crew familiarity occurred on this measure [$F(1,34) = 4.14$, $p < .05$]. Significantly more tension was released among crew members who had not flown together prior to the simulator sessions. This difference may be a reflection of the acquaintance process for crew members unfamiliar with each other. It was primarily evident in the low workload segment, and this type of behavior diminished significantly during the high workload flight segments [$F(2,64) = 8.0$, $p < .002$].

Frustration/Anger. Captains exhibited considerably more frustration and anger than did first officers regardless of experimental condition [$F(1,34) = 11.58$, $p < .002$]. Phase of flight was also a significant predictor as might have been expected [$F(2,64) = 3.76$, $p < .03$]. This may be attributable to the fact that more frustration occurred during the high workload phases of flight. The fact that captains are more prone to this type of behavior is no doubt strongly tied to the captain's authority role.

Embarrassment. This type of behavior typically consisted of apologetic remarks as a result of mistakes or oversights on the part of one crew member. None of the main effects for the experimental variables were significant.

Non-Task Related Communication. This category included crew interaction that was clearly not related to flight tasks. The main effect for crew familiarity was significant [$F(1,32) = 7.29$, $p < .02$]. Crews that had not flow together engaged in more non-task related interaction than crews that had flown together, and this may be related to the fact that they were probably becoming acquainted. This was particularly true during low workload periods of flight since the main effect for flight phase was also strongly significant [$F(2,64) = 7.18$, $p < .002$]. The two-way interaction between phase of flight and crew familiarity was also significant [$F(2,64) = 4.26$, $p < .02$], indicating that non-task related interaction was far more prevalent among crew members who had not flown together during low workload periods.

Repetitions. This category was intended to reflect instructions from one crew member to another that were repeated in quick succession. It was felt that communications of this type are typically utilized to convey a sense of urgency or to assure that an instruction had been received by the crew member to whom it was addressed. None of the main effects were significant, but the interaction between crew position and the fatigue variables was statistically significant [$F(1,34) = 4.59$, $p < .04$]. Post-Duty captains repeated instructions more often than either captains in the Pre-Duty condition or first officers in either condition. This may explain, in part, the apparently better coordination among Post-Duty crew members who were previously acquainted, since repetitions may assure that critical pieces of information are transferred between crew members at appropriate times.

Checklist Items. These communications were merely the challenges issued on standard procedural checklists required at various flight phases. No effects for the fatigue or crew familiarity variables were evident; however, the main effect for crew position was significant [$F(1,34) = 30.35$, $p < .001$]. First officers were responsible for most of the these communications, which is entirely logical since they were assigned non-flying pilot duties for the simulation.

Air Traffic Control Communications. Again, the main effect for crew position was significant [$F(1,34) = 256.93$, $p < .001$], with first officers almost entirely responsible for ATC communication. As with checklist duties, ATC communications are almost entirely the responsibility of the non-flying pilot.

Total Communication. It was expected that total communication, or the sum of all types of communication including noncodable verbal behavior throughout the simulated flight, would be related to overall performance (Foushee and Manos, 1981). Here the main effect for the crew familiarity variable was marginally significant [$F(1,34) = 3.55$, $p < .07$]. Overall, communication was more frequent in crews that had flown together than in crews that had not. This is particularly interesting in light of the significant performance differences between these groups. First officers exhibited more overall communication than captains [F(1,34) = 4.72, $p < .04$], and this is most likely due to the fact that first officers, in their non-flying role, were more involved in supplying task-relevant information for captains' use in decision making.

Communications Summary. In general, the communications variables as measures of group interaction and coordination reflected the same trends evident for the crew performance measures. Post-Duty crews and crews that had flown together engaged in more task-related communication and less non-task-related communication. As expected, instances of various communications behaviors increased with increasing task demands. These analyses support the notion that the performance differences are in large part due to differences in crew coordination. This conclusion is based on the assumption that crew communication patterns are, at least, partial reflections of the coordination process, since they are the means by which many individual efforts are coordinated. Crews that had flown together seemed able to coordinate their activities better than crews that had not flown together.

DISCUSSION

Overview of Findings

The issue of excessive flight fatigue as a result of trip exposure has been a primary concern of the aviation community for a long time, but there has been little tangible evidence with which to confirm or deny the extent or operational significance of fatigue associated with duty cycle exposure. We discussed how laboratory studies are of little use to those interested in aviation safety because of the difficulty of generalizing laboratory performance measures to the task of operating a complex aircraft. Thus, the operational significance issue was a pivotal part of this investigation.

The results of this study reveal that, as expected, Post-Duty crews were significantly more "fatigued" than Pre-Duty crews. The former averaged less sleep and reported higher levels of fatigue than the latter. However, fatigue did not affect the performance of flight crews in any operationally significant manner. As shown, Post-Duty crews performed better than Pre-Duty crews on a number of dimensions relevant to flight safety. While many measures did not discriminate between the two groups, in no case were Pre-Duty crews superior. Post-Duty crews flew more stable approaches, and they tended to make fewer significant operational errors than did Pre-Duty crews.

To some, this very consistent pattern of results may seem paradoxical. However, it is important to note, when considering how crews are usually assigned to flight duties, that there is a substantive difference between crews at the beginning and at the end of a trip, regardless of the fatigue factor. Obviously, after three days of flying with another crew member, one knows a considerable amount about his or her operating characteristics, personality, and communication style. Co-pilots, for example, learn when and how aircraft captains like to be assisted. Captains become familiar with the tendencies of their subordinates, how they supply information, and how best to elicit their input. Obviously, there is wide variation in human interaction, and the more individuals learn about their co-workers, the better they are able to tailor their behavior to the needs of a particular interaction.

This experiment was designed to evaluate the impact on performance of flight crew fatigue. However, the analyses suggested that the crew familiarity factor was more predictive than the level of fatigue. The data were re-analyzed based on who had or had not flown together on the most recent duty cycle (independent of the fatigue factor) and a striking pattern of results emerged. Performance differences were stronger, and it was apparent that crews in which the two pilots had flown together on the previous duty cycle made significantly fewer errors than crews who had not. This was particularly true for more serious errors—Type II and Type III errors. The same pattern was evident on other significant performance measures. Recent operating experience appears to be a strong influence on crew performance and may have served as a countermeasure to the levels of fatigue present in Post-Duty crew members. The process of gaining familiarity probably allows for the development of shared norms and behaviors associated with safety (Koch, this volume) and provides for increased standardization.

Examination of flight crew communication patterns as manifestations of the crew coordination process suggests that this dimension is in part responsible for the performance differences seen in this study. Crews that had flown together communicated significantly more overall, and the differences are in logical directions when compared with the significant performance results. Consistent with Foushee and Manos (1981), captains in crews that had flown together issued more commands, but so did co-pilots (even though the frequency of co-pilot commands was relatively low) and this was associated with high performance. This finding may reflect a better understanding and division of responsibility between familiar crew members. More suggestions and more statements of intent were made in crews that had flown together, also indicating more willingness to exchange information. This is the flip side of Hirschhorn's (this volume) discussion of how poor understanding and lack of communication impeded performance in a nuclear power plant.

Another replication of the Foushee and Manos results found acknowledgments associated with better performance. More acknowledgments of communications were made by both captains and first officers who had flown together. Foushee and Manos suggested that acknowledgments probably serve to reinforce the communications process, and the same phenomenon appears to have played a role in this study. A particularly interesting finding was the presence of more disagreement exhibited by first officers who had flown with the same captain during the preceding three days. This suggests that increased familiarity may be, at least, a partial cure to the frequently problematic hesitancy of subordinates to question the actions of captains.

There was significantly more non-task related communication in crews that had not flown together, which may well indicate that they spend more time attempting to get to know each other. There was also significantly more tension release among crews who had not previously flown together. Also interesting was the presence of more frustration among captains who had not flown with the same co-pilot during the preceding duty cycle.

These findings are consistent with information use in fast and slow decision organizations (Eisenhardt, this volume). In slow (poorer performing) decision organizations, less information is looked at and the information milieu is less rich than in fast decision (higher performing) organizations. The same seems to be true of high versus low performing teams here.

Operational Significance

The consistency of these results is particularly striking. Duty cycle exposure had no apparent effect on any measures of flight safety. It is also interesting to note that the positive effects on crew coordination of recent operating experience can be an effective countermeasure to the levels of fatigue associated with the duty cycles examined in this study. While fatigue tends to be more prevalent during the later stages of a given duty cycle, crew coordination may be better because of the increased familiarity of crew members.

One of the obvious limitations of this study is that we are unable to examine closely the interaction of fatigue and crew familiarity. For example, it would be enlightening to look at the performance of tired crews who are familiar with each other versus those who are not, and to repeat these comparisons for rested crews. Such an analysis could yield important insights into the effectiveness of crew familiarity as a countermeasure. Unfortunately, the sample included only two "fatigued" crews that had not flown together, while only one of the "rested" crews had flown together.

Another limitation is that we cannot determine from these data the amount or degree of familiarity necessary to produce a desired level of crew coordination. We can say that the recency of crew familiarity, not the absolute amount, seems to be the key component. Most crews that had not flown together (as operationalized in these analyses) did know each other, and had flown together at some point in the past, but not within the last two or three months.

Despite these rather compelling results, it would not be appropriate to suggest a policy establishing the creation of relatively permanent crew assignments. There may be negative aspects of flying with the same person over a long period of time, such as complacency, boredom, and so on. It could well be that continued pairing of the same individuals would ultimately lead to a reversal of this pattern—worse performance associated with increased familiarity. Although the operational community generally believes this to be the case, no research substantiates it.

What are the differences between this study and other research efforts that demonstrate performance deficits associated with fatigue? It is suggested (see Holding, 1983, for a review) that fatigue causes more minor types of errors because of its deleterious effect on the attentional process. This line of reasoning says fatigue lowers attentional capacity, and the cumulative effect of lower attentional capacity coupled with low motivation on "less exciting" tasks tends to produce more error. Since these non-engaging tasks tend to be of limited significance, performance deficits are often though not always minor. This study provided no real support for this notion. A slightly larger number of Type I (minor) errors was committed by Post-Duty crews, but the difference was not statistically significant. However, since traditional studies of fatigue effects have typically utilized laboratory or otherwise "artificial" performance measures of questionable motivational value, it remains a credible hypothesis.

The high levels of realism and workload associated with segments of the simulation scenario no doubt produced average arousal levels greater than those typically found in lower fidelity studies measuring psychomotor effects. Since the subjects in this investigation were highly skilled, professional pilots performing identical high workload tasks to those they perform in the real world, it is safe to assume that the motivation to perform well was quite high.

This is in striking contrast to the boredom and lack of motivation often associated with classic, low fidelity, psychomotor studies. Arousal may be a key moderator of fatigue effects. Optimal levels of arousal appear to be harder to maintain when the operator is fatigued, but task demands may override this difficulty to some as-yet-to-be-defined extent. However, when task demands are low, the effects of fatigue may more often be manifested in performance deterioration. There is fairly convincing evidence that monitoring and vigilance during boring tasks is substantially degraded when the operator is fatigued (Holding, 1983).

If arousal proves to be a key moderator of fatigue effects, it poses a complex puzzle for researchers interested in the implications of the fatigue-performance relationship for flight safety. On the one hand, during low workload segments, fatigue may affect performance since low task demands produce low arousal. But since task demands are low (and the effects of performance decrements likely to be minor), fatigue effects often may not be operationally significant. On the other hand, when task demands are high, if arousal effectively counteracts fatigue, performance may not be affected (as in the present study). Periods of high task demand are precisely the times when good performance is most important, and performance parameters during these periods are usually the primary concern of aviation safety specialists. Again, one is drawn to the conclusion that fatigue may be present, but that its effects may not necessarily be operationally significant. The Berkeley researchers find that performance degradation almost never happens when their organizations are at peak operational tempos (Weick and Roberts, submitted for publication).

The problem with this line of reasoning is that, occasionally, minor attentional or performance lapses during periods of low task demand can precipitate a sequence of events leading to a serious incident or accident. There was no evidence that fatigue produced such a sequence in this study, but as has been mentioned, the crew coordination process appeared to play a key role in eliminating the progression of minor errors into major problems. As we demonstrate here, coordination appeared to be better in short-haul crews at the end of the duty-cycle when they presumably experienced the highest effect of fatigue. These results clearly suggest that the system contains a "built-in" counter-measure.

REFERENCES

Bartlett, F. C. (1943). "Fatigue following highly skilled work." *Proceedings of the Royal Society*, Series B., 131, 247–257.

Brown, I. D. (1967). "Measurement of control skills, vigilance, and performance of a subsidiary task during 12 hrs. of car driving." *Ergonomics*, 10, 665–673.

Chiles, W. D. (1955). "Experimental studies of prolonged wakefulness." Dayton, OH: W.D.A.C. Tech. Report No. 55-395.

Cooper, G. E., M. D. White, and J. K. Lauber (eds), (1979). "Resource management on the flight deck." *NASA Conference Publication* 2120. Moffett Field, CA: NASA-Ames Research Center.

Dureman, E.I., and C. Boden (1972). "Fatigue in simulated car driving." *Ergonomics*, 15, 299–308.

Foushee, H. C. (1984). "Dyads and triads at 35,000 feet: Factors affecting group process and aircrew performance." *American Psychologist*, 39, 885–893.

Foushee, H. C., and K. L. Manos (1981). "Information transfer within the cockpit: Problems in intra cockpit communications." In C. E. Billings and E. S. Cheaney, (eds.), "Information transfer problems in the aviation system." *NASA Technical Paper* 1875. Moffett Field, CA: NASA-Ames Research Center.

Gagne, R. M. (1953). "Task variables in fatigue." In W. F. Floyd and A. T. Welford, (eds.), *Symposium on Fatigue*. London: H. K. Lewis.

Hart, S. G., V. Battiste, and P. T. Lester (1984). "Popcorn: A supervisory control simulation for workload and performance research." Sunnyvale, CA.: *Proceedings of the 20th Annual Conference on Manual Control*.

Holding, D. H. (1983). "Fatigue." In G. R. J. Hockey (ed.), *Stress and Fatigue in Human Performance*. New York: Wiley.

Klein, K. E., H. Bruner, H. Holtmann, H. Rehme, J. Stolze, W. D. Steinhoff, and H. M. Wegman (1970). "Circadian rhythm of pilots' efficiency and effects of multiple time zone travel." *Aerospace Medicine*, 41, 126–132.

Lauber, J. K., and H. C. Foushee (1981). "Guidelines for line-oriented flight training," (Vol. 1). *NASA Conference Publication* 2184. Moffett Field, CA: NASA-Ames Research Center.

McFarland, R. A. (1953). *Human Factors in Air Transportation*. New York: McGraw-Hill.

Moses, J. M., L. Lubin, P. Naitoh, and L. C. Johnson (1974). "Evaluation of the effects of sleep loss: The NPRU mood scale." *Technical Report* No. 74-75. San Diego, CA: Navy Medical Neuropsychiatric Unit.

Weick, K. E., and K. H. Roberts (submitted for publication). "Organization mind and organizational reliability: The case of flight operations on an aircraft carrier."

Wever, R. A. (1979). *The Circadian System of Man: Results of Experiments Under Temporal Isolation*. New York: Pringer-Verlag.

10

The Vulnerable System: An Analysis of the Tenerife Air Disaster

KARL E. WEICK
University of Michigan

Karl E. Weick, who is the Rensis Likert Professor of Organizational Behavior and Psychology at the University of Michigan, is the former editor of *Administrative Science Quarterly*. A social psychologist, trained at Ohio State University, Professor Weick studies the social psychology of improvisation, indeterminacy in social systems, the relationship between theory and practice, and collective mental processes. In 1990, the Academy of Management honored Professor Weick with the Irwin Award for Scholarly Contributions to Management and the award for Best Article of the Year published in the *Academy of Management Review*.

The Tenerife air disaster, in which a KLM 747 and a Pan Am 747 collided with a loss of 583 lives, is examined as a prototype of system vulnerability to crisis. It is concluded that the combination of interruption of important routines among interdependent systems, interdependencies that become tighter, a loss of cognitive efficiency due to autonomic arousal, and a loss of communication accuracy due to increased hierarchical distortion created a configuration that encouraged the occurrence and rapid diffusion of multiple small errors. Implications of this prototype for future research and practice are explored.

*T*here is a growing appreciation that large scale disasters such as Bhopal (Shrivastava, 1987) and Three-Mile Island (Perrow, 1981) are the result of separate small events that become linked and amplified in ways that are incomprehensible and unpredictable. This scenario of linkage and amplification is especially likely when systems become more tightly coupled and less linear (Perrow, 1984).

What is missing from these analyses, however, is any discussion of the processes by which crises are set in motion. Specifically, we lack an understanding of ways in which separate small failures become linked. We know that single cause incidents are rare, but we don't know how small events can become chained together so that they result in a disastrous outcome. In the absence of this understanding, people must wait until some crisis actually occurs before they can diagnose a problem, rather than be in a position to detect a potential problem before it emerges. To anticipate and forestall disasters is to understand regularities in the ways small events can combine to have disproportionately large effects.

The purpose of the following analysis is to suggest several processes that amplify the effects of multiple small events into potentially disastrous outcomes. These processes were induced from an analysis of the Tenerife air disaster in which 583 people were killed. The processes include the interruption of important routines, regression to more habituated ways of responding, the breakdown of coordinated action, and misunderstandings in speech-exchange systems. When these four processes occur in the context of a system that is becoming more tightly coupled and less linear, they produce more errors, reduce the means to detect those errors, create dependencies among the errors, and amplify the effects of these errors.

These processes are sufficiently basic and widespread that they suggest an inherent vulnerability in human systems that, up until now, has been overlooked. The processes suggest both a research agenda for the '90s as well as a managerial agenda.

DESCRIPTION OF TENERIFE DISASTER[1]

On March 27, 1977, KLM flight 4805, a 747 bound from Amsterdam to the Canary Islands, and Pan Am flight 1736, another 747 bound from Los Angeles and New York to the Canary Islands, were both diverted to Los Rodeos airport at Tenerife because the Las Palmas airport, their original destination, was closed because of a bomb explosion. KLM landed first at 1:38 P.M., followed by Pan Am which landed at 2:15 P.M. Because Tenerife is not a major airport, its taxi space was limited. This meant that the Pan Am plane had to park behind the KLM flight in such a way that it could not depart until the KLM plane left. When the Las Palmas airport reopened at 2:30, the Pan Am flight was ready to depart because its passengers had remained on board. KLM's passengers, however, had left the plane so there was a delay while they reboarded and while the plane was refueled to shorten its turnaround time at Las Palmas. KLM began its taxi for takeoff at 4:56 P.M. and was initially directed to proceed down a runway parallel to the takeoff runway. This directive was amended shortly thereafter and KLM was requested to taxi down the takeoff runway and at the end, to make a 180 degree turn and await further instruction.

Pan Am was requested to follow KLM down the takeoff runway and to leave the takeoff runway at taxiway C3, use the parallel runway for the remainder of the taxi, and then pull in behind the KLM flight. Pan Am's request to hold short of the takeoff runway and stay off it until KLM had departed was denied. After the KLM plane made the 180 degree turn at the end of the takeoff runway, rather than hold as instructed, it started moving and reported, "We are now at takeoff." Neither the air traffic controllers nor the Pan Am crew were certain what this ambiguous phrase meant, but Pan Am restated to controllers that it would report when it was clear of the takeoff runway, a communique heard inside the KLM cockpit. When the pilot of the KLM flight was asked by the engineer, "Is he not clear then, that Pan Am?" the pilot replied "Yes" and there was no further conversation. The collision occurred 13 seconds later at 5:06 P.M. None of the 234 passengers and 14 crew on the KLM flight survived. Of the 380 passengers and 16 crew on the Pan Am plane, 70 survived, although 9 died later, making a total loss of 583 lives.

A brief excerpt from the Spanish Ministry of Transport and Communication's investigation of the crash describes interactions among the KLM crew members immediately before the crash. These interactions, reconstructed from the KLM cockpit voice recorder (CVR), are the focus of the remainder of our analysis.

---

[1] All details concerning the Tenerife disaster are taken from two sources. The first source was the report of the Spanish Ministry of Transport and Communication, summarized in consecutive issues of *Aviation Week and Space Technology*: November 20, 1978, pp. 113–121 and November 27, 1978, pp. 69–74. References to this report are abbreviated Span. The second source was P. A. Roitsch, G. L. Babcock, and W. W. Edmunds, "Human Factors Report on the Tenerife Accident," Washington, D.C.: Airline Pilots Assn., 1979. References to this report are abbreviated Alpa.

Figure 10-1

Tenerife Airport Diagram

Accident between
KLM 4805 and PAA 1736
March 27, 1977
Elevation: 2073 feet
Runway : 3400 x 45 meters

T_1 = 1659:10 (GMT)
 Pan Am on range
 KLM enters runway

T_2 = 1702:08 (GMT)
 Pan Am enters runway
 KLM @ C3

T_3 = 1705:53 (GMT)
 Pan Am passing C3
 KLM receiving ATC
 clearance

T_4 = 1706:49 (GMT)
 Impact point near C4

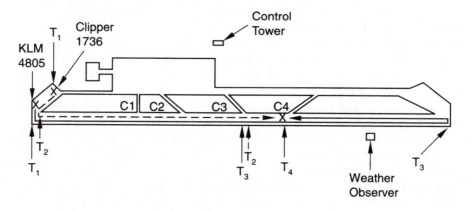

As the time for the takeoff approached, the KLM captain "seemed a little absent from all that was heard in the cockpit. He inquired several times, and after the copilot confirmed the order to backtrack, he asked the tower if he should leave the runway by C-1, and subsequently asked his copilot if he should do so by C-4. On arriving at the end of the runway, and making a 180 degree turn in order to place himself in takeoff position, he was advised by the copilot that he should wait because they still did not have an ATC clearance. The captain asked him to request it, and he did, but while the copilot was still repeating the clearance, the captain opened the throttle and started to takeoff. Then the copilot, instead of requesting takeoff clearance or advising that they did not yet have it, added to his read-back, "We are now at takeoff."

The tower, which was not expecting the aircraft to takeoff because it had not been given clearance, interpreted the sentence as, "We are now at takeoff position." (When the Spanish, American, and Dutch investigating teams heard the tower recording together and for the first time, no one, or hardly anyone, understood that this transmission meant that they were taking off.) The controller replied: "O.K., . . . stand by for takeoff . . . I will call you." Nor did the Pan Am, on hearing the "We are now at takeoff," interpret it as an unequivocal indication of takeoff. However, in order to make their own position clear, they said, "We are still taxiing down the runway." This transmission coincided with the "Stand by for takeoff . . . I will call you," causing a whistling sound in the tower transmission and making its reception in the KLM cockpit not as clear as it should have been, even though it did not thereby become unintelligible.

The communication from the tower to the PAA requested the latter to report when it left the runway clear. In the cockpit of the KLM, nobody at first confirmed receiving these communications until the Pan Am responded to the tower's request that it should report leaving the runway with an "O.K., we'll report when we're clear." On hearing this, the KLM flight engineer asked, "Is he not clear then?" The captain did not understand him and he repeated, "Is he not clear that Pan American?" The Captain replied with an emphatic "Yes." Perhaps influenced by his great prestige, making it difficult to imagine an error of this magnitude on the part of such an expert pilot, both the copilot and flight engineer made no further objections. The impact took place about 13 seconds later (*Aviation Week*, 1978b: 71).

TENERIFE AS A STRESSFUL ENVIRONMENT

Stress is often defined as a relation between the person and the environment, as in Holyroyd's and Lazarus's (1982) statement that "psychological stress requires a judgment that environmental and/or internal demands tax or exceed the individual's resources for managing them" (22). Their use of the word *judgment* emphasizes that stress results from an appraisal that imposes meaning on environmental demands. Typically, stress results from the appraisal that something important is at stake and in jeopardy (McGrath, 1976).

There were several events impinging on people at Tenerife that are likely to have taxed their resources and been labeled as threatening. These events, once appraised as threatening, had a cumulative, negative effect on performance (George, 1986). After we review some of the more prominent of these events, we look more closely at which concepts used in the stress literature help us most to make sense of the Tenerife disaster. It is these concepts that deserve closer attention in subsequent research on how crises are mobilized. The concepts to be discussed include size of discrepancy between demands and abilities, regression to first learned responses, and interruption as the occasion for stress. First, however, we review the demands at Tenerife.

Environmental Demands at Tenerife

The KLM crew felt growing pressure from at least three sources: Dutch law, difficult maneuvers, and unpredictable weather. Because the accident took place near the end of March, members of the KLM crew were very near the limits of time they were allowed to fly in one month. This was more serious than a mere inconvenience because in 1976 the Dutch enacted a tough law on "Work and Rest Regulations for Flight Crews" (Roitsch, Babcock, and Edmunds, 1979: 14) that put strict limits on flight and duty time. The computation of these limits was complex and could no longer be done by the captain, nor did the captain have any discretion to extend duty time. Therefore, the KLM crew faced the possibility of fines, imprisonment, and loss of pilot license if further delays materialized. The crew was informed that if they could leave Las Palmas by 7 P.M. their headquarters thought they could make it back to Amsterdam legally, but headquarters would let them know in Las Palmas.

Further pressure was added because the maneuver of turning a 747 around (backtracking) at the end of a runway is difficult, especially when that runway is narrow. It takes a minimum width of 142 feet to make a 180 degree turn in a 747 (Roitsch et al., 1979: 19) and the Tenerife runway was 150 feet wide.

Finally, the weather was unpredictable, and at Tenerife that creates some unique problems. Tenerife is 2073 feet above sea level and the sea coast is just a few miles away. This means that clouds rather than fog float into the airport. When KLM's crew backtracked, they saw a cloud 3000 feet down the runway moving toward them at 12 knots (Roitsch et al., 1979: 12), concealing the Pan Am plane on the other side. Pan Am was taxiing inside this cloud and passed its assigned runway exit because it could not see it. KLM entered that same cloud 1300 feet into its takeoff roll and that is where the collision occurred. The tower did not see the collision or the resulting fire because of the cloud, nor could the firefighters find the fire at first when they were summoned. The density of the cloud is further shown by the fact that when the firefighters started to put out the fire on one plane, the KLM plane, they didn't realize that a second plane was on fire nearby because they couldn't see it (*Aviation Week*, 1978a: 117–119).

The KLM crew was not the only group that was under pressure. Las Palmas airport had reopened for traffic at 2:30, barely 15 minutes after Pan Am had landed at Tenerife. Pan Am was ready to leave Tenerife immediately except that they were blocked by KLM 4805 and continued to be blocked for another 2½ hours. Reactions of the Pan Am crew to the lengthening delays undoubtedly were intensified by the fact that they had originally asked to circle over Las Palmas because they had sufficient fuel to do so, a request that was denied by Spanish controllers. The Pan Am crew also saw the weather deteriorating as they waited for KLM to leave. They had been on duty 11 hours, although they were not close to the limits of their duty time.

Controllers at Tenerife were also under pressure because they were short-handed, they did not often handle 747's, they had no ground radar, the centerline lights on the runway were not operating, they were working in English (a less familiar second language), and their normal routines for routing planes on a takeoff and landing were disrupted because they had planes parked in areas they would normally use to execute these routines.

Research Leads to Be Pursued

The events at Tenerife provide a pretext to think more carefully about discrepancy size, regression, and interruption as components of stressful environments. These three concepts figure prominently in the events we have just reviewed, and by implication, they may also be a source of system vulnerability in other environments.

McGrath (1976) has shown that the traditional formulation of stress as a discrepancy between demands and ability operates differently from what most people thought. The highest arousal occurs when abilities are only slightly less than what is demanded and there is a chance that the person can cope. Small discrepancies create the most intense stress.

Despite all of the pressures operating at Tenerife, and despite all of the ways in which demands were mounting, the people involved were nearly able to cope successfully. Abilities almost matched demands. When the KLM captain saw the Pan Am plane in front of him on the runway, he pulled back fully on the control column in an attempt to fly over it. The tail of his plane scraped the runway and left a 66 foot long streak of metal embedded in the runway. It was only the KLM's wheels that hit the right wing and rear cabin of the Pan Am Plane (which the Pan Am pilot had almost been able to steer off the takeoff runway) (Roitsch et al., 1979: 13), and when the KLM settled back on the runway after the collision, it was intact. Ignition of the extra fuel taken on to speed up departure from Las Palmas caused the KLM fatalities.

Tenerife is important, not just because it illustrates that small discrepancies can have large effects, but even more important because it seems to be an usually clear example of the much discussed, but seldom pursued idea that stress can produce regression to first learned responses (Allnutt, 1982: 11; Barthol and Ku, 1959). If there is a key to understanding the Tenerife disaster, it may lie in this principle.

The pilot of KLM 4805 was Head of the Flight Training Department of KLM. He was a training captain: the flights he was most familiar with were those which followed a script, had fewer problems, and were shorter in duration. Furthermore, he had not flown on regular routes for 12 weeks. The importance of this background becomes evident in the context of a footnote in the Spanish Ministry's report:

> Although the captain [KLM captain] had flown for many years on European and intercontinental routes, he had been an instructor for more than 10 years, which relatively diminished his familiarity with route flying. Moreover, on simulated flights, which are so customary in flying instruction, the training pilot normally assumes the role of controller: that is, he issues takeoff clearances. In many cases no communications whatsoever are used in simulated flights, and for this reason takeoff takes place without clearance. (*Aviation Week*, 1978a: 121)

Pressure leads people to fall back on what they learned first and most fully. In the case of the KLM pilot, this was giving himself clearance to takeoff. Giving clearance is what he had done most often for the last 10 years when sitting at the head of a runway and it is the response he may have reverted to as pressures mounted at Tenerife.

Both the Pan Am crew and the air traffic controllers seem also to show evidence of regression. The Pan Am captain wanted to hold short of the active runway, but he was asked to proceed down the active runway by a ground controller who spoke with a heavy accent and who did not seem to comprehend fully what Pan Am was requesting. Rather than attempt a potentially more complex negotiation to get permission to hold short, the Pan Am captain chose the more overlearned option of compliance with the controller's directive. Controller communiques also became more cryptic and harder to understand as controllers tried to cope with too many aircraft that were too big. These pressures may have made their use of English, a language which they used less frequently, more tenuous and increased the likelihood that more familiar Spanish language constructions would be substituted.

The more general implication of the disruptive effects of regression is that more recently learned complex rationales and complex collective responses are all more vulnerable to disruption than are older, simpler, more overlearned, cultural and individual responses. Requisite variety (Zeleny, 1986) is much harder to achieve than it looks. When people acquire more complex responses so that they can sense and manage more complex environments, they do not become more complex all at once. Instead, they develop their complexity serially. Under pressure, those responses acquired more recently and practiced less often should unravel sooner than those acquired earlier, which have become more habitual. Thus, requisite variety may disappear right when it is most needed. Hypothetically, the KLM pilot had high requisite variety because he was both a training pilot and a line pilot. In reality, however, his more recent habits of line flying disappeared under pressure and were replaced by his older habits of flying under training conditions.

Among the many theories of stress that could be applied to the incidents at Tenerife, one of the most fitting is Mandler's (1982) because it encompasses so many properties of Tenerife, including interruption, limited information processing, cognitive narrowing, interpretation, plans, and autonomic arousal.

The centerpiece of Mandler's theory is the idea that interruptions trigger activity in the autonomic nervous system. This autonomic activity absorbs information processing capacity, which then decreases the efficiency of complex thought processes. By way of background, the autonomic nervous system is the branch of the peripheral nervous system that regulates the body's internal environment and maintains homeostasis. The sympathetic branch of the ANS, through the secretion of adrenaline and noradrenaline, mobilizes the common symptoms of stress such as accelerated heart rate, increased blood pressure, and increased glucose secretion (Frankenhaeuser, 1986).

In Mandler's theory, autonomic activity is triggered by interruption, which he defines as "Any event, external or internal to the individual, that prevents completion of some action, thought sequences, plan, or processing structure" (92). Both action structures and intrapsychic cognitive structures can be interrupted, either when an expected event fails to occur or an unexpected event occurs.

The degree of autonomic activity that occurs following an interruption depends on two factors: first, the degree of organization of the action or thought process that is interrupted (invariant, habituated actions with high degree of expectancy among parts create a sharp increase in autonomic activity when interrupted); and second, the severity of interruption (high external demand to complete an action, coupled with repeated attempts to restart the action and repeated interruptions combine to facilitate arousal).

The autonomic activity triggered by an interruption focuses attention on two things, both of which consume considerable information processing capacity. Attention is focused on the interrupting event, and if it is not altered, on the internal autonomic activation itself. When autonomic arousal consumes scarce information processing capacity, this reduces the number of cues that can be processed from the activity that was underway at the time of the interruption.

In Mandler's model, stress is an interruption that signals an emergency and draws attention to events in the environment. In the short run, this signalling is adaptive and improves coping. Autonomic activity alerts people to the existence of threatening events, but if the threat is not dealt with and the arousal continues, then it registers in consciousness and interferes with ongoing cognitive activity. Thus, consciousness becomes the arena for troubleshooting, but unless the diagnosis and coping is swift and the response being interrupted is weak in its organization, the troubleshooting consumes information processing capacity and this leads to the omission of important cues for task performance and an increase in cognitive inefficiency.

If we apply Mandler's concepts to the situation of the KLM pilot, we pay closer attention to such aspects as the following. The diversion to Los Rodeos was an interruption of the plan to get back to Amsterdam legally. And the cloud moving down the runway toward the KLM plane represents a potential interruption of a lower order plan to leave Las Palmas. Because neither interruption can be removed directly, autonomic arousal increases, displaces more information processing capacity, and decreases attention to peripheral cues such as radio transmissions. The severity of the interruption should be substantial because a well organized takeoff routine is interrupted, but most of all because there is a continuing, intense demand to complete the interrupted action (there is no realistic substitute activity that will get the passengers to Las Palmas unless they leave Los Rodeos on KLM 4805).

The pilot's potential focus on the interruption created by the diversion to Los Rodeos and on the consequent lengthening of duty time, coupled with potential awareness of his own internal agitation (which would be hard to label as "pleasure" but easy to label as "frustration" or "fear"), all use up information processing capacity. This leaves little remaining capacity for the immediate task of taxiing the plane to a difficult takeoff position and then flying it safely off the runway. Furthermore, there would appear to be little remaining capacity available to process cryptic, non-standard, sometimes noisy transmissions from the tower and other aircraft.

Thus, to use Mandler's phrase, consciousness became "the arena for troubleshooting," but the troubleshooting was devoted to the question of a legal return to Amsterdam, a higher order plan, rather than to the immediate plan of leaving Los Rodeos. Attention devoted to interruption of the higher order plan used up the major share of attention that could have been allotted to the lower order, more immediate plan.

The point I want to demonstrate is that crises in general typically involve the interruption of plans or cognitive structures or actions that are underway. Because interruption is a generic accompaniment of crisis, a theory of stress and emotion that uses interruption as the point of departure is ideally suited for further investigation and application to settings involving crisis. Furthermore, susceptibility to interruption is an important predictor of system vulnerability.

THE BREAKDOWN OF COORDINATION UNDER STRESS

The phrase "operator error" is misleading in many ways, but among the most subtle problems is the fact that the term is singular (Hayashi, 1985). An operator error is usually a collective error (e.g., Gardenier, 1981), but it is only recently that efforts have been made to understand the ways in which team interaction generates emergent potentialities for and remedies of local failures (e.g., Hirokawa, Govran, and Martz, 1988). The crew in the KLM cockpit provides a unique glimpse of some ways in which crises become mobilized when crew interaction breaks down.

Individualism in the Cockpit

The setting in the KLM cockpit was unusual, not only because the captain was the head of flight training and a member of the top management team, but also because this captain had given the co-pilot (first officer) his qualification check in a 747 just 2 months earlier. This recently certified first officer made only two comments to try to influence the captain's decision during the crucial events at the head of the runway. The ALPA report of the crash describes those comments this way:

> The KLM first officer was relatively young and new in his position and appeared to be mainly concerned with completing his tasks so as not to delay the captain's timing of the takeoff. He only made two comments in order to try to influence the captain's takeoff decision. When the captain first began pushing up the thrust levers, he said, "Wait a minute, we do not have an ATC clearance." The captain, rather than admitting to an oversight, closed the thrust levers and responded by saying, "No, I know that, go ahead ask." The second occurrence was at the end of the ATC clearance readback. The KLM first officer observed that the captain had commenced the takeoff and finished the ATC clearance readback by stating, "We are, uh, taking off" or "We are at takeoff" over the radio. After many hours of replaying the tapes, it is difficult to be sure what statement the first officer made. For this reason, we assume that neither the approach controller nor

the Pan Am crew were positive about what was said. The Study Group believes that this ambiguous statement by the first officer was an indication that he was surprised by the KLM captain's actions in commencing the takeoff. We believe the first officer thought something was wrong with the takeoff decision by the captain, and tried to alert everyone on frequency that they were commencing takeoff. The KLM captain did not comment on his first officer's radio transmission but rather became immediately involved in setting takeoff power and tracking the runway centerline. (Roitsch et al., 1979: 18)

The first officer is not the only person acting in a manner that is more individual than collective (Wagner and Moch, 1986). The same was true for the engineer. The flight engineer was the First and current President of the European Flight Engineers Organization. There is an odd statement about him in the ALPA documents. It says that he was not in favor of integrating the functions of the engineering position with those of the pilot crewmembers, such as communication, navigation, and general monitoring of the operation of the flight. "He is said to have felt that flight engineering should consist of specialized emphasis on power-plant and systems analysis and maintenance consideration" (Roitsch et al., 1979: 5). Recall that the engineer was the last point where this accident could have been prevented when he asked, "Is he not clear then, that Pan Am?" Recordings suggest that he made this statement in a "tentative manner" (Roitsch et al., 1979: 22) just as the plane entered the thick cloud and the pilots had their hands full keeping the plane on the runway.

Research Leads to be Pursued

These several observations suggest that the KLM crew acted less like a team (Hackman, 1987) than like three individuals acting in parallel. That difference becomes important in the context of an important generalization suggested by Hage (1980): "Micro-sociological hypotheses usually require limits. The human scale is much smaller than the organizational one—at least as far as hypotheses are concerned. Beyond this the "world" of the individual appears to be dominated by normal curves where too much of a good thing is as bad as too little. In contrast, linearity appears to be a good first approximation in the organizational 'world' " (202).

We should expect that most microhypotheses are curvilinear and most macrohypotheses are linear. McGuire's (1968) model of individual persuasion, for example, is curvilinear and predicts that people with moderately high intelligence are more persuasible than are those who are higher or lower in intelligence. Daily (1971) argues that individual perceptual accuracy is curvilinear and reflects a tradeoff between increasing confidence in one's own judgment and decreasing openness to new information.

When we move from individual to group, we move from micro in the direction of macro and should expect to find fewer curvilinear relationships and more linear relationships. For example, the recurrent finding that the relationship between stress and performance is curvilinear holds for individuals, but when it is examined as a group phenomenon, the relationship is found to more linear (Lowe and McGrath, 1971). Thus, as we move from individual to group, increases in stress should lead to increases in performance, not decreases. However, this shift is dependent on whether individuals coalesce into a team that is a distinctive entity exhibiting distinctive functional relationships or whether they merely act in the presence of another and respond and fall apart, more like individuals than like groups.

A KLM crew that is not a team is subject to curvilinear relationships, whereas a crew that is a team is more subject to linear relations. It is conceivable that more stress improves team performance but degrades individual performance because teamwork lowers task complexity. A well functioning team may face a simpler task than does a poorly functioning team. And research on the Yerkes–Dodson (e.g., Bregman and McAllister, 1982) law shows that performance of simple tasks is less susceptible to the disruptive effects of arousal than is performance of complex tasks.

What Hage describes resembles what Hackman (1987) seems to have in mind when he describes group synergy: synergy "refers to group-level phenomena that (1) emerge from the interaction of group members, and (2) affect how well a group is able to deal with the demands and opportunities in its performance situation" (324). Group synergy creates outcomes that "may be quite different from those that would be obtained by simply adding up the contributions of individual members" (321–322). Synergy can be either positive or, as appears to be the case with the KLM crew, negative: negative synergy is described as "a failure of coordination within the group so severe that *nobody* knows what he or she is supposed to be doing" (322). Although it is true that the plane was accelerating in a mechanically correct manner and the crew had in hand a clearance routing them to Las Palmas, lingering uneasiness about pilot judgments was neither voiced nor resolved until it was too late. What is unclear is whether the KLM crew represents a case of negative synergy with a defective group interaction process, or a case of three individuals who never became a group in the first place, or a case where a group became transformed into a collection of separate individuals when stress led the three people to fall back on dissimilar idiosyncratic ways of responding (Lazarus and Folkman, 1984; 104).

Hackman's model seems to suggest that the KLM crew in the Tenerife disaster is an example of a group where there was a slight deficiency of knowledge and skill (pilot unfamiliar with route flying, first officer recently certified on 747) but mainly a deficiency in the performance strategies (328–331) they adopted to review their design and their process and to alter it to fit the abnormal demands created by the diversion.

Helmreich's continuing research on flightcrew behavior has direct relevance to our understanding of the Tenerife disaster. As part of this program, Helmreich has assessed the managerial aspect of flight operations using a 25-

item "Cockpit management attitudes survey" (Helmreich, 1984). The instrument, administered to more than 5000 pilots, has been validated on pilots classified as high and low in resource management (Helmreich, Foushee, Benson, and Russini, 1985) and covers such topics as personal reactions to stress (e.g., "pilots should feel obligated to mention their own psychological stress or physical problems to other flight-crew personnel before or during a flight"), interpersonal communication (e.g., "the pilot flying the aircraft should verbalize his plans for maneuvers and should be sure that the information is understood and acknowledged by the other pilot"), and crew roles (e.g., "There are no circumstances [except total incapacitation] where the first officer should assume command of the ship").

The items in the survey are of special interest in the context of Tenerife. It was found (Helmreich, 1984: 586) that Captains and First Officers differed significantly in their answers to item 5, which read, "First officers should not question the decision or actions of the captain except when they threaten the safety of the flight." The first officers agreed with the contention significantly more often than did the captains. However, on item 6, which read "Captains should encourage their first officers to question procedures during normal flight operations and in emergencies," captains were significantly less enthusiastic about encouraging input than were first officers. Thus, the idea of coordinated activity and coordinated decision making in the cockpit is a source of ambivalence and a potential source of errors that could enlarge.

These two items remained diagnostic in the validation study because they were two of the six items that discriminated most sharply between 114 pilots rated below average or outstanding by evaluators, who actually rode with these pilots and evaluated their flight crew performance. Pilots evaluated as outstanding felt more strongly that first officers should be encouraged to question their decisions and that the first officers should question decisions other than those that threaten the safety of the flight. Pilots with below average performance held the opposite attitudes. Parenthetically, it should be noted that the item that discriminated most sharply between the outstanding and the below average was the item that read, "My decision-making ability is as good in emergencies as in routine flying situations." Below average pilots agree with this item; outstanding pilots disagree with it. Thus, not only do the outstanding pilots realize that their ability to make decisions can change under stress, but in realizing this, they may become more receptive to inputs from others that will help the crew cope.

SPEECH-EXCHANGE SYSTEMS AS ORGANIZATIONAL BUILDING BLOCKS

KLM as an airline is in large part constituted by its speech exchanges. When people employed by KLM talk among themselves and with outsiders, not only do they communicate within an organization, they also construct the organization itself through the process and substance of what they say. As their talk varies, the solidity and predictability of the organization itself varies. Conversations with headquarters about duty time, conversations with the KLM agent at Las Palmas about ways to hasten the departure, conversations (or the lack of them) among crew members that construct the hypothesis that the runway is empty, all are the building blocks of the order and disorder that is the hallmark of organized activity.

The unfolding of the Tenerife disaster reminds us that macroprocesses such as centralization are made up of repetitive microevents that occur frequently and in diverse locations. Organizations are built, maintained, and activated through the medium of communication. If that communication is misunderstood, the existence of the organization itself becomes more tenuous.

The Tenerife disaster was built out of a series of small, semi-standardized misunderstandings, among which were the following:

1. KLM requested two clearances in one transmission (we are now ready for takeoff and are waiting for ATC clearance). Any reply could be seen as a comment on both requests.

2. The controller, in giving a clearance, used the words "after takeoff" ("maintain flight level niner zero right after takeoff proceed with heading zero four zero until intercepting the three two five radial from Las Palmas"), which could have been heard by the KLM crew as permission to leave. The ATC Manual (7110.650, October 25, 1984) clearly states, under the heading "Departure Terminology," that controllers should "Avoid using the term 'takeoff' except to actually clear an aircraft for takeoff or to cancel a takeoff clearance. Use such terms as 'depart,' 'departure,' or 'fly' in clearances when necessary" (heading 4-20: 4-5). Thus, the Tenerife controller could have said "right turn after departure" or "right turn fly heading zero four."

3. As we have seen, the phrase "We are now taking off" is non-standard and produced confusion as to what it meant.

4. When the controller said to KLM, "Okay . . . stand by for takeoff . . . I will call you," a squeal for the last portion of this message changed the timbre of the controller's voice. This may have led the KLM crew to assume that a different station was transmitting and that the message was not intended for them.

5. The controller did not wait to receive an acknowledgment (e.g., "Roger") from KLM after he had ordered them to "standby for takeoff." Had he done so, he might have discovered a misunderstanding (Hurst, 1982: 176).

6. Shortly before the collision, for the first and only time that day, the controller changed from calling the Pan Am plane "Clipper 1736" to the designation "Pappa Alpha 1736." This could sound like the controller is referring to a different plane (Roitsch et al., 1979: 22).

The point to be emphasized is that speech exchange and social interaction is an important means by which organization is built or dismantled. This is not to say that social interaction is a local, self-contained production that is unaffected by anything else in the setting. There clearly are "noninterpretational foundations of interpretation in social interaction" (Munch and Smelser, 1987: 367). The interpretation process itself is shaped by shared language, authority relationships that assign rights of interpretation, norms of communication, and communication. The meanings that actors co-construct are not self-created. So microanalysis cannot go it alone without macroinput. As Mead put it, people carry a slice of society around in their heads (Alexander and Geisen, 1987: 9). But to acknowledge that slice is also to acknowledge the carrier and the fact that the slice is realized, made visible, and given shape, in discourse.

Research Leads to be Pursued

We have already discussed several issues regarding communication and here will merely supplement those by suggesting that (a) communication is necessary to detect false hypotheses, and (b) crises tend to create vertical communication structures when, in fact, lateral structures are often more appropriate for detection and diagnosis of the crisis.

In any crisis situation, there is a high probability that false hypotheses will develop and persist. It is largely through open exchange of messages, independent verification, and redundancy that the existence of false hypotheses can be detected. There are at least four kinds of situations in which false hypotheses are likely to occur and in which, therefore, there is a premium on accuracy in interpersonal communication (O'Reilly, 1978). These four, identified by Davis 1958), are the following:

1. Expectancy is very high. If a pilot hears a distorted message and knows the tower would not say something meaningless, then the pilot tries to fill in the gaps and hears the message he or she "should" have heard. This tendency increases the likelihood that a dubious hypothesis will be preserved. Applied to Tenerife, because the crew was expecting takeoff clearance and because they wanted to hear takeoff clearance, it is probable that when the tower said, "Okay, stand by for takeoff, I will call you," and when a squeal accompanied the middle portion of that message, they could have heard "OK, takeoff," which is what they expected to hear.

2. The hypothesis serves as a defense. People interpret communiques in ways that minimize anxiety. In nuclear power plant control rooms, for example, "it is easy for each operator to assume the other knows best, and, in being a good fellow, to reinforce the other's misperceptions. Thus error probabilities for people working together may be better or worse than error probabilities for individuals working independently and not communicating" (Sheridan, 1981: 23). Occasionally, a pilot's

seniority and status "may be an even greater bar to admitting his mistakes—and he will only publicly reject his false hypothesis when it is too late" (Allnutt, 1982: 9). Applied to Tenerife, the hypothesis that there is no one on the runway, given the limited amount of current information present in the radio traffic that had been processed, could easily be bolstered if the pilot and the first officer both assumed that, if there were someone on the runway, surely the head of Flight Training would know it.

3. Attention is elsewhere. We have already encountered this explanation in the context of Mandler's theory. Allnutt (1982: 9) supplements the earlier discussion when he notes that, "if a pilot has a number of immediate tasks, and if one of those requires special attention, he is likely to be less critical in accepting hypotheses about other components of the work load." Thus a person may ignore information that conflicts with the prevailing hypothesis when it comes from instruments that are on the periphery of attention. Applied to Tenerife, the pilot was undoubtedly more focussed on the takeoff including the approaching cloud, the difficult backtrack maneuver, and tracking the centerline on the runway without the help of lights than he was on the radio communiques that were being handled by the first officer.

4. It is after a period of high concentration. There is often a let-up near the end of a journey, when the most difficult part of the procedure has been completed. False hypotheses can persist in the face of this decreased attentiveness. Applied to Tenerife, the Spanish Ministry report of the accident actually raised this possibility: "Relaxation— after having executed the difficult 180-degree turn, which must have coincided with a momentary improvement in the visibility (as proved by the CVR, because shortly before arriving at the runway approach they turned off the widescreen wipers), the crew must have felt a sudden feeling of relief which increased their desire to finally overcome the ground problems: the desire to be airborne" (*Aviation Week*, 1978a: 121). The false hypothesis that the runway was clear was something the crew expected to be true, something they wanted to be true, something they dimly felt might not be true, but in the context of hierarchical communications was something they jointly treated as if it were true.

The likelihood that crises impose hierarchical constraints (Stohl and Redding, 1987) on speech-exchange systems is a straightforward extrapolation from the finding that stress leads to centralization (see Staw, Sandelands, and Dutton, 1981). This finding traditionally has been interpreted in a way that masks a potentially key cognitive step that allows us to understand Tenerife more fully. Before stress creates centralization, it must first increase the salience of hierarchies and formal authority, if it is to lead to centralization. It is the increased salience of formal structure that transforms open communication among equals into stylized communications between unequals. Communication dominated by hierarchy activates a different mindset regarding what is and is not communicated and different dynamics regarding who initiates on whom. In the cockpit, where there is a clear hierarchy, especially when the captain who outranks you is also the instructor who trained you, it is likely that attempts to create interaction among equals is more complex, less well-learned, and changed in favor of hierarchical communication when stress increases.

What is especially striking in studies of communication distortion within hierarchical relationships (Fulk and Mani, 1985), is that the "types of subordinate message distortion [to please the receiver] are quite similar to the strategies used to address message overload. They include gatekeeping, summarization, changing emphasis within a message, withholding, and changing the nature of the information" (Stohl and Redding, 1987: 481). The similar effects of hierarchy and overload on communication suggests that one set of distortions can solve two different problems. A mere change in emphasis in a communication upward can both reduce message overload and please the recipient. These mutually reinforcing solutions to two distinct problems of crises—overload and centralization—should exert continuing pressure on communication in the direction of distortion and away from accuracy.

INTERACTIVE COMPLEXITY AS INDIGENOUS TO HUMAN SYSTEMS

As the day unfolded at Tenerife after 1:30 in the afternoon, there was a gradual movement from loosely coupled events to tightly coupled events, and from a linear transformation process to a complex transformation process with unintended and unnoticed contingencies. Human systems are not necessarily protected from disasters by loose coupling and linear transformation systems because these qualities can change when people are subjected to stress, ignore data, regress, centralize, and become more self-centered.

Thus it would be a mistake to conclude from Perrow's (1984) work that organizations are either chronically vulnerable to normal accidents or chronically immune from them. Perrow's (1984:63) structural bias kept him from seeing clearly that, when you take people and their limitations into account, susceptibility to normal accidents can change within a relatively short time.

Several events at Tenerife show the system growing tighter and more complex:

1. Controllers develop ad hoc routing of two jumbo jets on an active runway because they have no other place to put them. (Roitsch et al., 1979: 8).

2. Controllers have to work with more planes than they have before, without the aid of ground radar, without a tower operator, and with no centerline lights to help in guiding planes.

3. Controllers keep instructing pilots to use taxiway "Third Left" to exit the active runway, but this taxiway is impossible for a 747 to negotiate. It requires a 148 degree left turn followed by an immediate 148 degree right turn onto a taxiway that is 74 feet wide (Roitsch et al., 1979: 19). Thus, neither the KLM pilot nor the Pan Am pilot are able to do what the controller tells them to do, so both pilots assume that the controller really means for them to use some other taxiway. Nevertheless, the KLM pilot may have assumed that the Pan Am pilot had exited by taxiway third left (Roitsch et al., 1979: 24).

4. The longer the delay at Tenerife, the higher the probability that all hotel rooms in Las Palmas would be filled, the higher the probability that the air corridor back to Amsterdam would be filled with evening flights, occasioning other air traffic delays, and the greater the chance for backups at Las Palmas itself, all of which increased the chances that duty time would expire while the KLM crew was in transit.

5. Throughout the afternoon there was the continuing possibility that the terrorist activities that had closed Las Palmas could spread to Tenerife. In fact, when the tower personnel heard the KLM explosion, they first thought that fuel tanks next to the tower had been blown up by terrorists (Roitsch et al., 1979: 8).

Research Leads to be Pursued

Stress paves the way for its own intensification and diffusion because it can tighten couplings and raise complexity. Each of the several effects of stress that we have reviewed up to this point either increases dependencies among elements within the system or increases the number of events that are unnoticed, uncontrolled, and unpredictable. For example, the same stress that produces an error due to regression paves the way for that error to have a much larger effect by increasing the complexity of the context in which the error first occurred. As stress increases, perception narrows, more contextual information is lost, and parameters deteriorate to more extreme levels before they are noticed, all of which leads to more puzzlement, less meaning, and more perceived complexity. Not only does stress increase the complexity, it also tightens couplings. Threat leads to centralization, which tightens couplings between formal authority and solutions that will be influential, even though the better solutions may be in the hands of those with less authority. Notice how the same process that produces the error in the first place also shapes the context so that the error will fan out with unpredictable consequences.

Normally, individual failures stay separate and unlinked if they occur in a linear transformation system where they affect only an adjacent step and if they occur in a loosely coupled system where that effect may be indeterminate (Perrow, 1984: 97, characterizes "airways" as linear, modestly coupled systems). If the couplings become tighter (e.g., slack such as excess duty time is depleted) and if the linear transformation process becomes more complex through the development of a greater number of parallel events having un-known but multiple logical entailments (Douglas, 1985: 173), then more fail-ures can occur and they can affect a greater number of additional events.

Cost cutting at the Bhopal plant prior to the disastrous gas leak illustrates the subtle way in which minor changes can tighten couplings and increase complexity:

> "When cost cutting is focused on less important units [in Union Carbide], it is not just decreased maintenance which raises susceptibility to crisis. Instead, it is all of the indirect effects on workers of the perception that their unit doesn't matter. This perception results in increased inattention, indif-ference, turnover, low cost improvisation, and working-to-rule, all of which remove slack, lower the threshold at which a crisis will escalate, and in-crease the number of separate places at which a crisis could start. As slack decreases, the technology becomes more interactively complex, which means there are more places where a minor lapse can escalate just when there are more minor lapses occurring." (Weick, 1988: 313)

The point of these details is that "normal accidents" may not be confined to obvious sites of technical complexity such as nuclear power plants. Instead, they may occur in any system that is capable of changing from loose to tight and from linear to complex. As we have suggested, any system, no matter how loose and linear it may seem, can become tighter and more complex when it is subjected to overload, misperception, regression, and individualized response.

IMPLICATIONS AND CONCLUSIONS

Although we have examined closely only a single incident, we have done so in the belief that Tenerife is a prototype of system vulnerability in general. Among the generic properties of Tenerife that are likely to be found in other systems, we would include the interruption of important routines among and within interdependent systems, interdependencies that become tighter, a loss of cog-nitive efficiency due to autonomic arousal, and a loss of communication accu-racy due to increased hierarchical distortion. This configuration of events seems to encourage the occurrence and rapid diffusion of multiple errors by creating a feedback loop which magnifies these minor errors into major problems.

Implications for both research and practice of the processes observed in this prototype have been scattered throughout the preceding account and I conclude by reviewing some of those which seem especially important. The concepts that I found most helpful were concepts that have been around for some time. The good news is that much of the old news about crises and behavior remains viable news. What I have basically done is gather these bits and pieces of understanding in one place, sort through them for their relevance to a single dramatic event, and then propose that the resulting assemblage represents a plausible configuration that explains the genesis of a large crisis from small beginnings. The account I have assembled is as much a reminder of tools already in hand as it is a set of speculations about new variables.

Nevertheless, in assembling, editing, and reformulating existing ideas, several themes for future research were identified and I review seven of them below.

First, the concept of temporary systems (e.g., Bryman, Bresnen, Beardsworth, Ford, and Keil, 1987; Goodman and Goodman, 1976; Miles, 1964) has been around for some time but seems worth resuscitating because air crews, task forces, and project teams are both plentiful and doing increasingly consequential work. It is not just air crews with their constantly changing personnel that form an odd mix of the mechanistic and the organic. Any group with a transient population is subjected to some of the same dynamics (e.g., see Gaba, Maxwell, and DeAnda, 1987 on mishaps during anesthesia administration). Thus, it would be instructive to learn to what extent parallels of Tenerife occur in the larger category of organizational forms called temporary systems.

Second, it goes without saying that we must continue to refine and make more precise the concept of stress. The concept plays an important role. It blends together emotion, anxiety, strain, pressure, and arousal. This blending can be troublesome because of the resulting ambiguity, but the global concept of stress nevertheless serves the important function of reminding investigators that affect is a vital part of experience and the human condition (Kemper, 1987). That reminder is worth whatever terminological distress it may occasion.

Third, there appears to be an important but little understood tradeoff between cohesion and accuracy in groups (e.g., Weick, 1983). Janis's (1982) important research on groupthink demonstrates the many insidious ways that sensing and criticism can be sacrificed in the service of group maintenance. Tenerife reminds us again of how delicate this balance can be and of the necessity to see the conditions under which the dilemma can be accommodated.

Fourth, in a related vein, we may need to restudy the possibility that pluralistic ignorance (Miller and McFarland, 1987) is a potential contributor to early stages of crisis. Pluralistic ignorance applied to an incipient crisis means I am puzzled by what is going on, but I assume that no one else is, especially because they have more experience, more seniority, higher rank. That was the error with the *Enterprise* at Bishop Rock (Robert, in press) (i.e., "surely the captain knows that is a rock just ahead") as well as with the KLM takeoff (i.e., "surely the captain knows that the runway may not be clear").

The first officer, who is reluctant to takeoff for Las Palmas but assumes no one else is, may not be all that different from the person who is reluctant to ride to Abilene (Harvey, 1974) on a sticky Sunday afternoon but assumes no one else is. The conditions under which that paradox gets resolved before damage is done remain important to articulate.

Fifth, if the elements that form the pre-crisis context become tightly coupled and more complex, then failures occur more often because of complexity and spread farther and more quickly because of tighter couplings. That is important, but fairly obvious. What is less obvious, and what the analysis of Tenerife suggests, is that persistent failures (those that remain unresolved and lead to a buildup of autonomic arousal) can also tighten couplings and increase complexity. Failures use up information processing capacity. With less information processing capacity, people ignore more central cues, invoke simpler mental models that leave out key indicators, and become more tolerant of unexplained and unpredicted entailments. Failures make authority structures, divisions of labor, and assigned responsibilities more salient. This can tighten the coupling between assigned roles and role behavior in the crises, even though such in-role behavior may be dysfunctional. Notice that this tightening between assigned pre-crisis roles and action during crisis is especially likely if those pre-crisis roles are overlearned. Even though improvisation might reduce the impact of a crisis, it is difficult when arousal is high and when, as Helmreich (1984) demonstrated, captains are wary of the idea that there are times when first officers should override their judgment. This wariness surely does not get lost on ambitious first officers.

Special attention should be directed at systems that are either loose/ linear, loose/complex, or tight/linear because they all are potentially vulnerable to small failures that are difficult to contain. The fact that so many systems are included within these three categories is the basic point being emphasized.

If tightening and complication of systems can be blocked, slowed, or dampened, or if people can be trained and rewarded to redesign the performance strategies when both their context and their structure become tighter and more complex, then failures should stay small and local.

Sixth, we need to see whether, as group interaction improves, task complexity (Wood, 1986) decreases? If so, we then need to see if this is a plausible means by which cohesive groups are less susceptible to disruption from stress than are uncohesive groups? This may be one means by which cohesive groups continue to function productively even though they are subjected to very high levels of stress.

And seventh, we need to see whether an increment in stress increases the salience of formal structure and authority relations. If so, this may be a considerable deterrent to expertise rather than position controlling the content of an early diagnosis. Given the tendency for communication among equals to turn hierarchical under stress, it would appear necessary that those at the top of the hierarchy explicitly legitimate and model equal participation, if they are to override that salience of hierarchy.

Implications for Practice

Again, the implications for practice that emerge from an analysis of Tenerife are not unusual, but they bear repeating because we are likely to see many more situations in the future that assume the outlines of Tenerife.

First, part of any job requirement must be the necessity for talk. Strong, silent types housed in systems with norms favoring taciturnity can stimulate unreliable performance because misunderstandings are not detected. Of the four implications for managerial practice derived by Sutton and Kahn (1987) in their influential stress review, three concern talk: be generous with information, acknowledge the information functions of the informal organizations, do not hold back bad news too long. LaPorte, Rochlin, and Roberts (e.g., LaPorte and Consolini, 1989) find that reliable performance and amount of talk exchanged co-vary.

What our analysis of Tenerife has uncovered is the possibility that with communication a complex system becomes more understandable (you learn some missing pieces that make sense of your experience) and more linear, predictable, and controllable.

The recommendation that people should keep talking is not as simple as it appears, because one of the problems at Three-Mile Island was too many people in the control room talking at one time with different hunches as to what was going on. The din created by tense voices plus multiple alarms, however, would make it all but impossible to single out talk as uniquely responsible for confusion, misdiagnosis, and delayed responding. The crucial talk at TMI should have occurred in hours before the control room got cluttered, not after.

If things do not make sense, speak up. This is the norm that needs to be created. Only by doing so can you break pluralistic ignorance (i.e., "you too, I thought I was the only one who didn't know what was going on").

Second, cultivate interpersonal skills, select people on the basis of their interpersonal skills, and devote training time to the development of interpersonal skills (Helmreich, 1983). As technologies become more complex than any one person can comprehend, groups of people will be needed to register and form collective mental models of these technologies. Requisite variety is no longer an individual construct; it must be viewed as a collective accomplishment (Orton, 1988). But to create collective requisite variety, leaders must create a climate in which trust, doubt, openness, candor, and pride can co-exist and be rewarded.

Third, remember that stress is additive, and that off the job stressors cumulate with those that arise on the job. Encourage norms that people under stress should alert others who are dependent on them that their performance may be sub-par. That norm is hard to implant in a macho culture where coping is perceived as grounds for promotion and an admission of problems is seen as grounds for being plateaued.

Fourth, treat chaos as a resource and reframe crises into opportunities to demonstrate and reaffirm competence as well as to enlarge response repertoires. One of the most important contributions of chaos theory (e.g., Gleick, 1987) as well as the counsel to "thrive on chaos" (Peters, 1987) is that they suggest that disorder contains some order; therefore, prediction, if not control, is possible. If chaos theory is not convincing on those instrumental grounds, then at least it suggests that chaos is indigenous, patterned, normal, and to be expected. Appreciation of those aspects of chaos may cushion the arousal that occurs when it becomes the source of interruption. Any response is seen as susceptible to interruption: one never becomes wedded to a single strategy but instead repeatedly cultivates options and alternative routes by which projects can be completed.

Fifth, controllability makes a difference (Karasek, 1979; Sutton and Kahn 1987), which means discretion must be generously distributed throughout the system. The removal of the KLM pilot's discretion to extend duty hours increased the severity of the interruption occasioned by the diversion to Tenerife and may have produced more cognitive narrowing than would have occurred had the effects of that interruption been bypassed by an extension of duty time.

Sixth, if a strong case can be made that new complex skills should be learned to replace old skills that are no longer appropriate, then the new skills should be overlearned, but with a clear understanding of the tradeoffs involved. It is important to overlearn new skills to offset the tendency for that skill to unravel in favor of earlier learning under pressure of stress. But overlearning is a mixed blessing. It reduces the likelihood of regression, but in doing so it heightens the disruptive effects of an interruption because overlearning makes the sequence of the response more invariant. The remedy would seem to be to give people more substitute routes by which an interrupted response can be carried to completion and inoculate people against the disruptive qualitities of interruption. Help them expect interruption and give them a mindset and actions to cope with interruption.

And seventh, forewarn people about the four conditions under which they are especially vulnerable to false hypotheses. Remind people to be mindful when they are most tempted to act in a mindless fashion (i.e., when they expect something, when they want something, when they are preoccupied with something, and when they finish something).

In conclusion, small details can enlarge and, in the context of other enlargements, create a problem that exceeds the grasp of individuals or groups. Interactive complexity is likely to become more common, not less so in the 90s. It is not a fixed commodity, nor is it a peculiar pathology confined to nuclear reactors and chemical plants. It may be the most volatile linkage point between micro and macro processes we are likely to find in the next few years.

REFERENCES

Alexander, J. C., and B. Giesen (1987). "From reduction to linkage: The long view of the micro-macro debate." In J. C. Alexander, B. Giesen, R. Munch, and N. J. Smelser (eds.) *The Macro-Micro Link* Berkeley: University of California, 1–42.

Allnutt, M. (1982). "Human factors: basic principles." In R. Hurst and L. R. Hurst, (eds.), *Pilot Error*. New York: Jason Aronson, 1–22.

Aviation Week and Space Technology (1978a). "Spaniards analyze Tenerife accident." November 20: 113–121.

———— (1978b). "Clearances cited in Tenerife collision." November 27: 69–74.

Barthol, R. P., and N. D. Ku (1959). "Regression under stress to first learned behavior." *Journal of Abnormal and Social Psychology*, 59, 134–136.

Bregman, N. J. and H. A. McAllister (1982). "Motivation and skin temperature biofeedback: Yerkes-Dodson revisited." *Psychophysiology, 19*, 282–285.

Bryman, A., M. Bresnen, A. D. Beardsworth, and J. Ford, and E. T. Keil, (1987). "The concept of the temporary system: The case of the construction project." *Research in the Sociology of Organizations, 5*, 253–283.

Dailey, C. A. (1971). *Assessment of Lives*. San Francisco: Jossey-Bass.

Davis, R. D. (1958). "Human engineering in transportation accidents." *Ergonomics, 2*, 24–33.

Douglas, M. (1985). "Loose ends and complex arguments." *Contemporary Sociology, 14* (2), 171–173.

Frankenhaeuser, M. (1986). "A psychological framework for research on human stress and coping." In M. H. Appley and R. Trumbull (eds.) *Dynamics of Stress*. New York: Plenum, 101–116.

Fulk, J. and Mani, S. (1985). "Distortion of communication in hierarchical relationships." In M. McLaughlin (ed.), *Communication Yearbook*, 9: 483–510. Newbury Park, CA: Sage.

Gaba, D. M., M. Maxwell, and A. DeAnda (1987). "Anesthetic mishaps: Breaking the chain of accident evolution." *Anesthesiology, 66*, 670–676.

Gardenier, J. S. (1981). "Ship navigational failure detection and diagnosis." In J. Rasmussen and W. B. Rouse (eds.), *Human Detection and Diagnosis of System Failures*. New York: Plenum, 49–74.

George. A. L. (1986). "The impact of crisis-induced stress on decision making." In F. Solomon and R. Q. Marston (eds.), *The Medical Implications of Nuclear War*." Washington, D.C.: National Academy of Science Press, 529–552.

Gleick, J. (1987). *Chaos: Making a New Science*. New York: Viking.

Goodman, R. A., and L. P. Goodman (1976). "Some management issues in temporary systems: A study of professional development and manpower—the theater case." *Administrative Science Quarterly. 21*, 494–501.

Hackman, J. R. (1987). "The design of work teams." In J. W. Lorsch (ed.), *Handbook of Organizational Behavior*: Englewood Cliffs, NJ: Prentice-Hall, 315–342.

Hage, J. (1980). *Theories of Organizations*. New York: Wiley.

Harvey, J. B. (1974). "The Abilene paradox." *Organizational Dynamics, 3* (1), 63–80.

Hayashi, K. (1985). "Hazard analysis in chemical complexes in Japan—especially those caused by human errors." *Ergonomics, 28*, 835–841.

Helmreich, R. L. (1983). *What changes and what endures: The capabilities and limitations of training and selection*. Paper presented at the Irish Air Line Pilots/Air Lingus Flight Operations Seminar, Dublin.

—— (1984). "Cockpit management attitudes." *Human Factors, 26*, 583–589.

Helmreich, R. L., H. C. Foushee, R. Benson, and W. Russini (1985). *Cockpit resource management: Exploring the attitude–performance linkage*. Paper presented at Third Aviation Psychology Symposium. Ohio State University, Columbus.

Hirokawa, R. Y., D. S. Gouran, and A. E. Martz (1988). "Understanding the sources of faulty group decision making: A lesson from the *Challenger* disaster." *Small Group Behavior 19*, 411–433.

Holroyd, K. A. and R. S. Lazarus (1982). "Stress, coping, and somatic adaptation." In L. Goldberger and S. Breznitz (eds.), *Handbook of Stress*. New York: Free Press. 21–35.

Hurst, R. (1982) "Portents and challenges." In R. Hurst and L. R. Hurst (eds.), *Pilot Error*. Second edition. New York: Jason Aronson, 164–177.

Janis, I. R. (1982). *Victims of Groupthink*. Second edition. Boston: Houghton-Mifflin.

Karasek, R. A. (1979). "Job demands, job decision latitude and mental strain: Implications for job redesign." *Administrative Science Quarterly*, 24, 285–308.

Kemper, T. D. (1987). "How many emotions are there? Wedding the social and the autonomic components." *American Journal of Sociology*, 93, 263–289.

LaPorte, T. and P. M. Consolini (1989). *Working in practice but not in theory: Theoretical challenges of high reliability organizations*. Unpublished manuscript, Department of Political Science, University of California at Berkeley.

Lazarus, R. S. and S. Folkman (1984). *Stress, Appraisal, and Coping*. New York: Springer.

Lowe, R. and J. E. McGrath (1971). *Stress, arousal, and performance: Some findings calling for a new theory*. Project report, AF1161-67, AFOSR, University of Illinois.

Mandler, G. (1982). "Stress and thought processes." In L. Goldberger and S. Breznitz (eds.), *Handbook of Stress*. New York: Free Press, 88–164.

McGrath, J. E. (1976). "Stress and behavior in organizations." In M. D. Dunnette, (ed.), *Handbook in Industrial and Organizational Psychology*. Chicago: Rand-McNally, 1351–1395.

McGuire, W. J. (1968). "Personality and susceptibility to social influence." In E. F. Borgatta and W. W. Lambert (eds.), *Handbook of Personality Theory and Research*. Chicago: Rand-McNally, 1130–1187.

Miles, M. B. (1964). "On temporary systems." In M. B. Miles, (ed.), *Innovation in Education*. New York: Teachers College Bureau of Publications, 437–490.

Miller, D. T. and C. McFarland (1987). "Pluralistic ignorance: When similarity is interpr㏒ ㏒d as dissimilarity." *Journal of Personality and Social Psychology*, 53, 298–305.

Munch, R., and N. J. Smelser, (1987). "Relating the micro and macro." In J. C. Alexander, B. Geisen, R. Munch and N. J. Smelser (eds.), *The Macro-Micro Link*: Berkeley: University of California, 356–387.

O'Reilly, C. A. (1978). "The intentional distortion of information in organizational communication: A laboratory and field approach." *Human Relations*, 31, 173–193.

Orton, J. D. (1988). *Group Design Implications of Requisite Variety*. Unpublished manuscript, School of Business Administration, University of Michigan.

Perrow, C. (1981) Normal accident at Three Mile Island. *Society*, 18 (5), 17–26.

———— (1984). *Normal Accidents*. New York: Basic Books.

Peters, T. J. (1987). *Thriving on Chaos*. New York: Knopf.

Roberts, K. H. (in press). "Bishop Rock dead ahead: The grounding of U.S.S. *Enterprise*. *Naval Institute Proceedings*.

Roitsch, P. A., G. L. Babcock and W. W. Edmunds (1979). *Human Factors Report on the Tenerife Accident*. Washington, D. C.: Airline Pilots Association.

Sheridan, T. B. (1981). "Understanding human error and aiding human diagnostic behavior in nuclear power plants." In J. Rasmussen and W. B. Rouse (eds.), *Human Detection and Diagnosis of System Failures*. New York: Plenum, 19–35.

Shrivastava, P. (1987). *Bhopal: Anatomy of a Crisis*. Cambridge, MA: Ballinger.

Staw, B. M., L. E. Sandelands, and J. E. Dutton (1981). "Threat-rigidity effects in organizational behavior: A multilevel analysis." *Administrative Science Quarterly*, 26, 501–524.

Stohl, C. and W. C. Redding (1987). "Messages and message exchange processes." In F. M. Jablin, L. L. Putnam, K. H. Roberts, and L. W. Porter (eds.), *Handbook of Organizational Communication*. Newbury Park, CA: Sage, 451–507.

Sutton, R. I. and P. L. Kahn (1987). "Prediction, understanding, and control as anti-dotes to organizational stress." In J. W. Lorsch (ed.), *Handbook of Organizational Behavior*. Englewood Cliffs, NJ: Prentice-Hall, 272–285.

Wagner, J. A. and M. K. Moch (1986). "Individualism collectivism: Concept and measure." *Group and Organization Studies*, *11*: 280–304.

Weick, K. E. (1983). "Contradictions in a community of scholars: The cohesion-accuracy tradeoff." *The Review of Higher Education*, 6(4), 253–267.

——— (1988). "Enacted sensemaking in crisis situations." *Journal of Management Studies*, *25*, 305–317.

Wood, R. E. (1986). "Task complexity: Definition of the construct." *Organizational Behavior and Human Performance*, *37*, 60–82.

Zeleny, M. (1986). "The law of requisite variety: Is it applicable to human systems? *Human Systems Management*, *6*, 269–271.

11

Operational Reliability and Marine Systems

ROBERT G. BEA
University of California, Berkeley

WILLIAM H. MOORE
University of California, Berkeley

Robert G. Bea is a professor in the Department of Naval Architecture and Offshore Engineering and the Department of Civil Engineering, University of California at Berkeley. He started his engineering career with the U.S. Army Corps of Engineers in 1955. He then worked for Shell Oil and Shell Development Companies for 20 years in a variety of engineering, construction, and research assignments around the world. He later became Vice-President and Chief Engineer of the Ocean Services Division of Woodward-Clyde Consultants. In 1980, he joined PMB Engineering (a Bechtel subsidiary) as a Senior International Consultant and Vice President. He was appointed to the faculty at Berkeley in 1989.

The authors recognize the insights, guidance, and leadership in this work provided by Professor Karlene Roberts of the Haas School of Business Administration at the University of California, Berkeley, and Professor M. Elisabeth Paté-Cornell of the Department of Industrial Engineering and Engineering Management, Stanford University. Key items of data and information for the work were provided by the Marine Investigation Group of the National Transportation Safety Board and by the Marine Safety Group of the U.S. Coast Guard.

The work is a result of research supported in part by NOAA, National Sea Grant College Program, Department of Commerce, grant #NA89AA-D-SG138, project #R/OE-17, through the California Sea Grant College, and in part by the California State Resources Agency. The U.S. government is authorized to reproduce and distribute for governmental purposes.

The work was also sponsored in part by Chevron Corporation, Chevron Shipping Company, Amoco Production Company and Amoco Transport Company, Unocal Corporation, the California State Lands Commission, and the U.S. Minerals Management Service. The support and guidance of these sponsors is gratefully acknowledged.

Professor Bea's interests in offshore platforms and pipelines, reliability methods, environmental forces, and marine foundations have resulted in publication of more than 150 papers. He is the author of a recently published book titled *Reliability Based Design Criteria for Coastal and Offshore Structures*. He has received a number of awards including the J. Hillis Miller Engineering Award, the American Society of Civil Engineers Croes Medal, and the Bechtel Fellow Award. He is a member of the National Academy of Engineering.

William H. Moore is a graduate research engineer pursuing a Doctor of Engineering degree with the Department of Naval Architecture and Offshore Engineering at the University of California at Berkeley. He has an M.S. degree in Ocean Systems Management from the Massachusetts Institute of Technology and a B.A. degree in Statistics from the University of California at Berkeley. His current topics of research are examining human factors in operations of tankers and offshore platforms, and he has research interests in ship operations, port planning and operations, and shipping economics.

The source of a majority of high-consequence accidents associated with marine systems such as offshore platforms and tankers can be attributed to compounded human and organizational errors (HOE) (Bea, 1989; Paté-Cornell & Bea, 1989). More than 80 percent of these accidents are founded in problems that develop primarily during operations of these systems. Recent examples include the *Occidental Piper Alpha* North Sea platform explosions and fire in 1988 (167 men killed), the *Odeco Ocean Ranger* capsizing off Newfoundland in 1982 (84 men killed), and the grounding of the *Exxon Valdez* off the coast of Alaska in 1989 (258,000 barrels of crude oil spilled).

Traditional engineering of marine systems focus primarily on structure and equipment. It aims to ensure that the proper amounts of structural materials are in place, that suitable functioning equipment is provided, and that the structure is constructible and serviceable for its intended purposes. Given that something in excess of 80 percent of the failures of these systems are the result of HOE, it is timely for engineers, managers, and regulators to begin formally addressing people and organizational considerations in design, construction, and operations of marine systems.

At the present time, there is no structured quantitative method to assist engineers in identifying and evaluating effective strategies either to design more human-error tolerant systems or to include consideration of the potential for human and organizational errors as an integral part of reliability improvement assessments. Those critical of the use of reliability-based methods in engineering marine systems cite the omission of consideration of the "human aspects" as a primary obstacle to their meaningful application (Reid, 1989).

This chapter discusses the impact of human and organizational error on the operational reliability of offshore platforms and tankers. It examines how qualitative and quantitative probabilistic risk analyses can be used as a tool to help evaluate the impact of HOE and HOE management alternatives. Case histories based on several recent marine disasters are used to illustrate the insight developed as a result of such analysis.

MARINE SYSTEM RELATED HOE STUDY BACKGROUND

In 1989, after completing a reliability study for the *Occidental Piper Alpha* replacement platform *Piper Bravo*, the senior author and Professor Elisabeth Paté-Cornell initiated a cooperative year-long pilot project to develop a first-generation HOE-PRA analysis procedure. The procedure addressed errors involved in designing, constructing, and operating fixed offshore drilling and production platforms, with an emphasis on the organizational aspects and the design phase. The results of that work are summarized in Paté-Cornell and Bea (1989).

The authors have continued research to further develop and verify an HOE-PRA analysis procedure directed at marine structure *operations*, and specifically, at floating marine structures (tankers and floating drilling and production systems). The research addresses the interactions of four major elements: (1) the physical system (structure and equipment level), (2) the operating personnel (individual/s level), (3) the organization directly responsible for management of the operating personnel (company level), and (4) other organizations that are involved in and that influence the operations (societal level).

The approach used in this project is founded on five primary tasks, as follows.

Task 1. Identify, obtain, and analyze well-documented case histories of tanker and offshore platform accidents whose root causes are founded in HOE. Accident investigation reports by the U.S. Coast Guard, Minerals Management Service, and the National Transportation Safety Board, and information provided by U.S. ship and platform operators provide the majority of real-life case histories of operations-caused failures for this project. In addition, accident investigation reports by the Canadian Royal Commission (sinking of the *Ocean Ranger*), the U.K. Department of Energy (*Piper Alpha* fires and explosions), and the Norwegian Petroleum Directorate (*Alexander Kielland* sinking) are used to provide additional case histories.

Task 2. Develop an organizational and classification framework for systematically identifying and characterizing various types of human and organizational errors. Human-error organizational frameworks developed for operations of high reliability systems (e.g., aircraft, nuclear power plants) will be reviewed and applied as appropriate.

Task 3. Develop general analytical frameworks based on real-life case histories to characterize how the human and organizational errors interact to cause the accidents. It is anticipated that "influence diagrams" (Paté-Cornell and Bea, 1989; Bea, 1989) will provide the basic analytical frameworks.

Task 4. Formulate quantitive analyses for the case histories based on probabilistic risk analysis procedured using influence diagrams. Perform quantitative risk analyses to verify that the analyses can reproduce the results and implications from the case histories and general statistics of marine accidents. The real-life accident case histories used to create the analytical models will be different from the case histories used to test and verify the models.

Task 5. Investigate the effectiveness of various alternatives to reduce the incidence and effects of human and organizational errors. Evaluate the costs and benefits in terms of effectiveness of risk reductions (product of likelihoods and consequences). Case history-based evaluations of the alternatives and tradeoffs will be used to illustrate the processes associated with developing effective strategies for managing human and organizational errors in operations of tankers and offshore platforms.

This chapter summarizes some of the key observations, insights, and analytical procedures developed as a result of this work. They are based on findings from a large number of other researchers who have studied this problem for the last 10 years.[1]

There are two complimentary approaches to the evaluation and management of HOE in improving reliability: (1) *qualitative* and (2) *quantitative.* Both approaches have benefits; our work indicates that they both should be mobilized to identify how and where to improve HOE management. One approach (qualitative) can and should form the framework for the other (quantitative).

The structure and interactions of humans, organizations, and systems is very complex. Further, there is little definitive data to assist in the evaluation analysis of such problems. Data on human performance in different tasks under different constraints and environments are only beginning to be assembled.

Is what we have to work with ready for application? In the authors' opinions and experiences, the answer is a demonstrable yes! The principal objective of the explicit introduction of HOE considerations into conventional reliability analyses is to help identify potentially critical weaknesses in the human, organization, and systems that are designed, constructed, and operated, and then to give one a basis to evaluate and justify alternatives to improve the reliability of marine systems. Our record of marine safety attests to the fact that this must be done if the industry is to make major improvements in the reliability of its systems. It is the process of evaluation, assessment, analysis, and allocation of safety resources that can be dramatically improved with the present state of development in HOE reliability management procedures.

---

[1]The authors have been given significant directions and HOE data by a number of individuals and organizations with extensive backgrounds in marine safety, and in particular, the operations of HOE related aspects of safety. These include the U.S. Coast Guard, National Transportation Safety Board, Human Factors Group at NASA-Ames, and the High Reliability Organization Project at the University of California, Berkeley.

ACCIDENT ORIGINS

As shown in Figure 11-1, high-consequence accidents can be the result of a number of events. The first distinction is between *environmental* and *human factors*. Catastrophic accidents due to environmental factors can be the result of failures that exceed the "reasonable" demands of the structure during its lifetime. Two examples are experiencing the 1000-year wave event during the lifetime of a structure which has been designed for the 100-year wave event, or failure due to earthquake far in excess of the platform design capacity. These failures are unavoidable "acts of God."

High-consequence accidents resulting from human errors can be differentiated into those caused by *design*, *construction*, or *operations*. Accidents can be the result of improper design and construction of the system. For example, primary contributors to the capsizing of the *Alexander Kielland* (123 men killed)

Figure 11-1
Breakdown of Accident Origins

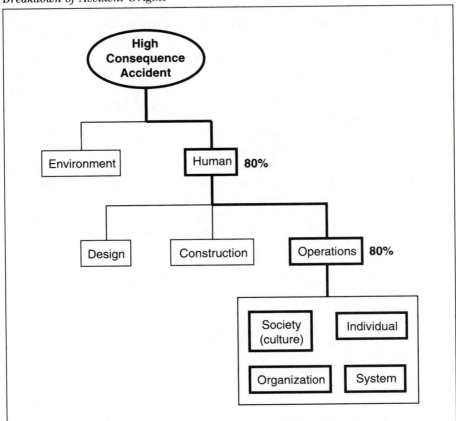

were the lack of redundancy (design) and cracks (construction) in the structure (Moan, 1981).

Accidents resulting from operations can be categorized into *societal* (cultural), *organizational, individual,* and *system* errors. Societal values can substantially influence the frequency of human and organizational errors. Expedient offshore development in the United Kingdom, resulting from the economic crises of the 1960s and 1970s, led to limited safety regulation and significantly high rates of marine accidents (Carson, 1982; Noreng, 1980).

Organizational factors have been shown to be associated with operational reliability for offshore platforms (Paté-Cornell and Bea, 1989; Paté-Cornell, 1990). For example, errors in management decisions resulted in the loss of the *Odeco Ocean Ranger* (Heising and Grenzebach, 1989; Royal Commission on the *Ocean Ranger* Marine Disaster, 1985) and the excessive loss of life aboard the drillship *Glomar Java Sea;* here 82 men were killed (National Transportation Safety Board, 1987).

Individual errors can also result in accidents. The chain of events that led to the *Occidental Piper Alpha* accident was initiated by events emanating from an unfinished maintenance job in the gas compression module (Lord Cullen Report, 1990; United Kingdom Department of Energy, 1988). Rochlin (this volume) provides extensive discussion of several ways human error can ramify into accidents.

Errors that occur because of human–system (equipment, structure) interfacing are system errors. System errors can be attributed to design errors and may result in an operator making improper decisions. System errors led to the loss of the ballast control aboard the *Odeco Ocean Ranger* (Royal Commission on the *Ocean Ranger* Marine Disaster, 1985) and emergency system failure aboard the *Occidental Piper Alpha* (Lord Cullen Report, 1990; United Kingdom Department of Energy, 1988).

Errors can be further categorized into *active* and *latent* errors. Active errors are those that have an immediate effect on the system (usually errors by front-line operators), while latent errors surface only once the active errors have occurred; these are primarily organizational and system errors (Reason, 1990). For example, the inadequacies of Alyeska's oil spill contingency plans (latent errors) only became blatantly apparent once the *Exxon Valdez* ran aground on Bligh Reef (active errors). Because Alyeska (a consortium of oil companies) was so ill-prepared for a spill of this magnitude, it took 14 hours to initiate a response to the spill (Davidson, 1990).

HUMAN ERRORS

Human errors are the basic cause of failure in many engineered systems (Bea, 1989; Heising and Grenzebach, 1989; Melchers, 1987; Moan, 1983; Offshore Certification Bureau, 1988; Paté-Cornell and Bea, 1989; Veritec, 1988; Wenk, 1986). Figure 11-2 (Bea, 1989) summarizes the causes of severe accidents

Figure 11-2
Severe Offshore Accidents, 1970–1984

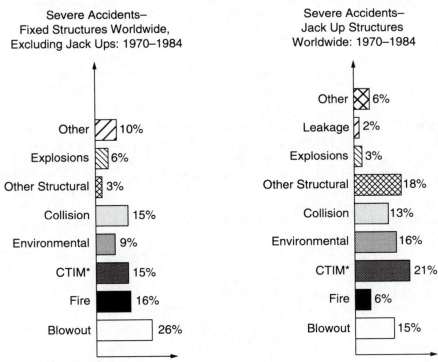

Severe Accidents–
Fixed Structures Worldwide,
Excluding Jack Ups: 1970–1984

Severe Accidents–
Jack Up Structures
Worldwide: 1970–1984

*Construction, Transportation, Installation & Mobilization

Source: Bea, 1989

involving fixed and mobile offshore structures used in the development of offshore hydrocarbons during the period 1970–1984 (Veritec, 1988). Less than 20 percent of the causes of severe accidents involving these marine structures can be attributed to the environment. The rest were due to initiating events such as groundings, fire, explosions, and collisions. In almost all cases, the initiating event can be traced to a catastrophic compounding of human and organizational errors (Heising and Grenzebach, 1989; Offshore Certification Bureau, 1988; Panel on Human Error in Merchant Marine Safety, 1976; Report of the Royal Commission on the *Ocean Ranger* Marine Disaster, 1985).

Table 11-1 shows a taxonomy of a number of factors that can result in human errors. The errors range from those of judgment to "ignorance, folly, and mischief" (Panel on Human Error in Merchant Marine Safety, 1976; Wenk, 1986). These errors are magnified and compounded in times of stress and panic (Heising and Grenzebach, 1989; Offshore Certification Bureau, 1988; Panel on Human Error in Merchant Marine Safety, 1976; Wenk, 1986). As shown in Figure 11-3, optimal performance levels are observed at an "appropriate level

Table 11-1
Human Error Factors

Fatigue	Wishful thinking	Bad judgment
Negligence	Mischief	Carelessness
Ignorance	Laziness	Physical limitations
Greed	Drugs	Boredom
Folly	Mischief	Inadequate training

of arousal" (Melchers, 1976). Human performance levels vary between individuals depending upon training, variability among individuals, organizational pressures, and complexity of the operating system. Performance deteriorates when pressure levels are either too low or too high. For example, stress or panic can produce high pressure while boredom or laziness produces low pressure. Both extremes can contribute to increased incidence of human errors. Foushee and Lauber (this volume) provide evidence of yet other forces that contribute to poor performance.

Figure 11-3
Human Performance Function

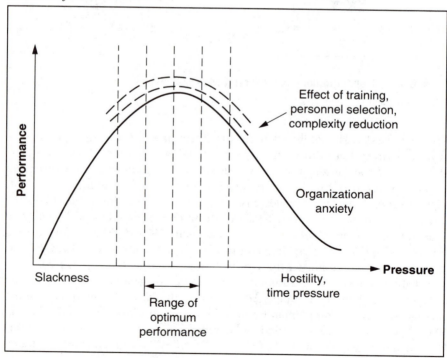

Source: Melchers, 1987

Modeling a Simple Mishap

Studies of the role of human errors in the reliability of engineered structures indicate that human errors and imperfections basically are inevitable (Bea, 1989; Ingles, 1985; Nowak, 1986). Figure 11-4 provides a schematic description of a simple mishap. Once a mishap is initiated, the objective is to return the system to normal before it reaches a critical threshold.

A mishap is differentiated into three psychological factors: *perceiving, thinking,* and *acting.* The danger threshold could be reached by lack of sufficient time to react, or errors in perception, thought, or action that would either lengthen the time between events or increase the magnitude of the danger buildup. The perception stage starts with a mishap and is followed by a warning signal (see Figure 11-5). The warning is then noticed and leads to recognition of the mishap source. The thinking stage begins with identification of the problem, and information (whether complete or incomplete) is processed at this stage to evaluate decisions for the best course of action. The mishap is acted upon with execution of a plan, and the system is returned to a normal operating status or escalates to a dangerous state.

Figure 11-4
A Simple Model of a Mishap

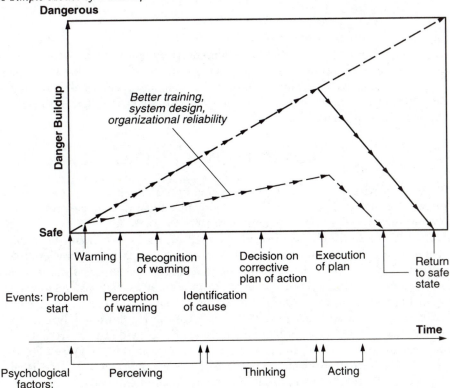

Figure 11-5
Danger Buildup Function

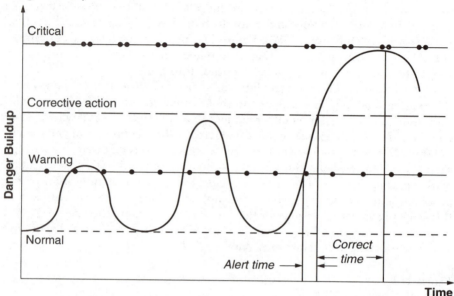

Source: Paté-Cornell, 1986

Though errors occur, they are influenced by cultural and moral values, corporate responsibilities and organizations, and individual training, craftsmanship, and integrity. The individual, organizations, and societies all play important roles in human errors that lead to dangerous states and that can result in catastrophic consequences.

ORGANIZATIONAL ERRORS

Analyses of past decisions regarding operating offshore platforms provide numerous examples of instances in which organizational deficiencies resulted in marine system failures (Heising and Grenzebach, 1989; Moan, 1983; Panel on Human Error in Merchant Marine Safety, 1976; Paté-Cornell and Bea, 1989; Report of the Royal Commission on the *Ocean Ranger* Marine Disaster, 1985; Veritec, 1988). Both collections of individuals (organizations, societies) and individuals (unilateral actions) contribute to accident situations. Failures can occur because of an organization's or an individual's willingness to take calculated risks (Arrow, 1951; Arrow, 1972). Failures can result from different types of inevitable errors that can be corrected in time, provided they are detected and recognized as errors, and corrective action is promptly taken (see Figures 11-4 and 11-5). Failures can also occur as the result of errors or bad decisions, most of which can be traced back to organizational malfunctions.

Table 11-2 shows a number of factors that can have negative effects on organizational reliability. For example, the goals set by the organization may lead rational individuals to conduct operations aboard a platform in a manner that corporate management would not approve if it were aware of their reliability implications (Howard, 1966; Kahneman, Slovic, and Tversky, 1982; Roberts, 1990). Similarly, corporate management, under pressure to reduce costs and maintain schedules, unknowingly may not provide the necessary resources required to promote safe operations. Hirschhorn (this volume) lays blame squarely on management's shoulders, as well as on required procedures for deteriorating performance in a nuclear power plant.

Generally, two classes of problems face an organization in making collective decisions that result from sequences of individual decisions: *information* (who knows what and when?), and *incentive* (how are individuals rewarded, what decision criteria do they use, how do these criteria fit the overall objectives of the organization?) (Arrow, 1972; La Porte, 1988). In developing programs to improve management of HOE, careful consideration must be given to information (collection, communications, and learning) and incentives, particularly as they affect the balancing of several objectives such as costs and safety under uncertainty in operations of offshore platforms (Foushee and Lauber, this volume; Weick, 1987; Wenk, 1986).

The structure, the procedures, and the culture of an organization contribute to the safety of its product (Kahneman, Slovic, and Tversky, 1982; La Porte, 1988; Schulman, this volume) and to the economic efficiency of its risk management practices (Royal Norwegian Council for Scientific & Industrial Research, 1979; Wenk, 1986). The organization's structure can be unnecessarily complex and may demand flawless performance. This can result in little or no credible feedback to upper levels of management (see Hirschhorn, this volume). The resulting safety problem may ensue because there are inconsistencies in decision criteria (e.g., safety standards) used by the different groups for various activities. This can result in large uncertainties about the overall system safety, about the reliability of the interfaces, and about the relative contribution of different subsystems to overall failure probability (Construction Industry Research and Information Association, 1977; Moan, 1983; National Bureau of Standards, 1985).

Organization and management procedures that affect system reliability include, for example, parallel processing such as developing design criteria at the same time as the structure is being designed, a procedure that may or may

Table 11-2
Organizational Error Factors

Time pressures	Culture	Incentives
Cost–profit incentives	Morale	Communications
Regulatory requirements	Promotion—recognition	Production orientation

not be appropriate in economic terms according to the costs and the uncertainties (Bea, 1989; Paté-Cornell and Bea, 1989).

The culture of the organization can also affect system reliability (Arrow, 1972; Roberts, Rousseau, and La Porte, in press; Weick, 1987; Wenk, 1986). For example, the dominant culture may reward risk-seeking (flirting with disaster) or superhuman endurance (leading to excessive fatigue), an attitude that in the long run may prove incompatible with the objectives of the organization. Another feature may be the lack of recognition of uncertainties leading to systematic biases towards optimism and wishful thinking (Panel on Human Error in Merchant Marine Safety, 1976; Paté-Cornell and Seawell, 1988).

SYSTEM ERRORS

Errors can also be exacerbated by poorly engineered systems that invite them. Such systems are difficult to construct, operate, and maintain (Ingles, 1985; Melchers, 1987; Moan, 1983). Table 11-3 shows a taxonomy of system flaws that can affect marine systems. New technologies compound the problems of latent system flaws. Complex design, close coupling (failure of one component leads to failure of other components) and severe performance demands on systems increase the difficulty in controlling the impact of human errors even in well-operated systems (Perrow, 1984). Emergency displays have been found to give improper signals of the state of the systems (Heising and Grenzebach, 1989; Lord Cullen Report, 1990; Perrow, 1984; Report of the Royal Commission on the *Ocean Ranger* Marine Disaster, 1985). Land-based industries often can spatially isolate independent subsystems whose joint failure modes would constitute a total system failure. System errors resulting from complex designs and close coupling are more apparent due to spatial constraints aboard ships and platforms. For example, spatially isolating the accommodations unit on *Piper Alpha* could have substantially reduced the loss of life aboard the platform: 82 men died in the accommodations unit (Lord Cullen Report, 1990).

Human performance is a function of the lead time available to respond to warnings in the system. Errors are compounded by the lack of effective early warning systems (Paté-Cornell, 1986). As observed in Figure 11-5, if the lead time is short, there is little time allowance for corrective action before the situation reaches a critical state. On the other hand, if the system is too sensitive, resulting in frequent false alarms, operators will eventually cease to respond to warning signals. The time differential between the normal and

Table 11-3
System Error Factors

Complexity	Latent flaws	Severe demands
Close coupling—non-redundancy	Small tolerances	False alarms

warning stages are dependent upon the sensitivity of the system to developing danger. However, as shown in the mishap model (see Figure 11-4), adequate human performance is critical at the initiation of an alert stage (warning) and in expedient execution of a plan (corrective action) to bring the system back under control.

ALTERNATIVES TO IMPROVE MANAGEMENT OF HOE

In many cases, a combination of human, organization, and technical (system) modifications can improve overall safety. Table 11-4 lists some effective human, organizational, and technical factors that can benefit operational reliability.

After a catastrophic failure, technical modifications are frequently proposed to "fix the problem." An example is the legislation requiring double-hull tankers following the *Exxon Valdez* disaster. (One wonders if this legislation took into account the reduction of cargo capacity of double-hull tankers. This will result in more tanker traffic to maintain capacities and increase the risk of other types of accidents such as collisions.) Technical modifications, however, represent only one class of risk management strategy. When a system's failure is studied after the failure occurs, it is often obvious that what resulted in a technical failure was actually rooted in a functional failure of the organization and the human operators (Arrow, 1972; March and Simon, 1958). Organizational modifications may address some of the reliability questions at a more basic level than at strengthening the engineering design alone. These include, for example, improving communications, setting effective warning systems, and ensuring consistency of standards across the organization. Rochlin and Schulman (this volume) focus specifically on organizational mechanisms to ensure safety in high reliability organizations. Creed, Stout, and Roberts (this volume) narrow in on the effectiveness aspect of these mechanisms.

There is a current misconception that new technologies are necessarily better than old ones. But new technologies create new sets of problems and additional risks (Wenk, 1986). As technological systems become more efficient and attractive (also more complex), we have a tendency to forget that these systems pose exceptional risks. The following examples demonstrate the need

Table 11-4
Error Management

Human	Organization	Systems
Selection	Resource allocation	Human tolerances
Training	Communication systems	Redundancy
Licensing	Decision making	Early warning systems
Verification	Process orientation	Damage tolerances
Incentives	Integrity	
Job design	Accountability	

for a combination of human, organizational, and system management to ensure operational reliability.

CASE HISTORIES

Development of accurate case histories of past marine accidents can provide a basis for defining how the interactions of systems, humans, and organizations can lead to such disasters. These interactions provide templates with which new and existing systems can be studied to determine how best to prevent catastrophic compounding of HOE ("Those who don't know history are destined to repeat it"). To illustrate the process, three case histories of marine accidents are developed.

Ship Pump Room Gas Detector

A shipping company operated its vessels with twenty-five crew members since 1955. In 1982, the first engineer and a pumpman were seriously injured in an accident in the pump room when a gas leak ignited. The company managers decided to place in a pump room gas detection and an emergency shutdown system that could be operated from the bridge. In addition, to cut costs and the chances of injury to crew members, the vessels were operated with a single day-shift engineer (instead of three or four engineers) and no pumpman since the pumping system was totally automated and operational from the bridge. The company also believed the new technology was attractive since pump and engine room maintenance crews could be brought aboard at ports of call and need not accompany the ships during transit, thus reducing operating costs (as well as ship maintenance).

No major problems developed with gas leaks aboard the vessel until 1991 when a leak again occurred in the pump room. The bridge operators, having not had any problems with this system over nine years, paid little attention to the gas detection gauge on the bridge console (early warning signal), and did not shut down the system before an explosion and fire occurred. In addition, over the last eight years, the company employed a day engineer whose specialties were not mechanical systems, but electrical systems to keep pace with the new automated technologies implemented over the years.

The day engineer, having little experience with these types of problems, could not control the fire automatically, nor was there manpower to fight the fire effectively since the size of the crew had been reduced. The ensuing fire escalated and reached the engine room. The result was a power plant failure while the ship transited an area with many navigational hazards. The ship sent a "mayday" for assistance since it was drifting towards a hazardous reef. Assistance did not arrive in time and the ship ran aground, spilling 200,000 barrels of oil in an environmentally sensitive area.

The point of this example is that new technological systems carry their own set of risks. This scenario demonstrates human errors (improper bridge monitoring, inadequate training), organizational errors (ship managers cutting back on manpower), and system errors (inadequate systems to prevent, detect, control and fight the fire). In addition, it exemplifies the overconfident trust placed on a technological system (gas detection, emergency shutdown systems, and automatic control from the bridge) without attention to the potential risks associated with it. The monitoring system had been changed from an active system (engineers and pumpmen working around the clock) to a passive system (gas detection and bridge control). Technological "fixes" did not control the problem but only created new failure scenarios.

Mobile Drilling Unit Ballast Control System

A floating mobile offshore drilling unit (MODU), operating off the east coast of Newfoundland, encountered a severe North Atlantic storm. As the intensity of the storm increased, the drilling unit suspended operations. Late in the evening, a large wave broke a port light in the ballast control room; the port light cover had not been put in place. Water entered the ballast control room, resulting in an electrical failure of the ballast control console. This made it difficult to assess the amount of ballast in the ballast tanks and to determine if the valves between tanks were open or closed. Manual ballast control could be conducted from the pump rooms at the stern of the pontoons that provided buoyancy to support this unit.

Valves between the ocean and ballast tanks could be operated manually from the control room in the event of an electrical failure. However, the ballast control personnel were under the assumption that the insertion of solenoid rods into the ballast control console closed the valves between tanks, when actually the rods opened them. As water entered the forward ballast tanks, the MODU began to list forward. By early morning, heavy seas began to break on the upper deck of the platform, resulting in water entering the mooring chain lockers; the unit slowly turned itself over and began to sink.

An SOS resulted in emergency rescue aircraft being dispatched to the scene. However, due to the severe weather, the emergency rescue aircraft could do little to help and had to return to land. Crewmen donned life jackets, but there were no exposure suits for protection against the cold 31-degree water. Personnel were clad in both light and heavy clothing; the order to abandon the MODU came at the last minute.

A standby support vessel in the vicinity of the MODU attempted to save the crew, but because of the vessel's inadequate design for rescues and the lack of formal rescue training of the ship crew, the attempt proved futile. Due to the extreme list of the MODU, only one lifeboat could be successfully launched. That lifeboat capsized alongside the rescue boat when water entered an open hatch and everyone moved to one side of the lifeboat to evacuate. In the water, the crewmen were quickly immobilized and died due to hypothermia. Nine hours after the port light had been broken, the MODU sank to the bottom of the North Atlantic. All eighty-four crewmen perished.

Not a single person aboard the MODU had a clear understanding of how to operate the ballast control system correctly. The organizational structure onboard the MODU was complex. The *tool pusher* is responsible for decisions regarding the safety of the rig, yet he had no experience with ballast control on floating drilling units. The *drilling foreman* is in charge when the rig is drilling and is the only person who has the authority to activate the standby support vessel and rescue aircraft. The *master* is responsible for supervising and training ballast control operators, loading and unloading operations, and general maintenance of the MODU. The particular master assigned to this MODU was a former mariner on temporary assignment who had no experience in ballast control. His *senior and junior ballast control operators* had no formal training in ballast control and were not familiar with the ballast control system onboard this particular MODU. Ten days prior to the accident, the master had made an error in the ballast control that resulted in a significant list of the rig. The shore-based operations management was aware of the situation; however, they chose not to replace the master since he was on temporary assignment. The senior and junior ballast control operators were placed onboard in response to regulations regarding the employment of local personnel.

This example illustrates the interrelationships of a complex and poorly designed system (ballast, evacuation), inadequate training, poor organization and supervision, and the lack of an effective rescue and safety contingency plan. Influences of the individual operators, the organization, and the society are clearly evident.

Platform Maintenance Operations

The night shift had just taken over operations onboard a fixed platform in the North Sea. The control room personnel were waking up and a contract maintenance crew had started working on one of the gas condensate pumps that was not working properly (there were two of these pumps). These pumps inject liquids or condensate from the produced gas into the oil production system.

The production superintendent was assisting the maintenance crew in determining the source of the problem. Gas being produced from the platform and from two adjacent platforms and sent via pipeline to the platform placed the platform on a code red status, indicating a maximum production situation. The production superintendent normally onboard the platform was on vacation. His position was filled by a replacement superintendent who had just come onboard the platform.

Earlier in the day, maintenance work was partially completed on the other condensate pump; it had been taken out of service to maintain its safety equipment, but the work had not been completed before the night shift took over. The control room personnel were unaware of the maintenance work. Also, earlier in the day, divers had been in the water working on the underwater portions of the platform, and the fire pumps and deluge system (similar to a sprinkler system in a building) had been placed on manual control to prevent divers from being sucked into the seawater intakes.

The malfunctioning condensate pump (which injects liquids from the gas stream into the oil pipeline) failed, and the order was given to the control room to turn on the other pump to avoid condensate from backing up into the gas compressors. The control room personnel did not realize that the other pump was not working and opened the valves to the pump, routing the gas condensate to the inoperable pump. Condensate and gas escaped into the module and ignited with a deafening explosion, killing the crew and production superintendent. Due to the containment of the explosion, the adjacent control room was decimated. Power was lost due to destruction of the primary electrical wiring system by the explosion. The automatic deluge and emergency power systems did not come on because they had been placed on manual control and could not activate the systems manually as a result of the fire.

The fire quickly spread to adjacent oil- and gas-producing vessels and piping. Unprotected fuel storage above the gas compression module was ignited, and thick, dense, toxic smoke engulfed the quarters where surviving crew members were being mustered for evacuation in life boats. While the crew was awaiting the orders from the production superintendent to evacuate, fresh air intake fans sucked the smoke into the quarters. Because the production superintendent was killed in the initial explosion, the evacuation orders never came, and in the dark and confusion the crew members were overcome by smoke and died.

Moored adjacent to the platform was an emergency support vessel. This vessel was designed specifically to provide emergency support to fight fires, kill well blowouts, accommodate divers and other field personnel, and provide emergency medical facilities. The vessel was instructed to fight fires at the order of the production superintendent. Again waiting for orders that could never come, and fearing for the safety of the vessel, the vessel master gave orders to pull back from the escalating fire. The fire fighting pumps were never used.

Pipelines bringing oil and gas from the adjacent platforms passed immediately under the platform. Subjected to intense heat, these lines softened and ruptured. A deafening explosion and fireball engulfed the entire platform. The emergency shut-in devices (to prevent the pipeline contents from escaping) were in the same area and were destroyed, allowing the pipeline contents to be emptied into the fire.

The result of these developments was total destruction of the platform and loss of 167 lives. The accident was the result of design flaws, human, organization, and societal factors. The platform owner was aware of the marginal situation onboard the platform before the incident; wishful thinking and shortsightedness (emphasis on present profitability) were evident. The regulatory body responsible for overseeing the operations was similarly aware of the situation but was unable or reluctant to force compliance with already lax safety guidelines. The operating personnel had operated the platform at its code red or maximum operating level only once before in the rig's lifetime; this occasion had occurred at a time when the experience level was marginal. The capacity of the equipment systems was stretched to the breaking point. What appeared to be redundant critical systems (the two condensate pumps, deluge system) were not really redundant. They could not be safety operated. Similarly, the onboard organization contained critical flaws that did not provide adequate backup or redundancy. Given the death of the production superintendent, the organization became dysfunctional in an emergency situation. Poor communications and work procedures (the day crew did not brief the night crew) exacerbated and eventually triggered the disaster.

PROBABILISTIC RISK ANALYSIS (PRA)

If HOE affects a subsystem whose functioning is not highly critical, its effect on overall system reliability may be minor and may not justify profound human or system changes. However, complex interactions of relatively independent subsystems can substantially affect overall system reliability due to system complexities and tight coupling (Perrow, 1984). If deficiencies affect a subsystem or a complex interaction of subsystems whose failure constitutes a system failure mode, it is urgent to address the problem at its human and system origins, as shown in the previous example. To permit evaluations of the interactions of the human and system components, it is desirable to organize and assess these features in a *probabilistic risk analysis* (PRA) (Moan, 1983). This allows one to develop insights into the urgency of remedial measures, to evaluate alternative remedial measures to improve safety, and to set priorities among HOE problems to be addressed.

A PRA for engineering systems allows identification of the weakest parts of a system through qualification of the probabilities of the different failure modes (Melchers, 1987). Event tree modeling, a form of PRA, has been found to be an effective method to analyze contributions of individual accidents to risk associated with offshore operations (Larocque and Mudan, 1982). This technique permits setting priorities among possible modifications aimed at the reduction of the failure risks and, therefore, optimal allocation of limited risk management resources.

The general method is to integrate elements of process analysis and organizational analysis in the assessment of the probability of system failure (Bea, 1989; Paté-Cornell and Bea, 1989; Paté-Cornell and Seawell, 1988). Figure 11-6 provides a schematic description of the structure of this integration model. The first phase (which does not appear in this diagram) is a preliminary PRA to identify the key subsystems or elements of the system's reliability. The second phase is an analysis of the process to identify the potential problems for each subsystem and their probabilities or base rates per time unit or per operation.

The next phase is to analyze organizational procedures and the incentive system to determine their influence on the occurrence of basic errors and the

Figure 11-6
Event Tree Showing the Structure of the Generalized Reliability Model

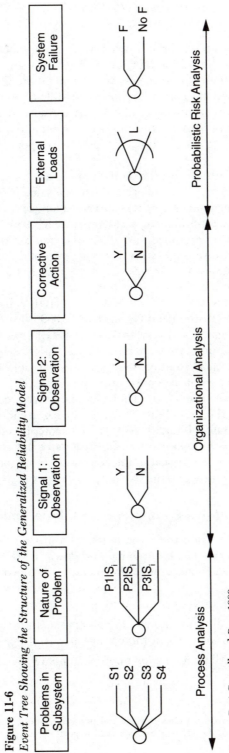

Source: Paté-Cornell and Bea, 1989

217

probability that they are observed, recognized, communicated, and corrected in time (i.e., before they cause a system failure).

The result of these three phases is a computation of the probabilities of the different system states corresponding to possible types of structural defects and, therefore, to different levels of systems capacity. The fourth phase involves a return to the PRA for the physical system and a computation of the probability of failure for each capacity level corresponding to the different system states.

The overall failure probability is then obtained. It explicitly includes the possibility of weaknesses in the different subsystems due to organizational structure. These different models (process, organization, and final PRA) are integrated using an event tree (Heising and Grenzebach, 1989; Nessim and Jordan, 1985) or influence diagram (Shachter, 1986) to compute the failure probability under different circumstances (such as occurrence and correction of a given problem in the process). We propose here to quantify the benefits of organizational measures, using PRA as a starting point.

One can quantify the costs and benefits of HOE reliability management measures using PRA (Heising and Grenzebach, 1989; Moan, 1983; Nessim and Jordan, 1985). The analysis of a system's reliability allows identification of its failure modes and computation of their probabilities. It permits a decision maker to choose technical solutions that maximize an objective function (costs and reliability) under resource constraints (Weick, 1987; Wenk, 1986). These solutions include, for instance, the choice of operating procedures and equipment that minimize the probability of failure during the lifetime of a structure under constraints of safety budgets, costs, time to completion, production level, structure location, and general type. The results of the analysis can provide valuable insights into where scarce safety resources can best be deployed to achieve the largest improvements in safety.

Operations Example: Event Tree Analysis

An example helps illustrate the basic tenets of a marine HOE PRA. The example is the installation of an emergency shut down (ESD) valve in an existing pipeline.[2] Three HOE management alternatives will be considered:

Alternative 1. Use the present system.

Alternative 2. Allow for modest improvements in the planning, training, and supervision involved in the operation.

Alternative 3. Allow for major improvements in planning, training, and supervision.

---

[2] A major fire recently destroyed a Gulf of Mexico platform during installation of an ESD into an existing pipeline (Minerals Management Service OCS Report, 1990).

Based on data developed on the performance reliability of each of these three alternatives, Table 11-5 summarizes the probabilities of a successful operation in each stage of installing the ESD.

The probabilities of successful operations of Alternatives 2 and 3 were based on one and two levels, respectively, of checking the normal operation characterized as Alternative 1. The probability of successful detection and correction of error signals developed in each phase of the operation in Alternative 1 (no checking) was assigned a probability of 0.5 and in Alternative 2 (one level of checking). The same probability of detection and correction was assigned in Alternative 3 (two levels of checking).

In an actual PRA, these probabilities are based on results from studies of operations comparable to those of Alternative 1 and of the likelihoods of checking and corrective action given specified procedures for such actions. At the present time, such data are generally lacking for HOE PRA, and this poses one of the major hurdles to the performance of realistic quantitative analyses. Some organizations have begun to develop such information (Veritec, 1988) and more will be developed in the course of the research summarized previously in this chapter.

Figure 11-7 shows an event tree for installing an ESD valve in an oil pipeline. The event tree distinguishes between decisions and events at various states of the system. Table 11-6 summarizes the results of the HOE PRA, indicating the probabilities that fires caused by the ESD installation operation are not extinguished before there is significant damage to the platform. In addition, the estimated costs associated with the installation of the ESD using each operation alternative is shown together with the expected total estimated costs associated with fires. The costs associated with the fires have been estimated at between one and two million dollars.

Table 11-5
Probabilities of Successful Operations

Phase of Operation	Alternative 1	Alternative 2	Alternative 3
Adequate planning of ESD installation	0.50	0.75	0.875
Adequate purging of pipeline	0.50	0.75	0.875
Detection of hazardous hydrocarbons	0.50	0.75	0.875
Suppression of explosion and fire	0.50	0.25	0.125
Extinguishment of fire before significant damage	0.50	0.75	0.875

Figure 11-7
Event Tree for Installation of ESD Valve in Oil Pipeline

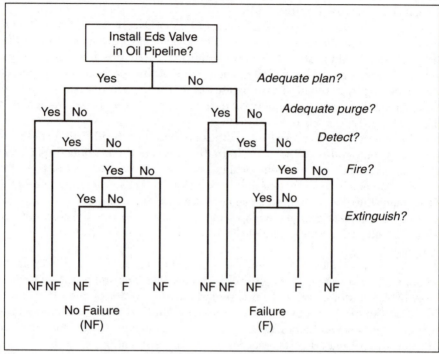

As shown in Figure 11-8, the increase in initial cost to make radical improvements to the operations to reduce the probability of fire during ESD installation ($30,000) does not appear to be economically justified. The $10,000 investment to make moderate improvements appears to be well-justified by the

Table 11-6
Probabilities for Expected Costs for Operational Alternatives

Operation Alternative	Probability of Fire During Operations	Estimated Initial Cost ($000s)	Expected Total Cost: $1 million damage cost ($000s)	Expected Total Cost $2 million damage cost ($000s)
Present system	0.0625	$50.0	$112.5	$175
Moderate improvements	0.0081	60.0	68.1	76.2
Major improvements	0.0001	80.0	80.1	80.2

Figure 11-8
Probability of Fire During ESD Installation versus Expected Cost

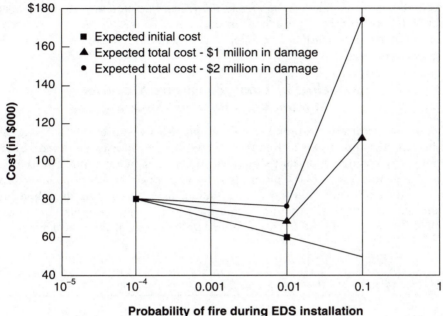

Probability of fire during EDS installation

range of reduction in expected total costs. Additional study could be performed to determine which of the changes in the operations phases are most effective at reducing the likelihoods of fires.

As a footnote to this example, after the platform disaster described in the previous section occurred, the industry quickly reacted and some operators began installing emergency shut-in valves on gas and oil import and export pipelines. One of these operations required cutting an existing pipeline prior to inserting an emergency shut-in valve. The pipeline had been purged of gas and oil prior to the start of the work. The inexperienced work crew (selected on the basis of low bid) ignored the warning work crew (selected on the basis of low bid) ignored the warning signs when oil and gas began to leak from the pipeline they were cutting. A fire started and was quickly followed by a massive explosion. The platform was engulfed by flames fed from the pipeline that had not been completely purged. The result was again total destruction of the platform and the loss of seven lives.

Influence Diagramming

Influence diagramming is a form of PRA modeling that allows flexibility in examining HOE and HOE management alternatives. There are distinct advantages for using influence diagramming for PRA. In standard decision tree analysis, decisions are based on all preceding aleatory and decision variables.

However, not all information is available to a decision maker, and information may come from indirect sources or not in the specific order in which the decision tree is modeled. When using influence diagramming, all nodes need not be totally ordered. This allows for decision makers who agree on common based states of information, but differ in ability to observe certain variables in the diagramming.

Modeling of Pump Room Fire Scenario: Manual vs. Automated System

Let us now return to the pump room example described previously. Using the influence diagram shown in Figure 11-9, we can consider two alternatives for emergency gas detection and shutdown in a tanker pump room: Alternative 1—manual monitoring of the pump room by an engineer and pumpman on duty around the clock, and Alternative 2—installing an emergency gas detection and shutdown system that is operated from the bridge. These alternatives are examined to determine the eventual failure probabilities of the power plant re-

Figure 11-9
Influence Diagram of Effects of Gas Leak in Tanker Pump Room

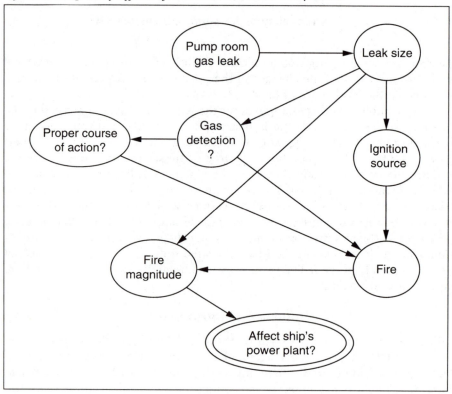

Table 11-7
Probability of a Pump Room Gas Leak

Gas leak (GL)	.005
No gas leak (NGL)	.995

Table 11-8
Probabilities of Pump Room Gas Leak Sizes

Small leak (SL)	.70
Moderate leak (ML)	.25
Large leak (LL)	.05

Table 11-9
Probability Distribution of a Pump Room Gas Leak Detection Before Ignition

Pump Room Gas Leak	Leak Size	Gas Detection	Probability of Detection (GDS)	Probability of Detection (operators)
Leak	Small	Yes	.90	0.75
		No	.100	0.25
	Medium	Yes	.990	0.85
		No	.010	0.15
	Large	Yes	.999	0.95
		No	.001	0.05
No leak	No leak	Yes	0.00	0.00
		No	1.00	1.00

sulting from fires initiated by pump room gas leaks. Each single-border oval or circular node shown in Figure 11-9 describes probabilistic nodes while double-border nodes describe deterministic values in the model. Table 11-7 shows the probabilities of a gas leak in the pump room.

A probability distribution is established for the magnitude of the leak and is represented by the "leak size" node. Table 11-8 shows this probability distribution for leak sizes. The leak size influences three factors: (1) the detection of gas, (2) the ignition of the leak, and (3) the magnitude of the fire. Gas detection is assumed to be dependent upon its concentration in the ambient atmosphere around either the pump room operators (detection by smell, sound, or gauging) (see Table 11-8) or the automatic gas detection system (GDS) (Table 11-9). Gas detection is a step process for both manual and automatic operations: it involves a warning signal followed by the problem recognition, identification, and execution of a plan (see Figure 11-4). The larger the leak, the greater the chance of detection. Table 11-9 displays the conditional probability distribution for gas detection dependent upon the initiation of the leak and its size. In addition, the gas must locate an ignition source for a fire to be

Table 11-10
Probabilities of Gas Leaks Finding Ignition Sources

Leak Size	Ignition Source	Probability of Ignition Source Being Located
Small	Found	.40
	Not found	.60
Medium	Found	.70
	Not found	.30
Large	Found	.95
	Not found	.05
No leak	Found	0.00
	Not found	1.00

Table 11-11
Probabilities of Controlling Gas Leak

Gas Detection	Leak Controlled	Probability Using Manual Operation	Probability Using GDS System
Yes	Yes	.90	.60
Yes	No	.10	.40
No	No	1.00	1.00

initiated. The model assumes that the greater the magnitude of the gas leak, the greater the probability it finds an ignition source, as shown in Table 11-10.

The "proper course of action?" node in Figure 11-9 models whether operators were able to return the system to a normal state by intervening to prevent the fire from occurring. The distributions shown in Table 11-11 demonstrate two factors: (1) the probability of manual control of a leak or fire is greater than that of automatic control since both manpower and mechanical expertise are available to extirpate the problem, and (2) passive monitoring from the ship's bridge can lead to a limited alert time before escalation to a state that is impossible to control (see Figure 11-5).

As shown in Figure 11-9 fire initiation, presented by the deterministic node "fire," depends on three factors: (1) whether the gas was detected, (2) whether a proper course of action was carried out to control the leak if detected, and (3) whether the gas located an ignition source. Table 11-12 shows the conditions in which a fire occurs.

As represented in Figure 11-9, "fire magnitude" is dependent upon both the size of the leak and fire occurrence. The larger the gas leak, the greater the chance of a large-magnitude fire. These assumptions are represented by the probabilistic distributions shown in Table 11-13.

Finally, due to the proximity of the pump room to the main engine room, the magnitude of the fire will have an effect on the probability of failure of the ship's power plant. The fire events represented by the fire magnitudes will

Table 11-12
Conditions to Initiate Fire Event

Ignition Source Located	Leak Controlled	Gas Detected	Fire Event
Yes	Yes	Yes	No fire
Yes	No	Yes	Fire
Yes	No	No	Fire
No	Yes	Yes	No fire
No	No	Yes	No fire
No	No	No	No fire

Table 11-13
Probability Distributions of Fire Magnitudes

Leak Size	Fire Event	Fire Magnitude	Probability of Fire Magnitude
No leak	Fire	No fire	1.0
	No fire	No fire	1.0
Small	Fire	Small	.75
	Fire	Moderate	.175
	Fire	Large	.075
	No fire	No fire	1.0
Medium	Fire	Small	.25
	Fire	Moderate	.5
	Fire	Large	.25
	No fire	No fire	1.0
Large	Fire	Small	.2
	Fire	Moderate	.4
	Fire	Large	.4
	No fire	No fire	1.0

Table 11-14
Probabilities of Plant Failures for Operational Alternatives

Manual operated system	Probabilities of failure
Fire	7.58×10^{-4}
Plant failure	3.11×10^{-4}
Automatic GDS	
Fire	1.33×10^{-3}
Plant failure	6.19×10^{-4}

determine whether the power plant is operational. It is assumed that if the fires are small, they can be effectively controlled and so pose no threat to the integrity of the power plant. If the fire is moderate or large, however, the integrity of the power plant is affected and the plant fails (this may be due to heat or flame moving from the pump room to the engine room).

Based on the assumptions of the probabilistic and deterministic variables discussed above, Table 11-14 summarizes both the failure probabilities of the power plants and the conditional failures of the power plants dependent upon fire events. Though the automatic GDS is better at detecting gas leaks than are human operators, the probabilities of fires for the manual system are approximately half those of the GDS system. This is primarily the result of the limited ability to control a fire due to limited manpower. Similarly, the probabilities of plant failures for the automated system are approximately twice that of the manual system. These results should lead decision makers to reevaluate the implementation of the automatic system. This scenario exemplifies the need for closer analysis of new technology systems.

CONCLUSIONS

In traditional reliability-based studies of ships and offshore platforms, HOE is implicitly integrated into the background of accident statistics and experience on which such studies are often based. The principal focus of these studies has been the structural aspects or the equipment aspects and how design may be modified to improve reliability.

Recently we have come to recognize that we may have been working on only a small part of the problem of marine system reliability. Given that some 80 percent of major accidents can be traced directly to HOE, it seems appropriate for engineers to evaluate explicitly how marine systems and the humans that are an integral part of them from their design to their decommissioning can be better configured to improve safety.

Our research and experience indicate that the majority of high-consequence, low-probability marine accidents have one common theme: *a chain of important errors made by people in critical situations involving complex technological and organizational systems. Many of these errors involve fatigue, carelessness, negligence, short sightedness, greed, lack of training, and wishful thinking.*

The errors go beyond individuals directly involved in the incidents. In some cases, organizations provide "cultures" that invite excessive risk taking, demand superhuman performance, and develop complacency that results in reactive risk management. Shortsightedness, with a central focus on present profitability, seems to be a primary factor in such cultures. Industry, government, and society all share in providing them. This is a far cry from organizational descriptions presented by Schulman and Rochlin (this volume), but it is close to the picture painted by Hirschhorn (this volume).

In some cases, we engineer marine systems that cannot be constructed and operated as they should, so field modifications and short cuts must be developed. The engineer rarely hears about these problems until they become critically evident. People are transferred so rapidly and in some cases retired so early that there is a loss of corporate memory of these mistakes. Unnecessary complexity in systems (physical and organizational) invites errors. When we engineer overly complex systems, and place them in the hands of improperly trained, unmotivated people, we ask for the trouble we have been experiencing.

The human and organizational elements of marine systems must be engineered and designed, just as we engineer the physical elements of these systems, and each of these needs to complement the other. We must learn how to engineer systems to be more forgiving and tolerant of errors and flaws: people tolerant systems. We must honestly recognize the potential blindness produced by our pride, our enduring trait of wishful thinking, our limitations (fatigue, boredom, confusion, ignorance), our reckless ways (drug abuse, greed, lack of integrity), and the differences between what we know we should do and what we actually will do.

The HOE problem must be attacked at the level of the individual: through training, testing, motivating, and by verifying to a degree commensurate with the job to be performed and the needs for safety in the job. People must be trained in managing crisis situations in the systems they operate. Reducing complexity of tasks, improving personnel selection procedures, providing for self- and external checking, planning and scheduling to reduce time pressures and excessive fatigue, and providing positive incentives for high-quality performance can all be effective in reducing the incidence of HOE. The same problems must also be attacked at the organizational level, recognizing the important roles of organizational strategy, structure, communication, decision making, and culture in fostering the reduction of HOE.

We need to develop practical and realistic risk management procedures to integrate HOE considerations with system performance considerations. These procedures are needed to allow engineers, managers, and regulators to understand the potential nature of critical problems, how they might best be cured, and the costs and benefits of alternatives for cures. While these procedures might not be perfect, nor the data and information that is used to implement them complete, the process of performing the assessments can provide substantial benefits. The objective of the qualitative and quantitative procedures being developed in this research is not prediction; it is improved risk management of marine systems.

REFERENCES

Arrow, K. J. (1986). *Social Choice and Individual Values*. New York: Cowles Foundation and Wiley.

———— (1972). *Decision and Organization*. Amsterdam: North Holland Publications.

Bea, R. G. (1989). "Human and organizational error in reliability of coastal and ocean structures." *Proceedings of the Civil College Eminent Overseas Speaker Program*, Institution of Engineers, Australia.

Carson, W. G. (1982). *The Other Price of Britain's Oil: Safety and Control in the North Sea*. Oxford, England: Martin Robertson & Company Ltd.

Construction Industry Research and Information Association (1977). *Rationalization of Safety and Serviceability Factors in Structural Codes*. London: CIRIA Report 63.

Davidson, A. (1990). *In Wake of the* Exxon Valdez: *The Devastating Impact of the Alaska Oil Spill.* San Francisco: Sierra Club Books.

Heising, C. D., and W. S. Grenzebach (1989). "The *Ocean Ranger* oil rig disaster: A risk analysis." *Risk Analysis, 9,* (1), 55–62.

Howard, R. A. (1966). "Information value theory." *IEEE Transactions on Systems, Man, and Cybernetics, SSC-2,* (1), 22–26.

Ingles, O. G. (1985). "Human error, and its role in the philosophy of engineering." Doctoral thesis, University of New South Wales, Australia.

Kahneman, D., P. Slovic, and A. Tversky (1982). *Judgment Under Uncertainty: Heuristics and Biases.* New York: Cambridge University Press.

La Porte, T. R. (1988). High Reliability Organization Project. Berkeley: University of California.

Larocque, G. R., and K. Mudan, (1982). *Costs and Benefits of OCS Regulations: Volume 3—Preliminary Risk Analysis of Outer Continental Shelf Activities.* Cambridge, MA: Arthur D. Little, Inc.

Lord Cullen Report (1990). *The Public Inquiry into the* Piper Alpha *Disaster.* United Kingdom Department of Energy. London: HMSO Publications.

March, J. G., and H. A. Simon (1958). *Organizations.* New York: Wiley.

Melchers, R. E. (1976). *Societal Options for Assurance of Structural Performance.* London: Final Report, 11 Congr, IABSE.

——— (1987) *Structural Reliability Analysis and Prediction.* Brisbane, Australia: Ellis Horwood Limited, Halsted Press: A division of John Wiley & Sons.

Minerals Management Service OCS Report (1990). "Investigation of March 19, 1989, Fire *South Pass Block 60 Platform B* Lease OCS-G 1608." MMS 90-0016. Washington, D.C.: U.S. Department of Interior.

Moan, T. (1981). "The *Alexander Kielland* Accident." *Proceedings from the First Robert Bruce Wallace Lecture,* Department of Ocean Engineering. Boston: Massachusetts Institute of Technology.

——— (1983). "Safety of offshore structures." *Proceedings, Fourth International Conference on Applications of Statistics and Probability in Soil and Structural Engineering.*

National Bureau of Standards (1985) "Application of risk analysis to offshore oil and gas operations." *Proceedings of an International Workshop,* NSB Special Publications 695. Washington, D.C.: U.S. Department of Commerce.

National Transportation Safety Board (1987). Capsizing and Sinking of the United States Drillship *Glomar Java Sea* in the South China Sea 65 Nautical Miles South-Southwest of Hainan Island, Peoples Republic of China, October 25, 1983. Washington, D.C.: NTSB/MAR-87/02.

Nessim, M. A., and I. J. Jordan, (1985). "Models for human error reliability." *Journal of Structural Engineering, 111,* 6, 1358–1376.

Noreng, Ø. (1980). *The Oil Industry and Government Strategy in the North Sea.* London: Croom Helm.

Nowak, A. S. (1986). "Modeling human error in structural design and construction." *Proceedings of a Workshop Sponsored by the National Science Foundation.* New York: American Society of Civil Engineers.

Offshore Certification Bureau (1988). "Comparative safety evaluation of arrangements for accommodating personnel offshore." Report OTN-88-175.

Panel on Human Error in Merchant Marine Safety (1976). "Human Error in Merchant

Marine Safety." Maritime Transportation Research Board Report. Washington, D.C.: National Academy of Sciences.

Paté-Cornell, M.E. (1986). "Warning systems in risk management." *Risk Analysis*, 6, 2, 223–234.

————(1990). "Organizational aspects of engineering system safety: The case of offshore platforms." *Science, 250*, 1210–1217.

Paté-Cornell, M. E. and R. G. Bea, (1989). "Organizational aspects of reliability management: Design, construction, and operation of offshore platforms." Research Report No. 89-1. Department of Industrial Engineering and Engineering Management. Palo Alto: Stanford University.

Paté-Cornell, M. E., and J. P. Seawell (1988). "Engineering reliability: The organizational link." *Proceedings of the ASCE Specialty Conference on Probabilistic Mechanics and Structural and Geotechnical Safety*, Blacksburg, Virginia.

Perrow, C. (1984). *Normal Accidents: Living with High Risk Technologies.* New York: Basic Books, Inc.

Reason, J. (1990). *Human Error.* New York: Cambridge University Press.

Reid, S. G. (1989). "Guidelines for risk based decision-making." Investigation Report No. S726, School of Civil and Mining Engineering. Sydney: The University of Sydney.

Roberts, K. H. (1992): "Top Management and effective leadership in high technology." In L. Gomez-Mehia and M. W. Lawless, (eds.), Vol. III. *Top Management and Effective Leadership in High Technology Firms.* Greenwich, CT: JAI Press.

Roberts, K. H., D. M. Rousseau, and T. R. La Porte (in press). "The culture of high reliability: Quantitative and qualitative assessment aboard nuclear powered aircraft carriers." *Journal of High Technology Management Research.*

Royal Commission on *Ocean Ranger* Marine Disaster (1985). Report of the Royal Commission of the *Ocean Ranger* Marine Disaster. Ottawa, Ontario, Canada.

Royal Norwegian Council for Scientific & Industrial Research (1979). Risk Assessment Report of the Norwegian Offshore Petroleum Activities. Oslo, Norway.

Shachter, R. D. (1986). "Evaluating influence diagrams." *Operations Research, 34*, 6, 1210–1222.

United Kingdom Department of Energy (1988). "*Piper Alpha* Technical Investigation: Further Report." London: Crown.

Veritec (1988). *The Worldwide Offshore Accident Data Bank (WOAD) Annual Reports through 1988.* Oslo, Norway.

Weick, K. E. (1987). "Organizational culture as a source of high reliability." *California Management Review, 29*, 112–127.

Wenk, E., Jr. (1986). *Tradeoffs: Imperatives of Choice in a High-Tech World.* Baltimore: The Johns Hopkins University Press.

12

Bligh Reef Dead Ahead: The Grounding of the Exxon Valdez

KARLENE H. ROBERTS
University of California, Berkeley

WILLIAM H. MOORE
University of California, Berkeley

For biographical information about Karlene H. Roberts, see page 1.

For biographical information about William H. Moore, see page 199.

The authors thank various members of the United States Coast Guard and the Exxon Shipping Company for their help and informative comments. We also thank Walter Parker and Edward Wenk, Alaska Oil Spills Commission; and William Shrenk, Natural Resources Defense Council.

*L*ike Meyer and Starbuck, Hirschhorn, and Weick's contributions to this volume, this chapter tells a story of organizational failure. It is an unfolding analysis of management processes operating with pilotage, at the Coast Guard, aboard the *Exxon Valdez*, and in the Exxon Shipping Company before and at the time of the *Exxon Valdez* misfortune. The analysis is based on a review of the literature and on numerous interviews with marine industry experts. While much discussion of the grounding has focused on crew activities prior to and during the accident, it is generally agreed that the mishap was the result of a number of forces coming together in a disastrous way just after midnight on March 24, 1989. The ship's course is diagrammed in Figure 12-1.

When the *Exxon Valdez* hit Bligh Reef, the vessel was holed in eight of eleven cargo compartments and two ballast tanks. Most of the cargo loss occurred during the first eight hours after the grounding. Thirty minutes after the grounding, 115,000 of the ship's 1,263,000 barrels were lost. A total of 258,000 barrels, or eleven million gallons, were lost in all.[1]

Ironically just three months before this accident, the only other major spill in the 12 years of the Trans-Alaska Pipeline operation occurred when the *Thompson Pass* released 1700 barrels of oil. More than 8800 successful oil shipments had passed through Prince William Sound (PWS) without serious incident by March 24, 1989 (Alaska Oil Spill Commission, personal communication).[2]

One of the requirements of the Trans-Alaska Pipeline Authorization Act (TAPS) of 1973 was to establish and operate a Vessel Traffic Service (VTS) for PWS. The PWS VTS was the only federally mandated VTS in the country. The Port and Tanker Safety Act of 1978 authorized operations, surveillance and communication, routing systems, and fairways for supervising vessels in transit, and gave the Coast Guard the authority to establish routing schemes and specific times of entry, movement, and departure.

Unlike other VTSs across the country, Valdez VTS personnel could be utilized in non-VTS duties at the discretion of the Commanding Officer (CO). In a letter to the CO of the U.S. Coast Guard (USCG) headquarters in 1985, he stated, "What MSO [Marine Safety Office] Valdez does is much larger than just having a few people watch radar screens in the least-trafficked, yet fully federally mandated, VTS in the country." Watchstanding was reduced at the same time that the potential for problems due to ice floes in the sound increased. Procedures for certain eventualities were not well spelled out, or if they were spelled out were not implemented.

The VTS consisted of a Vessel Traffic Center (VTC), a radar surveillance system, and a communication system. The VTC was manned 24 hours around

---

[1] This information is from the National Transportation Safety Board (NTSB) report. However, L. Z. Katcharian, Marine Accident Investigator for the Marine Accident Division of the NTSB, provided the following figures in his report to the NTSB, dated May 8, 1989. "The vessel lost about 250,000 barrels (10,400,000 gallons) of its 1,264,164 barrels (53,094,510 gallons) of cargo of North Slope crude oil.

[2] Two to three major ships pass into and out of PWS daily.

the clock by two watchstanders (one radar watchstander and one radio watchstander). The radar watchstanders' responsibilities were to maintain vessel positions, while the radio watchstanders established and monitored radio contact for PWS. The radar surveillance system had initially been able to maintain contact with vessels from Port Valdez to areas south of Bligh Reef. Three hours before entering PWS, vessels were required to give VTS general information about vessel name, position, estimated time of arrival (ETA) to navigation in the VTS area, speed, cargo type, towing assistance, vessel impairments, and additional requested information. Once in VTS waters, vessels were required to report at various reporting points, and when changing speed and crossing and clearing the Traffic Separation Scheme (TSS).

The VTS was reorganized in 1982, making four of the five watch supervisors department heads who had little to do with supervising watches. In 1986, the CO of MSO Valdez proposed that the Marine Safety Office be downgraded to the Marine Safety Detachment (MSD). The proposal eliminated five VTS officer watchstander billets. In 1987 the watches were discontinued and replaced by a Command Duty Officer (CDO) or Officer of the Day (OOD). The CDO was not required to be at the VTS during routine vessel transits.[3]

In 1988 the VTS lost five billets. As a result, remaining personnel took on additional functions that had little to do with VTS, and by default the senior watchstander became responsible for supervising the day-to-day operations of the VTS. This person worked days and stood watches when anyone called in sick. Several of the OODs were enlisted personnel, junior to the civilian watchstanders they supervised. On the day of the accident only one OOD was a qualified watchstander. The station OOD on duty prior to the accident had never qualified as a watchstander. Reduction in personnel may have caused communication between the VTC and senior MSO/VTS personnel to decline. No officer's primary duty was to be in charge of the VTS.

Despite the fact that ships regularly deviated from the TSS, the CO of MSO Valdez reported to the National Transportation and Safety Board (NTSB) (Woody, 1989) that if a vessel knew its position and was maneuvering, no further radio contact was required. He continued, "There is no good reason for a ship to deviate from the TSS; a vessel requesting deviation is requesting something out of the norm." VTC watchstanders do not have the authority to allow vessels to leave the lanes, and if a vessel requests deviation the request is forwarded to the Operations Officer (OO) who forwards it to the CO or Executive Officer (XO) for a reply. Neither the CO nor the OO appeared to be aware that vessels regularly departed the TSS

In 1980, after the *Prince William Sound* lost power in the Sound, the Coast Guard recommended installing reinforced tow lines on tankers and requiring tugboats to escort them to Hinchinbrook Island. The lines were in-

---

[3] However, it was required that he be contacted in the event that vessels deviated from the TSS. The CDO could be contacted 24 hours a day if conditions arose in which vessels needed to deviate from the traffic scheme.

stalled. In 1981, James Woodle, the CO of Valdez, recommended that the Coast Guard radar system be improved in response to the break up of the Columbia Glacier (Davidson, 1990). Nothing was done. According to the NTSB Report (Woody, 1989) in 1984 the Coast Guard requested the installation of an additional radar site on either Glacier or Bligh Island. In 1984, the Coast Guard and oil companies met to talk about the increasing ice. In neither case was anything done. For a time the oil companies ordered their vessels to operate at reduced speed or only during daylight. In 1986, the Coast Guard issued a series of recommendations and directives that made pilotage so complicated that no one knew what was required (Davidson, 1990, p. 72).

A study done after the accident showed that the existing radar was incapable of reliable radar coverage of Valdez Arm. The number one (master) radar that synthetically displayed the TSS boundary lines was burned out. The Coast Guard was warned in 1984 that the system would begin deteriorating in the next two years without attention. After the accident, the OO testified that he noted its deterioration over the last two years. The contractor did not keep the system well maintained, and as a result it was inoperable up to 28 percent of the time. Between 1981 and 1984, 18.9 percent of the vessels transiting the VTS area deviated from the TSS because of ice.[4]

The *Exxon Valdez's* bridge complement consisted of four deck officers (captain, chief mate, second mate, and third mate), and two able bodied seamen (ABs, one a helmsman and the other a lookout). The mates and able bodied seamen stood two four-hour watches each day with eight hours off in between. The day before the accident, Captain Hazelwood was off the ship while it was loading crude oil in Valdez. By his own confirmation he was drinking that day. The NTSB report (Woody, 1989) states that extrapolating from a blood test taken ten hours after the accident, his blood alcohol level would have had to be approximately 0.285 at the time he boarded the ship. A person boarding the ship this inebriated would have shown some evidence of physical impairment or would have needed some assistance. Additionally, a cab driver and an Alyeska (oil-company consortium) guard interviewed by the Board investigators reported that none of the *Exxon Valdez* crew members returning to the vessel were "under the influence of alcohol." According to Keeble (1991), no one on the ship observed any deficiency in Captain Hazelwood's behavior. The blood alcohol test gave a reading of 0.061, or a little more than over half of the drunk driving limit of 1.0 in Alaska and 50 percent higher than the 0.04 percent limit set by the Coast Guard for seamen operating ships.

---

[4] In August 1984, a meeting was called of operators, Coast Guard, state pilots, and Alyeska to discuss ice conditions. A Coast Guard representative mentioned their concern for ice conditions in PWS, though representatives at the meeting tried to downplay the problem (NTSB Factual Reports—Ice Conditions, p. 226). An Exxon representative said he was confident of the abilities of the masters of their vessels to handle the situation and would like to see operations continue as they were. An Arco representative agreed, saying he believed in preliminary planning reports but saw no need for further controls. Pilots concurred that masters would not transit if they felt the ice was too dangerous.

The ship left port at 2054. Federal and Alaska state law require that ships be under the control of a federally licensed pilot when transiting in U.S. pilotage waters (inside the three-mile territorial seas). In 1977, the state pilot association established a pilot station at Cape Hinchinbrook, using a converted fishing vessel, the *Blue Moon.* In 1980 the *Blue Moon* foundered. Due to the dangers involved in embarking and disembarking pilots in the outer Prince William Sound, the pilot station was moved to Rocky Point at Valdez Arm. The Alaska Board of Marine Pilots eliminated the state requirement for state pilotage between Cape Hinchinbrook and the pilot station at Rocky Point. The Federal Pilotage requirements still were in effect, though there were no transport pilots between Cape Hinchinbrook and Rocky Point. This created few problems since most trade masters held federal pilotage between Cape Hinchinbrook and Rocky Point.

In June 1985, proposed changes in pilotage regulations were introduced. The Coast Guard reduced the areas of required pilotage. In September 1986, the Coast Guard began to issue requests for pilotage on a case-by-case basis for tank vessel masters without pilotage endorsements. The major change was in the requirement of two-mile visibility in the sound with potential reassessment of this proposal during adverse weather conditions. The night of the *Exxon Valdez* accident a state pilot was aboard the ship until it reached Rocky Point. During the time he was aboard, Captain Hazelwood was off the bridge for approximately one hour and thirty five minutes. The pilot smelled alcohol on his breath.

Captain Hazelwood decided to take the ship out of the outgoing TSS and into the incoming TSS to avoid ice.[5] This was not an unusual course, and Hazelwood informed the Coast Guard that he was making this deviation. Only a short time before, the *Arco Juneau* had taken a similar course out of the Sound. Sylvia Gil and John Rush were the first to see *Exxon Valdez* on Bligh Reef. Their house at Ellamar overlooks Bligh Reef. According to John Rush, "Actually . . . there was no surprise to it whatsoever. We knew it was a question of time. They've been cutting that corner for years." (Keeble, 1991, p. 162) One speculation is that by cutting the corner out of the sound, tankers could cut a half hour from their exit time and perhaps four hours from their sailing time.

Shortly prior to his relief at 2355, the helmsman responded to an order from the master to sail the ship 180 degrees and put it on automatic pilot. Helmsman Harry Claar was puzzled by this order. He didn't check it with the master. The third mate was unaware that the ship was on automatic pilot. For the captain to put the ship on automatic pilot in confined waters and not tell the third mate was inconsistent with normal practice. The master left the bridge but not before asking the third mate, Gregory Cousins, if he felt comfortable

---

[5] This decision was probably made to increase reliable performance. Often decision makers are unable or unwilling to examine the unintended unsafe consequences of decisions made with the goal of increasing safety.

Figure 12-1
Trackline of Exxon Valdez

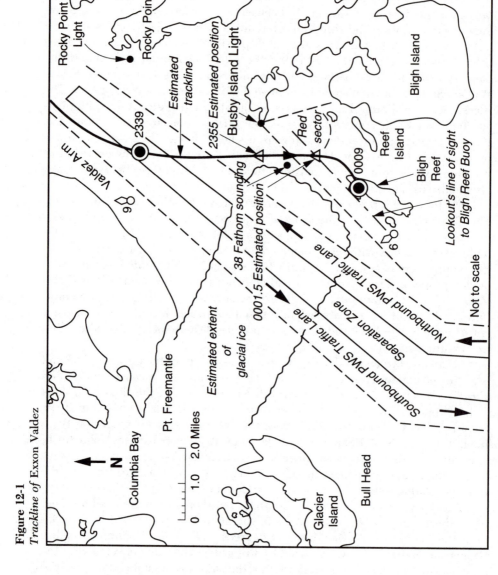

Source: National Transportation Safety Board (1990): "Grounding of the U. S. Tankship *Exxon-Valdez* on Bligh Reef, Prince William Sound, near Valdez, Alaska, March 24, 1989." PB90-916405 MTSB/Mar-90/04.

sailing the ship under these conditions. Cousins replied that he did. The master left the bridge at 2352.

At 2347, the ship left the outbound (TSS) going into the inbound lane to avoid the ice. At 2355, the helmsman was relieved by Robert Kagan (Davidson, 1990). The ship was on "load program up," which meant it was increasing its speed while exiting the harbor. One account has it that the *Exxon Valdez* was traveling at 12 knots and on automatic pilot just prior to hitting Bligh Reef (Davidson, 1990).[6] At his relief, the helmsman reported to the third mate that the ship was on automatic pilot. The third mate did not discuss the reason for the automatic pilot with the master. Keeble (1990) states that Cousins took the ship off automatic pilot when Kagan relieved Claar as helmsman.

At 2355, the third mate plotted the ship as 1.1 miles from Busby Island. Before midnight, the AB reported to the third mate a red light flashing every five seconds on the starboard side of the ship.[7] Kagan acknowledged this and stated he knew the light to be Bligh Reef, Light 6. The third mate ordered a right ten degree rudder, but the vessel did not move to this position. There was a six-minute delay before the third mate and helmsman responded to the fact that the ship did not begin to turn.

> The frequent fixing of the vessel's position could have taken a substantial amount of the third mate's time and would have limited his ability to concentrate on other important functions, such as watching for ice and conning the vessel. Conning also requires careful supervision of the helmsman. Under normal conditions, when a master or a pilot is conning a vessel, the watch officer assists by carefully observing the actions of the helmsman in response to orders from the master or pilot. This enables the officer conning the vessel to concentrate on observing and directing the vessel's movements. In this instance, the helmsman had limited steering experience and required additional supervision. The master was aware of the helmsman's limitations and should have considered them before leaving the bridge (National Transportation Research Board, 1989, p. 115).

Watch Condition C (Exxon Bridge Organizational Manual) states that two officers must be on the bridge during this transit. The third mate testified that normally two officers served on the navigation watch when Exxon vessels were maneuvering in confined or congested waters.[7]

About this time, the AB reported the light flashing every four seconds. The third mate ordered a right twenty-degree rudder. Moving at twelve knots while the ship was still engaged in maneuvering evolutions to avoid ice violated

---

[6] According to Keeble (1990), this ship maneuvers best at eleven knots. According to Exxon Shipping Company, sea speed for this ship is sixteen knots.

[7] All mariners know the phrase *red light returning*. It means always keep red buoys and red markers on the right when returning to port, and keep them on the left when departing. There is an exception to this. At a given point a ship might find a red light on its right, by virtue of its distance and angle from the marker.

prudent ship handling practices while it increased the risk of damage to the ship if an ice floe had been struck. Cousins then ordered a hard right rudder.

When the ship hit the reef, the third mate ordered a hard left rudder to get the vessel to stop swinging to the right and prevent the stern from swinging around. The ship had clearly skidded into Bligh Reef. The helmsman was confused about some aspects of the situation. According to Keeble (1991), when testifying at the master's trial the helmsman "would blurt out almost endearingly, 'I get so confused.' " (p. 41) He also reported that the third mate was panicky. The chief engineer stopped the engines at 0020. It is not clear from the NTSB report what time the ship hit the reef. According to Keeble (1991), it was probably eleven or twelve minutes after midnight.

Kagan obtained the unrated Able Bodied Seaman (AB) rating in 1981. Since that time, however, he had worked about seven and a half months documented time as an AB. He worked primarily as an ordinary seaman in unrated positions. No performance appraisals referred to an AB specific job. In 1986, the performance evaluator noted severe deficiencies in his ship handling skills. None of the performance evaluations were good.

The third mate held a second mate's license and first sailed as the third mate on an Exxon tanker in January 1987. He had sailed on five tank vessels owned by the company and had been employed by Exxon for nine years. According to Davidson (1990), he had completed approximately eighteen voyages in and out of Valdez, sailing in both unlicensed and licensed categories. At the time of the grounding, he had approximately 199 days of at-sea experience as a third mate. According to Keeble, Cousins made the passage through Prince William Sound twenty-six to thirty times, three of them on the *Exxon Valdez*.

The night before, Cousins slept from 0100 to 0720; after lunch he took a cat nap (1300 to 1350), relieved the chief mate for supper, and worked through to the grounding. The situation is further complicated because the chief mate had worked the entire time of the loading, was asleep, and was unavailable as an additional resource.

The third mate decided not to call his relief, the chief mate, until after they cleared the ice.[8] The third mate determined there was 0.9 mile between Busby Island and the ice floe and felt he could pass around the ice. He relied considerably on the radar, but did not correlate radar information with the navigation charts through position fixing. The submerged reef was not displayed on the radar.

The lack of vigilance with which the VTS handled operations the night of the accident is another factor behind the misfortune. Only one civilian watchstander and one enlisted radioman were on duty. But the accountability and

---

[8] The error might have been detected through the watch relief procedures. However, Keeble (1991) noted that crew members were attempting to help each other out by standing longer watches so their co-workers could get some sleep. Captain Hazelwood, himself, planned to take an extra watch.

responsibility rested with people who were not there. Neither the CO nor the XO were at the VTS. The VTC manual requires the watchstander to advise the OOD when a vessel deviates due to ice in the lanes. The 1600 to 2400 watchstander failed to do this. He said he believed the radar did not detect the *Exxon Valdez* because the radar was not working properly. However, he did not report a malfunction to his relief or to the electronics technician on duty. The watchstander's relief came on at 2333.

Thus, both the VTS and *Exxon Valdez* watches changed at approximately the same time. Neither watchstander knew that the *Exxon Valdez* had altered course from 200 degrees to 180 degrees. The *Exxon Valdez* was lost on the radar but could have been picked up. The 0000–0800 watchstander said he did not try to do this because he had been told by the other watchstander that the *Exxon Valdez* was no longer visible on radar. At the time of the accident, the watchstander was away getting a cup of coffee. That the radar was operating appropriately is evidenced by the fact that the watchstander had no difficulty detecting the grounded ship.

The ship previously leaving the port reported heavy ice to the VTS, but the VTS saw no reason to report this to the *Exxon Valdez* or to more carefully monitor it. At about 1930, a passenger ship approached Valdez. Its captain said the ice was some of the worst he had ever seen, and he reduced speed. He did not report this to the VTS. At 1930, the outbound *Arco Juneau* reported ice in the TSS. The VTC operator said he was concerned about the heavy ice reported by the *Arco Juneau*, but that factor did not motivate him to have the ship report its position more frequently, nor did he report that to the *Exxon Valdez*. Both ships transited during the day and neither had as far outside the TSS to go as the *Exxon Valdez* because when the latter ship transited, the ice was much further to the northeast.

The *Exxon Valdez* remained on course 180 degrees for nearly 18 minutes. The VTC operator had ample time to call the vessel and ascertain its intentions. Any inquiry from the VTC regarding the vessel's intentions probably would have alerted the third mate to turn earlier or apply more rudder. The VTS communication system failed to meet the Coast Guard's requirement of 99.9 percent operational status. During the event of March 23, the Naked Island and Cape Hinchinbrook remote communication sites were inoperable. The system was old, requests for money had been denied, and the harsh Alaskan climate degrades the system easily. At 0027, the master let the VTS know the ship had run aground. Only then did the VTS watchstander know it had gone aground. He then adjusted the radar and picked up this information.

At 0035, the master ordered the main engine restarted. According to Keeble (1991), he gave the following orders: "Half ahead, full ahead, slow ahead, dead slow ahead, stop." A number of accounts stated that he tried to get the ship off the reef, which might have resulted in its capsizing. These orders are inconsistent with that theory. According to Keeble (1990), the captain stabilized the ship and protected his crew, and his actions were the best that could possibly have been taken. According to NTSB documentation, the record fully supports the fact that had the master gotten the ship off the reef it would have capsized. Other evidence suggests it might not have (Brady, 1960).

Chief Mate Kunkel was awakened by the grounding. He went to the cargo control room to assess damage. He determined that the stress on the ship exceeded acceptable limits and took this information to the master, arriving on the bridge at 0030 or 0035. Between 0035 and 0100, Kunkel performed further analyses and concluded that if the vessel were not supported by the reef it would capsize. He relayed this information to the master. At 0107, the master was still advising the Coast Guard that the ship's stability was acceptable. At 0141, the engine was shut down.

Some of Exxon's policies contributed to the accident, while others were efforts to avoid such accidents. Two federal statutes cover Exxon's behavior. One says that an officer cannot take charge of the deck watch on a vessel when leaving a port unless he has been off duty for at least six of the twelve hours immediately before leaving. Another statute says a licensed individual or seaman is not required to work more than eight hours a day except for safety related functions.[9] Apparently Exxon had no provision for giving six hours of rest to any deck officer before getting underway.

Manning schedules were conceived when tankers were making longer journeys, thus allowing sea time for both maintenance and catching up on rest. Crew member tours were lengthened from sixty to ninety days. During 1988's senior officer's conferences, Exxon management discussed demanning with senior officers. It was recognized that a growing number of companies operated their vessels with significantly fewer personnel than Exxon. Exxon provided data to the NTSB that reduced manning was associated with better, not poorer crew performance. More recent study shows no negative impact on safety by demanning practices within the maritime industry (National Research Council, 1990).

Exxon stated, "It is our conclusion that, when addressing improved safety performance, management focus, leadership and effective supervision are more critical elements than crew size." In 1986, the company instituted a safety initiative: "As part of this effort, management teams, frequently accompanied by officials of the unlicensed union, visited every ship in the fleet to train personnel in new safety concepts. This was supplemented by one full day of safety training provided to all senior officers during each of the next two fleet management conferences. . . ."

However, there is no evidence that Exxon had policies or procedures to compensate for the risks of using smaller crews. No supervisory training recognized such factors as tiredness, social isolation, longer hours at sea, and so on. There was no company program to monitor officer's work in excess of eight

---

[9] The average workday is about ten hours, which includes voluntary overtime.

hours a day. There is evidence that officers do deck work that unlicensed workers did previously. Exxon continued to increase crew work load after the accident, and plans to further reduce crew size and to lower qualifications.

The policies Exxon had in updating fleet and reducing crew were consistent with those of the industry. Exxon's Seaman's Union officers expressed concern that maintenance was regularly deferred on the ships because of insufficient manning levels and because of Exxon's attempt to convince the Coast Guard that existing manning levels included too many crew by not authorizing overtime.

In June 1988, Frank Iarossi (then president of Exxon Shipping Company) presented a paper titled "Surrendering the Memories" in which he stated that it was Exxon's policy to reduce its standard crew compliment to sixteen by 1990. He noted that other ships (mostly foreign flag) successfully operated at such levels. The paper makes little mention of considerations of ship safety and crew fatigue, and it focuses solely on economic issues. The NTSB came to possess three memos to Exxon Shipping Company masters ordering them to reduce overtime purposefully to satisfy Coast Guard overtime concerns and to argue better for reducing manning levels.

The company's written policies about alcohol and drug abuse were not taken very seriously. The policy instructed supervisors to report to the medical department employees whose performance was unsatisfactory due to alcohol use. Crew members were not to perform job duties within four hours of having a drink. Hazelwood entered an alcohol rehabilitation program in 1985; the company learned about this when his supervisor tried to contact him. No supervision was involved in making sure that he continued with some sort of support group. The NTSB concluded that Hazelwood should have been confined to shore duty until there was ample proof that this problem was under control. His performance evaluation of 1988 was more than satisfactory.

Exxon had fleet managers and port captains (later, ship group coordinators) who monitored Hazelwood in port. It was stated that Hazelwood was also monitored at social functions. The company was unaware of the revocation of his driver's license in 1985 and 1988. No attempt was made by the Exxon personnel to visit Hazelwood when he was in Valdez. The company had alcohol testing equipment aboard the *Exxon Valdez* but had no indication the master had been drinking. Hence, no testing was ordered.

Exxon's performance appraisal system appeared to leave something to be desired. Annual performance appraisals for the master are not available for every year. The company made no statement about how it follows up on appraisals. Are they only done for salary increases or are they done as part of a larger performance improvement effort? Does anyone provide feedback to the person evaluated? A number of statements about Hazelwood's performance lead to the conclusion that he had difficulties managing people. These difficulties emerged as early as 1974 (NTSB). One could ignore one or two such statements, but they appear repeatedly through the years.

OVERALL ANALYSIS

In general, the *Exxon Valdez* collision looks like a story of organizational atrophy (system entropy) over time. The pilots reduced piloting requirements, the ship operated with two few officers on the bridge, and the Coast Guard had reduced force in the VTS over the years. While the accident lends itself to analysis along many different lines (e.g., failure to recognize the importance of the interdependent nature of organizations simultaneously working with complex technologies, lack of on-line information processing with real time feedback, and so forth), we highlight only three issues here: the operational culture of the participating organizations, training, and requisite complexity.

Culture

The culture of any organization is often subtle and often operates just below the surface of the everyday consciousness of its employees. As pointed out by Koch (this volume), organizations in which safe operations are mandatory in the prevention of behaviors with catastrophic consequences must develop cultures in which sensitivity to safety awareness and safety issues is paramount. It appears that the state pilots, the Coast Guard, and the Exxon Shipping Company were all characterized by weak cultures with regard to safety. Schulman (this volume) describes how safety-related interactions and behaviors are constantly renegotiated in a high-reliability organization. Over time, any organization moves to states of lesser organization unless this occurs.

In this situation, such renegotiations failed to occur. Over time, the pilots had reduced pilotage requirements for PWS, and there did not appear to be agreed-upon procedures for a pilot to engage in when he confronted a master who had been drinking. Pilot associations could develop standard procedures for such an event (including reporting it to the Coast Guard and the shipping company). The relationship established between pilots and masters since the days of Henry VIII does not favor such activity and should be re-examined.

The same weak culture with regard to safety appeared on both the *Exxon Valdez* and in the Exxon Shipping Company. In hindsight, one can say that the *Thompson Pass* incident three months earlier should have acted as a wake-up call. Such a response could prevent worse accidents in the future. The U.S. Navy exhibited this kind of response with its one-day standdown to focus on safety in 1989 after the occurrence of five serious accidents in a very short period of time. While that standdown may have been largely politically driven, it no doubt focused attention on safety for Navy personnel.

Greater attention to safety, at the possible expense of profit, would have been difficult to obtain at Exxon. First, the most serious accident the oil industry had previously incurred was the *Amaco Cadiz* spill in March 1978, a considerably less costly misfortune. That, in itself, likely influenced management's perception of the seriousness of tanker spills and influenced what it felt it had to be ready to deal with.

Second, the company, indeed the maritime industry, is in the grips of discussion about demanning. Demanning poses a tension against building in redundancies that can spot and prevent some kinds of catastrophes. When an organization suspects that the nature of error in it is such that the next error may be the last trial in a trial-and-error sequence, it engages in activities to avoid error, one of which is usually redundancy. If one has redundancy in observation and thinking, one can rely less on constraining written procedures and more on local expertise. Some organizations require high degrees of both, such as the nuclear power plant discussed by Schulman (this volume).

Another aspect of the culture is the development of corporate and operational goals that are synchronous with regard to maintaining safety. A situation in which bridge watchstanders are rewarded (if only in terms of having their buddies similarly help them later) for standing longer watches and helping shipmates get additional sleep is possibly consistent with a profit goal and is inconsistent with a safety goal. The goal of an alcohol-free culture is inconsistent with lackadaisical compliance procedures. Cultures take a long time to build (Schein, 1990; Trice and Beyer, 1984) and organizations that suddenly can become volatile need to think about what they have built and whether their cultures are sufficient for the safety task.

The Coast Guard culture, too, seems to have shifted over the years. Perhaps the years of refusals of requests to replace and repair equipment alone were enough to send a strong message to the Valdez VTS about the Coast Guard's and maybe its financial underwriter's (the Congress) expectations of its operations. When staffs are reduced and equipment is allowed to deteriorate, employees cannot avoid having the feeling that they and their mission do not have top priority. Allowing shift changes at the same time as they occurred in the organizations the VTS serviced, and having personnel with authority and responsibility for deviations in the TSS completely unhooked from the TSS decision-making process, are two examples of a system that can only respond to a potential disaster with a loose confederation.

Training

Training is an issue closely related to culture and is often used to stamp into employees the desired culture of an organization. The first aspect of the *Exxon Valdez* situation that strikes one is the apparent overall lack of emergency simulations or drills. Drills must include all parties so that in the event of a true surprise (and surprises will always happen) the parties will have worked out the relationships among themselves. Such drills must be conducted frequently enough so that turnover across the organizations does not erase all organizational memory, and so that new responses can be devised for changing technologies and environmental circumstances.

Though not a perfect model, one potential prototype is followed by some nuclear power plants. Every two years, the Pacific Gas and Electric Company (PG&E) conducts a full-scale drill for a problem at its nuclear power plant at

Diablo Canyon in California. Representatives from state agencies, the parent company, Diablo Canyon, the city of San Luis Obispo, local fire departments, and others participate. Each time the drill is conducted, a different scenario is presented. In many respects no simulation can appropriately map an accident because a day has to be decided upon to conduct the drill, and adrenalin may not be flowing. However, people play their own roles from the locations in which they would be at the time of an accident (i.e., San Francisco, Diablo Canyon, Sacramento, etc.). This procedure at least recognizes the importance of agency interdependence in case of an accident. When asked why such drills are not conducted more frequently, company representatives state that the cost is prohibitive.

Participation in such a drill is one way to ascertain an approximate hierarchy across agencies for decision making and control. In drills, players can work these things out, and they may discover what information, authority, responsibility, and materials they lack in order to do their jobs in an emergency.

As well as being a device to work out relationships, simulation is about the only kind of training that simultaneously involves all possible participants in emergency responses. Following simulations, written training materials can be sent to all participants. While our analysis here only includes the Coast Guard, the pilots, and the Exxon Shipping Company, in reality the situation included many more players who should also be included in simulation training. In this situation, we see no evidence of training in emergency response.

While system-wide training is important, so, too, is individual training. Here, if the Coast Guard thought it was important for watchstanders to check on traffic frequently, to keep records of traffic moving into and out of the TSS, and so on, it either failed to train or to motivate the watchstanders to do so. Similarly, while the Exxon Shipping Company stated that leadership and supervision were more important than crew size in maintaining safe operations, and indicated that it trained crews aboard its ships, either the training was insufficient, or inappropriate motivators produced the conditions that led to the events of March 24. Performance evaluations are often used to identify training needs. In this case, it was noted that Hazelwood had some difficulties managing people. These difficulties might have been corrected with appropriate training. The helmsman also had deficiencies in doing his job and had been assigned mostly nonrated jobs by the company. The combination of few redundancies and skills deficiencies on the bridge contributed to the situation.

Requisite Complexity[10]

Perrow (1984) discusses tight coupling as a major factor in "normal accidents." Normal accidents are events brought on in systems by tight coupling and complex interactions that cause enormous damage. Perrow discusses the im-

---

[10]Our thanks to Karl Weick for his inputs to this section.

portance of tight coupling in creating such accidents. Here it appears we have a disaster *without* tight coupling and complex interactions. Weick (1987) discusses the importance of the requisite variety of an organization matching the requisite variety of its environment in highly reliable organizations. This appears to be a situation in which the requisite variety of the organizations involved did not match the requisite variety of the situation that required managing.

Both the shiphandling requirements and the nature of the environment prescribed the use of a more tightly coupled system in which players in various organizations recognize their interdependence with one another. An under-elaborated mechanistic, nondifferentiated system; rather than a fluid, changing, organic, organizational system; was put in place to respond to a fluid, unstable, and complex environment (Burns and Stalker, 1961).

The ship's crew were only loosely coupled with one another. The master was away from the bridge when the accident happened and the three watchstanders on the bridge were only loosely interconnected. Tight interconnections would have been represented by continuous feedback and checking with one another about the meaning of orders, placement of warning lights, and other factors.

The ship's crew was only loosely connected with the pilot, who apparently spotted a danger signal and failed to raise a question about it on the ship. The pilot, the Coast Guard, and the Exxon Shipping Company were also only loosely, if at all, connected with one another.

Coast Guard officers and watchstanders were only loosely connected with one another, as evidenced by the fact that the people with authority and accountability for ship activities were not at the VTS, and the two watchstanders at the VTS and their shift replacements did not exchange important information about ship traffic and ice floe conditions. A further disconnect took place when one watchstander left the VTS to get coffee at the time of the accident.

Exxon Shipping Company policies, too, were in a state of disconnect. Its drug and alcohol policies were apparently only casually monitored. The company's performance appraisal system appeared to be largely independent of how it managed employees. Whatever the training of shipboard personnel was seemed either largely disconnected from behavior, or perhaps reinforced the very behaviors that occurred on the bridge.

CONCLUSIONS

Many of the issues discussed in this volume are relevant when one must consider the prevention of accidents such as occurred to the *Exxon Valdez*. As indicated previously, both Koch (this volume) and Schulman (this volume) emphasize the development and nurturance of safety cultures in organizations in which errors can lead to catastrophic outcomes.

Organizations can apply the theoretical perspectives offered by Rochlin (this volume) and Creed et al. (this volume) in answering their own questions about the degree to which performance is guided by some underlying understanding of what the organization wishes to accomplish. Does the organization have a theory about what constitutes reliability (Rochlin), and about the appropriate way for it to view and improve its effectiveness (Creed et al.)?

It appears that linkages within and, surely, between organizations in this situation contributed to the accident. Hirschhorn (this volume) alerts us to the importance of building a system in which people can act in a healthy manner.

Foushee and Lauber (this volume), Weick (this volume), and Eisenhardt (this volume) all suggest that in addition to system characteristics, the cognitions, actions, and interactions of the organization's members must be examined and thought about. If people carry inappropriate cognitions (as perhaps the bridge team did), the probability is higher than an accident will occur than it is if they have correct mental representations of their situations (Weick and Daft, 1983). People perform best when the glue of social interaction plays a hefty role in their organizations (Schulman, this volume; Foushee and Lauber, this volume). Trusted counselors (Eisenhardt, this volume) may also play a key role in organizational action. Basically, pilots and VTSs are the trusted counselors of the maritime industry. However, they can only serve this role in a limited capacity, and in this case the VTS was absent from service.

As pointed out by Meyer and Starbuck (this volume), organizations' actions and inactions are heavily tied to their political systems. Management would do well to assess these systems carefully because it may be, as Creed et. al. speculate, that if technologically advanced organizations are to operate safely and reliably in uncertain environments, they must minimize political activity so the organization is not overwhelmed by political behavior when it needs to attend to potentially very damaging activities. In this case, it is impossible to know the degree to which political behaviors may have influenced field operations.

Finally, several basic research programs that model risk are alive and well in various industries (Bea and Moore, this volume; Paté-Cornell, 1990, among others). While such research is useful in identifying causal factors in accidents, one should not just complacently use the results of such work. Users need to think about whether the weight given various factors is appropriate to their situations and whether the models they use are sufficiently inclusive.

REFERENCES

Brady, E. M. (1960). *Marine Salvage Operations*. Centerville, MD: Cornell Maritime Press.

Burns, T., and G. M. Stalker (1961). *The Management of Innovation*. London: Tavistock.

Davidson, A. (1990). *In the Wake of the Exxon Valdez*. San Francisco: Sierra Club.

Keeble, J. (1991). *Out of the Channel: The Exxon Valdez Oil Spill in Prince William Sound*. New York: HarperCollins.

Davidson, A. (1990). *In the Wake of the Exxon Valdez*. San Francisco: Sierra Club.

Keeble, J. (1991). *Out of the Channel: The Exxon Valdez Oil Spill in Prince William Sound*. New York: HarperCollins.

National Research Council (1990). *Crew Size and Maritime Safety*. Washington, D.C.: National Academy Press.

National Transportation Research Board (1989). *Exxon Valdez Casualty Factual Reports*.

Paté-Cornell, M. E. (1990). "Organizational aspects of engineering system reliability: The case of offshore platforms." *Science*, 250, 1210–1217.

Perrow, C. (1984). *Normal Accidents: Living with High Risk Technologies*. New York: Basic Books.

Schein, E. H. (1990). "Organizational culture." *American Psychologist*, 45, 109–119.

Trice, H. M., and J. M. Beyer (1984). "Studying organizational culture through rites and ceremonials." *Academy of Management Review*, 9, 653–659.

Weick, K. E. (1987). "Organizational culture and high reliability." *California Management Review*, 29, 112–127.

Weick, K. E., and R. L. Daft (1983). "The effectiveness of interpretation system." In K. S. Cameron and D. A. Whetton (eds.), *Organizational Effectiveness: A Comparison of Multiple Models*. New York: Academic Press.

Woody, W. (1989). National Transportation Safety Board. *Grounding of the U.S. Tankship* Exxon Valdez *on Bligh Reef, Prince William Sound near Valdez, Alaska*. PB90-916405. Washington, D.C.: NTSB/MAR90/04.

13

Epilogue

KARLENE H. ROBERTS
University of California, Berkeley

W. E. DOUGLAS CREED
University of California, Berkeley

For biographical information about Karlene H. Roberts, see page 1.

For biographical information about W. E. Douglas Creed, see page 55.

*T*he increased use of advanced technologies is changing, perhaps forever, the way we must think about the catastrophic potential of organizational processes. Not so long ago, it was simply impossible to blunder into an accident with the far reaching and long-term consequences of a Chernobyl. While in many industries the incidence of mishaps has declined over time, the potential for immediate and enduring environmental devastation and for enormous economic costs stemming from a single accident has risen. Naval aviation statistics provide a good example of this trend over time. Figure 13-1 shows how Class A aviation accidents (those costing over a million dollars or involving loss of life) have declined over time. This decline has been accompanied by increased costs of accidents to the Navy. Larger and larger oil tankers can cause more and more dramatic spills. In arenas less frequently associated with the need for high reliability than potentially catastrophic technologies, the possibility of enduring calamity appears greater. The tight coupling of banks, known for their small profit margins with their client industries, can lead to economic disaster.

The amount of research devoted to issues of how organizations organize and manage their people to avoid disastrous outcomes is minuscule. The existing work is about individual differences and group processes, rather than about organizational processes that influence safe operations. Most of what exists is laboratory research (see, for example, Driskell and Salas, 1991) that cannot possibly capture the characteristics of the complex situations found in organizations that should be giving primary attention to issues of reliability. Thus, the generalizability of the work is questionable.

Some research attention has been devoted to the organizational dynamics of airline flight crews (see, for example, Gregorich, Helmreich, and Wilhelm, 1990). In addition to moving the focus to issues of how training, socialization, and cultural norms regarding authority influence safe performance, this research has greater face validity because much of it involves the simulation of actual processes and interactions that enhance or undermine safety.

Within some of the industries most prone to severe accidents, some management has heard the wake-up call, though perhaps too late. The American nuclear power industry and the American oil tanker industry, both of which have experienced severe accidents, are examples. Both industries initially attempted engineering solutions to safety problems: Individual operator error, perceived as the most likely source of mishaps, was ostensibly engineered out of the system. Human factors in the form of organizational systems remained for the most part neglected until it was inescapably clear that further tweaking of engineering solutions produced little benefit. Only then were human systems considered. This consideration has yet to be born or is still in its infancy in many parts of both of these industries as well as in other industries.

A problem here is the lack of institutional structures to support the necessary basic management research. Often there is no source of research support at all, while for some industries, what little research has taken place has been supported by regulators. Organizations in regulated industries are inherently distrustful, however, of both research and researchers sponsored by their reg-

Figure 13-1

Navy/Marine Class A Aviation Flight Mishap Rates

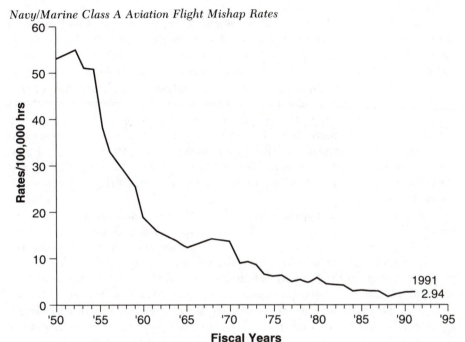

Source: Navy Aviation Safety Center, Norfolk, Virginia

ulators. One way around this dilemma would be to create industry consortia, the members of which would support the necessary basic research.

The absence of basic research creates an obvious gap in knowledge on which to base management policies, training, and the like. Such gaps are quickly filled with snake oil and people to sell it. A number of more specific research needs and management issues are suggested by the state of the situation in general and by the chapters in this book in particular.

RESEARCH NEEDS

Most clearly, we need to know which aspects of existing organizational research and theory are applicable to organizations in which errors can produce catastrophes. Much more attention needs to be devoted to framing theory that can drive future research. While much of the field research on HROs is compelling in its depiction of how these organizations are unusual, it is not persuasive in the claim that HROs cannot be understood at all within the context of existing theory. Rochlin, Schulman, Creed et al., and Weick all contribute to the task of identifying where existing theory may serve and suggesting how theory can be advanced. Much more work is needed because good theory is the basis of good measurement. Koch and Bea and Moore address the measurement issue, but more research needs to be done in this arena.

Much of the work on reliability-enhancing organizations, as well as much of the other work represented in this volume, involves inductive research. As this book makes clear, case studies can illuminate important organizational processes that serve the organization well. They can also help identify important processes that *are missing* within organizations (Schulman, Meyer and Starbuck, Hirschhorn, Eisenhardt, Foushee and Lauber, Weick, and Roberts and Moore). Case studies are possibly the only way to uncover organizational paradoxes. Paradox plays an important role in most of the organizations discussed here. For example, reliability-enhancing organizations must simultaneously centralize and decentralize (Roberts, 1992; Roberts, Stout, and Halpern, in press). The findings from this work should drive deductive research in the future.

A number of the papers here make explicit or imply more specific research needs. Rochlin notes that those descriptions that characterize organizations in terms of performance fail to specify the unending processes through which high reliability organizations attempt to reduce risk through dynamic management. He and Schulman agree that more attention must be given to identifying these processes. Schulman adds that the comparative framework he offers is only a rudimentary step in the analysis of contrasting approaches to achieving high reliability. He finds it useful to recognize a variety of approaches that can be adopted in managing failure-critical systems. The specific character of the technical hazard, identifying what system states must be avoided to maintain safety, determines appropriate organizational structures and strategies.

Creed et al. state that we need to find the place on a continuum of organizations where HROs fall. These authors speculate that if effectiveness is culturally derived, reliability is a higher-order manifestation of HROs' core cultural assumptions, including technological constraints. Reliability, as a cultural value, is oriented against ineffectiveness rather than toward effectiveness. If this is true, it may be that these organizations—existing as they do in an era of continuous technological change—can enjoy no equilibrium state and are characterized by continually changing cultures striving to avoid a non-goal.

Both Koch and Schulman lay groundwork for distinguishing among organizations at different points on a reliability-seeking continuum of the sort posited by Creed et al. Their work suggests arraying other organizations against those they discuss. In her discussion of common themes observed in fast decision making and high reliability organizations, Eisenhardt alerts us to look for the presence or absence of and utility of specialization, extensive rich and real time information, and the dynamic balancing of centralization and decentralization in other organizations. Based on her work, we might do well to broaden effectiveness to include reliability and speed rather than to focus almost solely on profit and growth.

Foushee and Lauber point to the need to examine more closely positive and negative consequences of work team fatigue and familiarity. Teams are important in all reliability-enhancing organizations. These authors point out that we need to determine the amount of crew familiarity necessary to produce a desired level of coordination. If arousal is the key moderator of fatigue, a complex puzzle is posed for researchers. It is possible that low work load fatigue affects performance that is not important because task demands are low, and high work load arousal counteracts the impact of fatigue.

Weick makes a number of suggestions about future research. First, he says that assessing the extent to which processes, analogous to those which operated at Tenerife, arise in other temporary systems would be instructive. From a team perspective, refining the concept of stress is important, as are understanding the tradeoff between cohesion and accuracy, examining whether ignorance is a potential contributor to early crisis stages, and assessing whether improvement in group interaction decreases task complexity. From an organizational perspective, it is important to direct attention to systems that are what Weick characterizes as *loose/linear, loose/complex,* or *tight/linear.* Because of their potential vulnerability to small failures that are difficult to contain, it is important to see whether increased stress increases the salience of formal structure and authority relationships in such systems.

Within the broad area of organizational behavior, future research needs to tie issues of reliability enhancement more tightly to work being done on quality enhancement. It also needs to address the relationship of organizational learning to improved reliability.

MANAGEMENT ISSUES

A number of general management issues are suggested by this collection of papers. Many managers probably do not take an analytic perspective that encourages them to think about potential catastrophe in their organizations. Pauchant and Mitroff (1992) provide the example of a company manager who thought the worst thing that could happen to him was that his product might not be available on store shelves. But his product could have been Tylenol. Managers in many industries need to ask themselves how likely it is that errors in their organizations can lead to cataclysmic outcomes for organizational members, innocent bystanders, future generations, and/or the environment.

Estimating the cost of an accident is often very difficult to do. For example, the most costly accident the oil industry had to deal with prior to the *Exxon Valdez* accident was the considerably less destructive *Amaco Cadiz* accident. The cost of oil industry compliance with the Oil Pollution Act of 1990, written because of the *Exxon Valdez* accident, would be the equivalent of the cost of two *Exxon Valdez* cleanups per year for every company in the industry. By not having faced squarely the potential for catastrophe earlier, the oil industry now finds itself in a very costly position.

For one reason or another, many organizations engage in "head in the sand" behavior when it comes to thinking about potential calamity. An example is the Bulgarian government's operation of its nuclear power plant in Kozloduy, said by experts to be the worst-run nuclear power plant in the world (Anonymous, 1990). The plant supplies 40 percent of Bulgaria's electricity. Bulgaria has no other means to supply that 40 percent and no money to buy power from its neighbors. In the long run, however, it may be cheaper to turn the lights off than to deal with the outcomes of an accident in this plant which, after all, can cause harm to future generations of all living things. The nuclear power plant accident at Chernobyl is another example. The Russian government sent relatively unprotected scientists into that plant to find a loose rod in what is a crumbling sarcophagus. The scientists were engaging (if sometimes voluntarily) in suicide missions in a situation with unknown and potentially very dangerous outcomes. When will the price be deemed too high for organizations to ignore issues concerning reliable operations?

Once managers decide to confront the potential for hazardous outcomes in their organizations, the hard work begins. They then have to find ways to diagnose the potential for such outcomes. They need to recognize that people as well as mechanical systems contribute to those situations. Diagnostic tools must include measures sensitive to people issues as well as to hardware and software issues. To be of any value, these tools must have a firm theoretical and measurement foundation.

Diagnosis is futile and often harmful if managers are unprepared to attempt to fix the problems they uncover. Often "fixes" are quite expensive. But again, they may be less expensive than would be the cost of responding to an accident. One can see depicted in Schulman the efforts of one company to remain constantly vigilant concerning the development of problems that can lead to catastrophe. In this firm, great attention is focused on human factors. Should this company fail to engage in vigilant behavior, the probability of serious consequences increases dramatically. As Schulman's illustration shows, reliability-enhancing organizations identify sets of outcomes they continually work never to experience.

Managers in technologically sophisticated companies can no longer operate as though they are "iron men in wooden ships." The organizational reality has changed. It requires the smooth operation of interdependent, skilled teams of people who develop the social glue appropriate to their situations. While one might not ask a platoon of soldiers to vote on whether to attack, today it is not possible to operate smart weapons systems and other technologically complex hardware without using the combined expertise, vigilance, and teamwork of a number of people.

Specific management issues are discussed by several of this volume's authors. Meyer and Starbuck list a number of lessons learned from the NCR experience. To recapitulate: Discrete technologies and distinct industries are ephemeral; cohesion can pay off between reorientations; success and failure have the same roots; ideologies both stabilize and change organizations; industry revolutions confound organizations; and finally, managing reorientations requires good timing and political acumen.

Hirschhorn entreats managers to adopt a four-part model of an effective organization that is hierarchical in structure. In it, delegation is broad and deep and management develops two classes of procedures, guiding and detailed, with methods for integrating the two.

Bea and Moore have a very clear message for industry: Devote as much time to human and organizational error as is devoted to engineering. They state that most accidents result from a chain of errors involving fatigue, carelessness, negligence, shortsightedness, greed, lack of training, and wishful thinking. Errors go beyond people in the system when organizational cultures "invite risk shortsightedness." Engineers too frequently design systems that cannot be constructed or, if they can be built, cannot be effectively operated. Engineers and management experts need to work *together* to design *both* technological and human/organizational systems that are compatible with one another. In so doing, they must attack simultaneously human and organizational error at the levels of individual, group, and organizational behavior, as well as from the perspective of technology.

Roberts and Moore make a plea for increased attention to training as a whole and to the explicit connecting of performance evaluation to training. They also encourage scrutinizing company policy to assess whether it encourages risky behavior and developing policies that discourage risk.

CONCLUSION

Our hope is that the diverse perspectives on reliability-enhancing organizations presented in this book will stimulate further research of both theoretical and practical significance. Clearly, HRO research is moving apace from its earliest stages of primarily inductive and descriptive work to hypothico-deductive and prescriptive work. The importance of this line of inquiry—related as it is to interactions of technological and organizational complexity—cannot be overstated. While the work has obvious implications for safe operations of potentially hazardous technologies, it also contributes to other increasingly important areas of organizational behavior.

REFERENCES

Anonymous (1990). "Nuclear Morning." *New Scientist, 128,* 1740.

Driskell, J. E., and E. Salas (1991). "Group decision making under stress." *Journal of Applied Psychology, 76,* 473–478.

Gregorich, S. E., R. L. Helmreich, and J. A. Wilhelm (1990). "The structure of cockpit management attitudes." *Journal of Applied Psychology, 75,* 682–690.

Pauchant, T. C., and I. I. Mitroff (1992). *Transforming the Crisis Prone Organization: Preventing Industrial, Organizational, and Environmental Tragedies.* San Francisco: Jossey Bass.

Roberts, K. H. (1992). "Structuring to facilitate migrating decisions in reliability en-
    hancing organizations." In L. Gomez-Mehia and M. W. Lawless (eds.) *Top Man-
    agement and Effective Leadership in High Technology Firms.* Greenwich, CT: JAI
    Press.
Roberts, K. H., S. Stout, and J. J. Halpern (in press). "Decision dynamics in two high
    reliability military organizations." *Management Science.*